Praise for
Where Is the Lone Ranger?

"A timely assessment of America's ability to develop and field an essential component of stability operations—constabulary forces, also known internationally as 'formed police units.' Perito demonstrates their importance by drawing on American experience, particularly in Iraq and Afghanistan, and explains why America has been slow to arrive at this solution, as well as why its governmental system inhibits its implementation."
—**David Bayley**, distinguished professor emeritus and former dean, School of Criminal Justice, State University of New York, Albany

"Our men and women in uniform can face greater danger from drug traffickers, violent mobs, and lawlessness than from enemy tanks, planes, and ships. Robert Perito has given us a blueprint for building capable and sustainable institutions to provide the rule of law . . . this is a mission we WILL perform again."
—**William B. Caldwell IV**, Lieutenant General, United States Army

"The second edition of *Where Is the Lone Ranger? America's Search for a Stability Force* remains the 'go to' text for those wishing to learn how the security gap was tackled in peace and stability operations involving U.S. forces. Perito writes with the flair of an academic, the accuracy of a seasoned practitioner, and the passion of someone who cares deeply about establishing the rule of law in postconflict environments. *Realpolitik* doesn't get realer. Perito convincingly illustrates the enduring requirement for an international expeditionary police force—as well as the limitations of police deployed under a military mandate and the problems of soldiers training police. He courageously reminds us that the proverbial masked lawman is now needed more than ever in the crisis zones across the globe."
—**Andrew Carpenter**, Chief of the Strategic Policy and Development Section, Police Division, Department of Peacekeeping Operations, United Nations

where is the
LONE RANGER?

where is the
LONE RANGER?

AMERICA'S SEARCH FOR A STABILITY FORCE

SECOND EDITION

Library Commons
Georgian College
825 Memorial Avenue
Box 2316
Orillia, ON L3V 6S2

Robert M. Perito

UNITED STATES INSTITUTE OF PEACE PRESS
WASHINGTON, D.C.

UNITED STATES INSTITUTE OF PEACE
2301 Constitution Avenue, NW
Washington, DC 20037
www.usip.org

© 2013 by the Endowment of the United States Institute of Peace.
All rights reserved.

First published 2013

To request permission to photocopy or reprint materials for course use, contact the Copyright Clearance Center at www.copyright.com. For print, electronic media, and all other subsidiary rights email permissions@usip.org.

Printed in the United States of America.

The paper used in this publication meets the minimum requirements of American National Standards for Information Science—Permanence of Paper for Printed Library Materials, ANSI Z39.48-1984.

Library of Congress Cataloging-in-Publication Data

Perito, Robert, 1942-
  Where is the lone ranger? : America's search for a stability force / Robert M. Perito. -- 2nd ed.
      pages cm
  Includes bibliographical references and index.
  ISBN 978-1-60127-153-2 (pbk. : alk. paper)
  e-ISBN 978-1-60127-165-5
  1. Peacekeeping forces. 2. International police. 3. Military police. 4. Peace officers. 5. Constables. 6. Law enforcement--International cooperation. 7. United States--Armed Forces--Foreign countries. I. Title.
  JZ6377.U8P47 2013
  341.5'84--dc23
                              2012049702

In memory of
Patricia Campbell Perito

Contents

Foreword by Lieutenant General James M. Dubik   xi

Introduction   1
Overview   2

1. Brcko: SFOR vs. the Rent-a-Mob   5
The Police Station   11
Evacuation of the IPTF   12
The Brcko Bridge   14
Status of Brcko   18
The U.S. Reaction   22

2. Constabulary   25
Constabulary Forces in Europe   29
History of Constabulary Forces in the United States   33
U.S. Experience with Constabulary Forces Abroad   37
Post–World War II Experience   44
The Contemporary U.S. Experience   52

3. Test Case: Creating Postconflict Security in Bosnia   61
Signing the Dayton Agreement   65
Implementing the Dayton Accords   66
Support of the Police in Bosnia   72
The U.S. Debate on Extending SFOR   75
A Decisive December   77
Planning for the Deterrent Force   83
Creating the MSU   85

4. Blue Box: The Multinational Specialized Unit in Bosnia   95
MSU Mandate and Organization   98
Command and Control   100
Public Order and Refugee Returns   103
Combating Organized Crime   108
Counterterrorism   115
Training Bosnian Police   117
MSU Expansion   118

5. Odd Jobs: Constabulary Forces in Kosovo 121
   The Kosovo Force 122
   The Kosovo Police Service 125
   UNMIK Police 128
   Special Police Units 128
   Command and Control 130
   Financial Arrangements 131
   Deployment 132
   Crime and Ethnic Conflict 134
   Mitrovica 136
   Two Years of Violence 141
   The "Odd Jobs" Unit 142
   A Campaign for Law and Order 147
   Lessons Identified in Kosovo 152

6. Biting the Bullet in Iraq 155
   A Larger Debate on Nation Building 156
   The Global War on Terrorism 157
   The U.S. Decision to Intervene in Iraq 159
   Planning for the Postwar Period 161
   Postconflict Chaos in Iraq 164
   A False Start on Reconstruction 169
   The Department of Defense Takes Over the Police Training Program 172
   The Onset of Civil War 174
   The Crest of Sectarian Violence 177
   The U.S. Military's Effort to Control Iraqi Police Abuses 178
   The U.S. Surge to Reverse the Tide of Battle 181
   The Future Role of the Iraqi National Police 186

7. Police Building under Fire: The Afghan National Civil Order Police 191
   U.S. Retaliation for September 11 Routs the Taliban 193
   The International Effort to Rebuild the Afghan Police 195
   The U.S. Police Assistance Program 197
   The Department of Defense and the Combined Security
   Transition Command 200
   Kabul Riots Highlight the Need for a Constabulary Force 201
   Police Failures Dictate the Need for a Revised Training Program 202
   Resurgent Taliban Target the Afghan Police 205

The United States Announces a New Policy for Afghanistan 206
ANCOP Has an Expanded Role as a Counterinsurgency Force 209
NTM-A Initiates a Program to Improve ANCOP's Performance 211
Kandahar Provides a Battlefield Test for ANCOP 215
After a Difficult Start, ANCOP Finally Hits Its Stride 217

3. Where Is the Lone Ranger When We Need Him? 219
    The Model for a U.S. Stability Force 224
    Special Police Units 224
    Civil Police 225
    Judicial and Penal Experts 226
    Summing Up 227

Index 231

Foreword

Complex Contingency Operations: Assessing Our Past and Preparing for Our Future

"**A** fiery horse with the speed of light, a cloud of dust, and a hearty 'Hi-Ho, Silver!'" So began each episode of the *Lone Ranger*. With his faithful companion, Tonto, the Lone Ranger stood against lawlessness and injustice. After a decisive shootout, peace was restored and justice reestablished. The masked man and his sidekick then rode off, more work to be done elsewhere. *Where Is the Lone Ranger?* reminds us that reality isn't like a television show. The international community has no Lone Ranger to restore peace and establish justice; it has only governments, coalitions, and alliances.

The United States, its allies, and potential coalition partners may not want to undertake the kinds of nation building, peace operations, or complex contingencies that have characterized the strategic environment since the end of the Cold War. Who would? Reality has a way of imposing itself on our lives; the same is true for nations. America must work toward the future it wants but deal with reality as it is.

The United States Institute of Peace is publishing a second, updated edition of *Where Is the Lone Ranger?* to help the current U.S. strategic review deal with reality. As much as the United States would like to avoid involvement in complex interventions, failed and failing states with shifting demographics, diminishing resources, growing integration, and nefarious actors empowered by new technologies dictate otherwise. A solid strategic review, including an objective examination of the military and nonmilitary capabilities from the last eleven years of wartime experiences—as well as other historical experiences—is vital. The current U.S. debate, however, is likely to miss that mark by overly focusing on military capabilities.

In four major case studies—Bosnia, Kosovo, Iraq, and Afghanistan—Perito looks at one of the most essential activities associated with restoring peace and justice in a fractured society: creating and improving police. Although each nation's case is unique, common conditions existed in each that differ only in degree: the breakdown of civil order; high levels of violence; the rise of black markets, illicit trafficking, gang activity, and corruption; porous borders; weak governments; conflicted loyalties; and sectarianism. Further, in each case, political leaders, governing bodies, judges, critical infrastructure, and elections all needed protection, and the intervening force in each case had to raise a police force while it established security.

The commonalities that emerge in Perito's case studies match my personal experience. I commanded an infantry brigade in the 10th Mountain Division during Operation Uphold Democracy in Haiti in 1994–95. Part of my unit's responsibility was to impose security and reestablish the police, courts, and jails in Haiti's second largest city, Cap Haitien. In 1999, I was the deputy commanding general of Task Force Eagle and Multinational Division–North in Bosnia-Herzegovina. During my tour, our command helped Ambassador Robert Farrand implement the Brcko Arbitration Decision. We also helped seat the Srebrenica government, and we were involved in several other incidents mentioned in Perito's case study. During the "surge" period in Iraq, June 2007–July 2008, I was the commanding general of the Multi-National Security Transition Command–Iraq. Our command helped accelerate the growth—in size, capability, and confidence—of all Iraqi security forces, as well as the Ministries of Defense and Interior and the Iraqi Joint Force headquarters. We were involved in assisting the Iraqi Ministry of Interior to reform the Iraq National (now Federal) Police. Some of these activities are also mentioned in Perito's case studies. Finally, in 2009–10, I helped Generals Stanley McChrystal and David Petraeus as well as Lieutenant General William Caldwell IV in restructuring NATO's approach to developing the Afghan national security forces. So I read *Where Is the Lone Ranger?* not just out of an academic interest but as one who served in the operations that Perito describes. I found his discussion of the cases engaging, well balanced, and informative.

At the end of the book, Perito recommends that the United States establish "an effective U.S. stability force" that includes "civilian police constabulary units, civil police, judicial teams of judges, lawyers, and court administrators, and corrections officers." He further states that these "public order and law enforcement components are essential . . .[and] must be assembled and ready at the outset of military operations. They should be under the control of U.S. military authorities because unity of command in the initial phase of an operation is paramount. Civilian control of the civilian elements of the force should, however, be restored as quickly as possible." As a former practitioner, I drew four major conclusions from squaring the case studies in *Where Is the Lone Ranger?* with my personal experiences.

The United States—alone or as part of a coalition or alliance—will be involved in these kinds of operations again. Call them what we will—peace operations, complex contingencies, nation building, reconstruction, stability operations—the United States has been involved in the kinds of actions Perito describes for much of its history. Moreover, if the megatrends, game-changers, potential worlds, and black swans of the National Intelligence Council's *Global Trends 2030: Alternative Worlds* are any indication of the strategic environment and the United States' role in it, these actions will be part of our future as well.[1]

All societies have a degree of violence, criminality, corruption, and instability; no nation's governance is perfect. The tolerance in each society for these activities and imperfections varies. For each, however, there is a threshold which, when crossed, triggers a negative spiral that can result in the collapse of trust and governance. Sometimes this collapse necessitates external intervention. Given America's global interests, future intervention in some cases is inevitable. When—not if—it happens, the chorus of "never again" will change to "why aren't we ready?"

In 1990, while a student in the Army's School of Advanced Military Studies program at Fort Leavenworth, Kansas, I participated in a command post exercise in which the United States was part of a NATO peacekeeping mission in a collapsed Yugoslavia. In the exercise, the U.S. commander had a Russian subordinate unit. Many thought the scenario unrealistic. Reality demonstrated that it was not.

Both military and nonmilitary forces are needed in the kinds of crises that are likely in our future. One of the ultimate goals in such interventions is to move the levels of violence, criminality, corruption, and instability back below that society's threshold in order to provide "space" to improve its governance. Military force is often necessary in these cases, but insufficient. Also necessary is a suite of other forces—governmental, judicial, economic, and police. The essential characteristic of the future is uncertainty. Preparing for the inevitable "next time" requires developing the suite of military and nonmilitary capabilities and the ability to use them. Now, while our experience is fresh, is the time to identify and create these capabilities.

Imposing security and enforcing security are related but distinct activities. Imposing security is the first key task in interventions like most of those executed since the end of the Cold War. Without security, the levels of violence, criminality, corruption, and instability will remain above the threshold of acceptability, prolonging the intervention, delaying the ability to address the underlying issues, and increasing the duration and cost of the intervention.

---

1. National Intelligence Council, *Global Trends 2030: Alternative Worlds* (www.dni.gov/nic/globaltrends: December, 2012).

Police forces may be an essential element to final success, but initially, because of predatory behaviors and other conditions, local police are more likely to be part of the problem than part of the solution. On the other hand, whether part of a larger intervention force consisting of military forces or alone, constabulary police forces are immediately useful, for they are a mix of military and police capabilities. They help impose security and begin immediately to set the conditions for enforcing security—ultimately the job of police forces. Enforcing security requires a set of minimum conditions: the constabulary forces must be large enough and capable enough to handle the existing level of violence and criminality; a body of law must exist, and the judicial and confinement systems must work adequately well; and a sufficient social agreement to obey the law must be present in the citizenry.

Often these conditions emerge over time, and they commonly develop unevenly under the umbrella of imposed security. For example, training a constabulary may proceed faster than developing a local police force; improving a judiciary system usually takes longer than improving confinement capacity. And if a body of laws must be passed and promulgated, that will take longer still. As these conditions develop, trust returns to the social fabric. Slowly, the umbrella of imposed security can be lifted in areas of a country where these minimum conditions emerge, and the composition of the intervention force can change accordingly. Given enough patience and progress, the imposed-security umbrella can close altogether, and security can be enforced by the nation's police forces.

The United States as part of a multinational coalition employed a large enough force to impose security in Haiti in 1994; NATO did so in Bosnia-Herzegovina in 1995 and Kosovo in 1998. None of these interventions was perfectly executed, but all moved violence and instability below the threshold, setting up the conditions not only for force reductions but also for the long process of improving governance. Neither in Afghanistan nor in Iraq did the United States, NATO, or coalition partners initially employ sufficient force to impose security. The result prolonged each war, delayed the ability to address the underlying issues, increased the cost of the intervention, and risked ultimate success. Too light a footprint is as unhelpful as one that is too heavy.

Preparing for the inevitable "next time" requires understanding the difference between imposing and enforcing security, having the right mix of capabilities to do both, and knowing how to transition between the two effectively.

Raising police is not a "stand-alone" activity; it requires a campaign-style and enterprise approach. Simply put, raising police forces and creating the associated conditions that allow for law enforcement in the kinds of intervention operations Perito describes takes concerted effort over time.

The approach, therefore, requires "campaign-like" thinking—that is, a form of thinking in which individual decisions and actions have meaning only in relation to the larger, future goal. Raising police forces, developing a judicial system, and creating a confinement program are not discrete activities—they are related. Each of these activities is the cumulative result of many smaller tasks accomplished over time—hence requiring a campaign plan. Further, success in the three major activities entails success at the local, provincial, and national levels—hence requiring an enterprise approach.

As Perito's Afghan case study shows, neither a campaign nor an enterprise approach was present in NATO's lead-nation methodology to police, judicial, or confinement development, or to the minimum conditions required for law enforcement. Nor is a campaign or an enterprise approach reflected in the belief that one merely must contract out the parts of each major activity and then just "supervise the contracts." Adopting a campaign-like and enterprise approach increases the likelihood of coherence over time; a lead-nation or contracting methodology results in more incoherence.

We can prepare now for the inevitable "next time" by adapting the professional training and education requirements in the military and nonmilitary agencies responsible for orchestrating police, judicial, and confinement development—an inherently interagency activity. We could also conduct more interagency exercises that force the development of campaign-like and enterprise approaches. Finally, we could, as *Where Is the Lone Ranger?* suggests, figure out how to have ready and available capabilities that we know will be required.

Time matters: costs in lives and treasure, as well as in political will, demand progress and continual improvement. I remember a conversation that I had in Iraq during the summer of 2007 with several members of the Jones Commission, a group led by retired Marine general Jim Jones, tasked by the U.S. Congress to evaluate the Iraqi Security Force development effort. Several of the senior police leaders in the group said that the best way to develop high-quality police was to have high entry-level requirements and an extended training program, followed by an apprentice period—in total, about a yearlong program. Ideally, I agreed. Practically, however, I completely disagreed.

As Perito notes in his Afghan case study, the initial German approach to police development would have taken decades to succeed, if ever. Generations are required to complete a transformation of police who had been viewed as pariahs and enforcers of a dictatorial regime. One of the ways to accomplish police transformation includes the slow process of selecting, training, and promoting the right people for police leadership positions. But this approach cannot be used alone. If it is, the intervention plays into the hands of those seeking to destabilize the country, discredit the government, and protract the crisis situation long enough for intervention forces to lose interest.

Augmenting the slow process must be a faster one, a way that recognizes that quality is an iterative characteristic of both people and institutions. This faster process initially uses sufficient selection criteria, training standards, and promotion requirements. Then, it employs continual training to improve the initial product—police, leaders, processes, and institutions—over time. The U.S. police, judiciary, and confinement systems did not emerge fully mature overnight; they won't emerge quickly anywhere else either.

Leaders of an intervention must look for ways to accelerate the slow process. In Iraq, for example, the minister of interior tripled the capacity of the Baghdad Police College by opening extension campuses in Mosul and Basrah; this expansion allowed for almost three times the number of cadets to receive the full three-year training and education program. Then he increased the capacity yet again. First, he added a program for those Iraqis who already had a college education. Second, he introduced a program for long-serving police with adequate education to become limited-duty officers. Finally, he created a program to convert army officers who wanted to become police officers.

The slow process with the kind of accelerants the Iraqi minister of interior introduced and the fast process that recognizes quality as an iterative characteristic can work together. Similar approaches establishing both "alternative adjudication methodologies" as well as a formal judiciary and rule-of-law program are also possible. Time matters in the kinds of contingency operations *Where Is the Lone Ranger?* is focused upon.

Now, before the "next time," we should review the assumptions on which we base our approaches for police, judicial, and confinement development. In *Where Is the Lone Ranger?*, Perito makes it clear that U.S. efforts to create police forces, as well as the systems and institutions necessary to sustain them, have a mixed record of successes and failures. Perhaps more important, his case studies show that many of the failures resulted from repeated erroneous assumptions and strategies.

U.S. policymakers currently are undertaking a strategic review of the capabilities the United States will need to deal with future contingencies. *Where Is the Lone Ranger?* reminds us how we should prepare for when, not if, reality imposes itself on the United States again. Bob Perito has written a timely and useful book. Every security professional—governmental, military, private contractor, and non-governmental agency—would do well to study what *Where Is the Lone Ranger?* has to say and participate in changing the way the United States approaches the kinds of complex situations that are certain to be in our future.

—James M. Dubik
Lieutenant General, U.S. Army, Retired
Senior Fellow, Institute for the Study of War
31 December 2012

Introduction

In the emerging literature on the challenges of establishing sustainable security in fragile states and postconflict environments, much has been written about the role of the military, but there are few works on the role of nonmilitary security forces. This study examines the past roles and future potential of constabulary forces in peace and stability operations, looking at the issue of sustainable security from a U.S. perspective.

The United States has a unique and troubled history with foreign interventions, particularly since the end of the Cold War. It has developed and deployed the world's most effective military forces but has struggled to provide police and constabulary. Under the Clinton administration, the United States played a primary role in peace operations in Somalia, Haiti, Bosnia, and Kosovo, but Congress, the U.S. military, and the George W. Bush administration had a deep aversion to peacekeeping. Perhaps for that reason, the United States was ill prepared to deal with the civilian mobs that looted Baghdad in 2003 and the demonstrators that threatened U.S. forces in Kabul in 2006. The United States did not have civilian constabulary forces trained in riot control; it used commercial contractors as police advisers and had no program to provide the operational constabulary, police, and judicial specialists that were required to establish the rule of law in Iraq and Afghanistan.

The need to create nonmilitary security forces for peace and stability operations was compelling. In the wake of the terrorist attacks on September 11, 2001, the United States could no longer afford the luxury of ignoring turmoil in war-torn societies. Weak and dysfunctional states had become the primary source of international instability. Washington recognized its strategic interest in preventing failed states from providing breeding grounds for extremists and safe havens for terrorist organizations. By the spring of 2003, the United States was involved in a global war on terrorism, fighting two ground wars against extremist-based insurgencies in Iraq and Afghanistan. In the Balkans, the United States had faced the need to control civilian mob violence and ethnic cleansing that threatened the viability of peace operations in Bosnia and Kosovo, and turned to its European allies for constabulary trained to deal with civil disorder. This required a prolonged diplomatic effort, and the forces took years to arrive. In Iraq and Afghanistan, allied constabulary forces were not available, and the United States was forced to create indigenous constabulary forces to control urban rioting and assist in the battle against insurgents. This effort proved costly in battlefield reverses, casualties, and unintended consequences.

In future interventions, the United States needs to create the forces required to deal with civil disorder and counterinsurgencies in order to establish a safe and secure environment. To accomplish this mission, a U.S. stability force is required that includes civilian constabulary forces that can deal with violent demonstrations, armed gangs, and militias and assist military forces in countering insurgencies. Constabulary forces straddle the line between military and police and have characteristics and capabilities of both. Constabulary units can deploy rapidly in response to situations that require greater force and firepower than civil police can provide but do not need the firepower of infantry or armored units. Constabulary forces are trained to deal with civilians and are skilled at using the minimum amount of force necessary to control the situation. Constabulary can serve as a bridge between the military and civil police and can handle tasks that do not clearly fall within either camp. They have proven effective in the hold and build phases of counterinsurgency operations, working in areas that military forces have cleared of main force insurgent groups.

While soldiers and civil police have participated in peace operations since the early 1960s, constabulary forces have appeared only recently. This is surprising since the United States has turned to such forces repeatedly throughout its history. During the colonial period, English and Spanish settlers drew on their respective European traditions to organize local militias that performed both military and police functions. In the Civil War, the Grand Army of the Republic both preserved the Union and dealt with riots and sedition. On the American frontier, settlers banded together to defend their homes against marauders and provide a rough form of justice. The best-known example of an American constabulary was the Texas Rangers, which fought Native American tribes, patrolled the Mexican border, and brought law and order to the frontier; from the stories of the Texas Rangers, scriptwriters at a Detroit radio station in the 1930s created the Lone Ranger, a fictional character who, in hundreds of radio episodes and later television shows and motion pictures, always came to the rescue.

OVERVIEW

This study looks at the evolution of U.S. policy toward peace and stability operations through the prism of the U.S. experience with police and constabulary forces. Chapter 1 describes a riot in Brcko, Bosnia, on August 28,

1997, that had far-reaching implications for U.S. policy on creating sustainable security. After armed U.S. soldiers were nearly overrun by an unarmed mob, the Defense Department determined that European constabulary forces were needed to handle civil disorder in Bosnia. Chapter 2 examines the nature of constabulary forces, providing a working definition of such forces and detailing the early history of U.S. experience with constabularies. Chapter 3 returns to the story of the U.S. effort to create a European constabulary force for Bosnia. It describes the political and diplomatic process through which the United States reached a tacit understanding with its European allies to maintain troops in Bosnia in return for deployment of a European Multinational Specialized Unit (MSU) as part of the North Atlantic Treaty Organization (NATO) Stabilization Force (SFOR).

Chapter 4 recounts the checkered history of the MSU in Bosnia. Trained to provide crowd control, the MSU was misunderstood by SFOR commanders and improperly utilized. Chapter 5 details the use of both military and civilian constabulary forces in Kosovo, where they performed a variety of critical functions but were almost never used for crowd control. Chapter 6 chronicles the U.S. intervention in Iraq and the trial-and-error process of creating indigenous constabulary forces that assisted U.S. brigade combat teams in stabilizing Baghdad during the surge. Chapter 7 brings the story of the U.S. experience with constabularies to its most recent chapter in Afghanistan. In response to deadly rioting in Kabul, the United States created an Afghan constabulary that assisted U.S. military forces during some of the heaviest fighting of the war. Finally, chapter 8 summarizes the U.S. experience with constabulary forces in peace and stability operations and makes the argument for creating a permanent U.S. stability force that includes constabulary, police, and judicial teams. This force would give the United States the capacity it now lacks to control civil disorder, restore sustainable security, and establish the rule of law in future peace and stability operations.

1

Brcko: SFOR vs. the Rent-a-Mob

The old air raid siren sounded at 4:30 A.M. on August 28, 1997. Soon it was joined by a cacophony of church bells. In a well-planned and carefully prepared assault, buses loaded with Bosnian Serb women, children, and paramilitaries in civilian clothes rolled into the slumbering market town of Brcko, Bosnia. As sleepy residents emerged from their homes, they were told that NATO forces had occupied the police station. When the mob reached the police station, they found it surrounded by heavily armed U.S. troops. The demonstration spiraled rapidly out of control, with the mob venting its fury against the soldiers, the Office of the Deputy High Representative, UN vehicles, and the UN police. The radio station in Brcko added vitriol, urging the population to attack the "occupiers."[1] As the day unfolded, U.S. soldiers and UN police faced the most serious incident of mob violence directed against peacekeeping forces in Bosnia.

The reasons for the incident were complex. The members of the ethnic Serb rent-a-mob were supporters of Radovan Karadžić, indicted war criminal and hard-line former president of the Republika Srpska (RS), one of two entities that composed the Republic of Bosnia and Herzegovina. The U.S. troops were from Camp McGovern, the military facility that housed one thousand U.S. soldiers on the outskirts of Brcko. They were members of Task Force Eagle, the U.S. contingent of NATO's Stabilization Force (SFOR), which was responsible for the Multinational Division (MND)–North sector, which included the Brcko region. The UN police officers were members of a special Brcko unit of the International Police Task Force (IPTF), which was created under the Dayton Accords to monitor the local police.

The mob's ostensible target was the Brcko police station, which had been subjected to an attempted takeover by Serb police officers loyal to Biljana

---

1. David Bosco, "After Genocide: Building Peace in Bosnia," *The American Prospect*, July 1998, 16.

Plavšić, the RS president. Plavšić was a former Serb nationalist who was receiving international support for her defiance of Karadžić, and the president of Yugoslavia, Slobodan Milošević. With municipal elections scheduled for September 13 and 14, President Plavšić had sought to expand her influence by seizing control of police stations across northern Bosnia. SFOR and the IPTF assisted in this effort by helping to expel policemen who remained loyal to Karadžić. SFOR also had seized a television transmitter that the former Serb leader had used to broadcast propaganda against the international community. The goal of these unusual actions was to break the iron grip that hard-liners in the Serb Democratic Party (SDS) retained more than a year and a half after the first NATO peacekeepers arrived in Bosnia.[2]

Already a political and strategic flashpoint, Brcko thus was at the epicenter of the conflicts between Serb political factions. Police stations in towns west of Brcko largely fell to pro-Plavšić forces. Police in towns to the east remained loyal to Karadžić. In Brcko, the local police chief, who was aligned with Plavšić, intended to take over the local police station, which was held by Karadžić loyalists. The police chief had alerted the American SFOR commander at Camp McGovern but asked him to stand by. There was a standoff between opposing groups of Serb police, but the pro-Plavšić group ultimately lost its nerve and capitulated. During this confrontation, SFOR troops took up positions at the police station, allegedly to "prevent violations of the Dayton Accords, which among other things barred police from carrying rifles."[3] SFOR subsequently issued a public statement that it had entered Brcko to deter an outbreak of violence after receiving indications that forces loyal to President Plavšić would try to take control of the police station and local media.[4] The pro-Karadžić authorities who controlled Brcko, however, saw these actions as support for Plavšić, and the arrival of the Serb mob was the hard-liners' response to the SFOR intervention into Serb politics.

The senior international official in Brcko was a U.S. diplomat, Ambassador Robert "Bill" Farrand, deputy high representative and international supervisor of Brcko. He was awakened by the early morning siren; his bedroom was just down the corridor from his office on the second floor of an unassuming building in the center of town, and, having slept with the windows open on a hot August night, he first thought there had to be a fire. It then struck him that he had never heard a siren during his four months in Brcko. Moving to the window, Farrand first heard and then made out the darkened forms of numerous people "shuf-

2. Edward Cody, "Bosnian Serb's Backers Stone American Troops: U.S. Support for Rival Angers Karadzic Allies," *Washington Post,* August 28, 1997, A1.

3. Wesley Clark, *Waging Modern War* (New York: Public Affairs, 2001), 86–87.

4. Misha Savic, "NATO Troops, Serbs Clash," *Stars and Stripes,* August 29, 1997, 1.

fling" toward the part of town where the police station was located. From earlier reports, he knew the local police commander was a Plavšić loyalist and was intent on removing pro-Karadžić officers from the station. Farrand had expected trouble.[5]

Pulling on his clothes, Farrand went down the hall to his office, where the single guard assigned to watch the building was on duty. The building housing the Office of Brcko Supervisor was a security officer's nightmare. It was right on the street with large glass windows and no protection. Only the window in the supervisor's office had bulletproof glass, a contribution from the Swedish government. The building had a good-sized meeting room on the first floor and offices for Farrand's twelve-member international staff. The IPTF was previously located in the building but had recently moved its headquarters. Figuring no one would be awake at the Office of the High Representative (OHR) in Sarajevo, and doubting he could get through by telephone, Farrand logged on to e-mail. From Brcko the electronic signal went via NATO headquarters in Brussels before returning to Bosnia. In Brussels there was a construction crane on a worksite adjacent to NATO headquarters. When the crane was pointed in the wrong direction, radio and satellite transmissions to NATO headquarters were disrupted and Farrand's e-mail did not work. In the wee hours of August 28, the crane was pointing in the right direction and the message went through.

Sitting in front of his antiquated computer, Farrand sent a report alerting the OHR in Sarajevo that there was trouble in Brcko and describing what he could see from his window. He concluded the first e-mail by promising to send a similar situation report every fifteen to twenty minutes. For the remainder of the day, Farrand stayed in his office, following events by telephone and through reports from staff members who managed to elude the demonstrators and reach the office. The mob vented its wrath on UN and OHR vehicles parked in front of the building but did not attempt to enter. With a bird's-eye view of the growing mayhem below, Farrand had not seen a single police officer.[6]

Donald Grady, the chief of the UN IPTF unit in Brcko, had also been awakened by the siren and the church bells. Grady was a former chief of police of Santa Fe, New Mexico, with a Ph.D. in applied management, and his six-foot-six-inch athletic frame made him an imposing figure. An African American from Wisconsin, Grady faced the tough challenge in Santa Fe of reforming a police force run by a Hispanic old-boys' network. In Brcko he had the more daunting task of turning a local police force of Serb thugs

5. Interview with Ambassador Robert Farrand, Washington, DC, November 7, 2001.

6. Interview with Farrand.

into a multiethnic police service.[7] Under the Dayton Accords, the IPTF was responsible for reorganizing, retraining, and monitoring the performance of the local police. Unarmed and without executive authority to conduct investigations, make arrests, or use force, the IPTF depended on SFOR and the local police for protection.[8] The 257 IPTF officers in Brcko were members of a special unit with the primary task of reforming the local police and protecting returning refugees. Chief Grady reported directly to the UN IPTF commissioner in Sarajevo.

At 5:00 A.M., Grady left his residence and headed for the IPTF station in the center of Brcko. He discovered that SFOR troops, supported by armored personnel carriers, had taken up positions in front of the local police station, while SFOR helicopters flew overhead. The station was already surrounded by a mob. A week earlier, IPTF headquarters in Sarajevo had instructed Grady to make a weapons inspection of the Brcko police station at ten o'clock that morning. Just before 7:00 A.M., Grady received the first of a number of increasingly frantic calls from IPTF Sarajevo ordering him to start the inspection as quickly as possible. In other towns, SFOR had used the alleged need to protect IPTF weapons inspectors as a pretext to surround local police stations and remove pro-Karadžić police officers. Grady tried to plan a snap inspection, but with only the IPTF overnight duty staff available and the streets filling with demonstrators, he quickly realized it would be impossible to comply with the order. At this point, it occurred to Grady that the IPTF headquarters in Sarajevo had advance knowledge of the planned takeover of the Brcko police station, and he had not been informed.[9]

From the IPTF station, Grady made the first of many calls that day to Farrand to brief him on the demonstration. He also sent out vehicle patrols in an effort to determine what was happening in various parts of the town. Demonstrators were moving quickly through the streets, congregating in front of the U.S. military checkpoint on the bridge leading to Croatia and the deputy high representative's office, as well as at various key crossings and access points to the town. They were also blocking roads by building barricades of debris, Dumpsters, scrap wood, and destroyed cars, making it impossible to enter or leave town. The barricades channeled SFOR and IPTF vehicles into cul-de-sacs or directly into crowds, which climbed on the vehicles and attacked them with stones. Before the riot, the Office of the

---

7.   Daniel Pearl, "A Tough U.S. Cop with a Daunting Beat: Peace in the Balkans," *Wall Street Journal*, December 9, 1999.

8.   General Framework Agreement for Peace in Bosnia and Herzegovina, Annex 11 (International Police Task Force).

9.   Telephone interview with Donald Grady, January 16, 2002.

Supervisor and the IPTF had developed a comprehensive plan to evacuate all internationals, including the IPTF, in case of an emergency. This plan had been compromised, as one of the IPTF local language assistants had passed a copy to hard-liners in the Serb police. Knowing the plan, the demonstration's organizers had sent protesters to control the designated rallying points and escape routes. There were also well-coordinated mobile teams of rioters with instructions to block roads and prevent SFOR, IPTF, and other internationals from moving.

On the streets, white IPTF police vans with the initials "UN" painted on their sides were magnets for violence. The mob threw rocks, smashed windows, and dented the sides of the vehicles with two-by-fours. With no means of self-defense, those IPTF officers who could flee did so, driving through gauntlets of people throwing rocks and bottles at their vehicles. Excepting three officers who suffered bruises and cuts from flying glass, none of the IPTF officers was injured.[10] The media reported that "IPTF officers in blue helmets and flak jackets" were seen fleeing Brcko in "white UN pickups with smashed windows" toward the safety of Camp McGovern.[11]

The IPTF station also came under siege by rock-throwing demonstrators, who quickly shattered all the windows. The crowd attacked UN police vehicles in the station's parking lot, removing the radios and then turning over the vehicles and setting them on fire. Altogether, thirty UN vehicles were destroyed and seventy others were vandalized and damaged. Inside the IPTF station, the thirty officers on duty barricaded the doors and windows and hid under their desks, but the crowd made no attempt to enter the building. Telephone calls from IPTF officers and other internationals began to come to the station. Most of the IPTF officers, like other members of the foreign community, were trapped in their homes by hostile crowds that prevented them from leaving.[12] Two IPTF officers, Bill Aycock and Joe Jordan, were protected by their Serb landlord, who put the officers' UN vehicle in his garage and hid the officers in his attic. The landlord told the officers they would be safe, but their vehicle would be destroyed if the mob discovered it. When an opportunity to escape presented itself, a group of elderly neighbors formed a protective ring around the UN officers' van as they drove out of the neighborhood.[13]

10. Jerry Merideth, "International Police Had to Flee Bottle-Throwing Mobs," *Stars and Stripes*, August 30, 1997, 1.

11. Chris Stephen, "Farrand Reportedly 'Marooned' in Brcko Town Center," Agence France-Presse, August 29, 1997.

12. Stephen, "Farrand Reportedly 'Marooned.'"

13. Merideth, "International Police Had to Flee."

At about 8:00 A.M., Grady made the first of several attempts to get the RS police to control the disturbance. He found the head of the regional police, Chief Bjelosivic, at the headquarters of the Ministry of Interior's special police unit. Grady was unaware Bjelosivic had already tried but failed to take over the main police station and was now completely discredited in the eyes of nearly all the RS police officers. Bjelosivic told Grady only that there was nothing he could do. Two hours later, the frightened Bjelosivic fled Brcko for the safety of Camp McGovern. After his departure, Grady's subsequent efforts to rally the RS police also failed because the few pro-Plavšić officers who remained in Brcko were too frightened to intervene.[14]

By midmorning, the mood in Brcko had become even uglier. Shops were shuttered. Angry people roamed the streets. Truckloads of shouting men, some carrying Karadžić posters, roared around town. Roving mobs smashed cars belonging to international agencies. In incendiary broadcasts over the local radio station, Serb authorities accused the United States of assisting in the takeover of the police station and called for the townspeople to oppose the action. Speaking over Radio Pale, the voice of Bosnian Serb authorities, Momčilo Krajišnik, the Serb member of the tripartite Bosnian presidency, congratulated the mob, saying, "I hope you will repeat this feat a hundred times."[15] A Serb Orthodox priest broadcasted an appeal for those who housed UN personnel to throw them out. The broadcasts also falsely accused SFOR troops of wounding four civilians and killing local people. These messages continued until General David Grange, the commander of MND-North, ordered a helicopter to direct its downdraft at the station's antenna and blow it down.[16]

Grady drove into Brcko convinced that the demonstrators were highly disciplined and under instructions to frighten representatives of international agencies and destroy their property, but not to directly harm them. To prove the point, Grady, in uniform and accompanied by his female interpreter, left his UN vehicle and walked into a crowd of demonstrators. His UN vehicle was overturned and burned, but Grady and his assistant were virtually ignored. At about the same time, a small group of IPTF officers outside of Brcko had a similar experience. The officers were pursued by a rock-throwing mob, which stopped abruptly and allowed them to escape to the safety of an SFOR vehicle.[17]

---

14. Interview with Grady.

15. The constitution contained in the Dayton Accords established a three-member presidency, with one ethnic Serb, Croat, and Bosniak (Bosnian Muslim) member.

16. Savic, "NATO Troops, Serbs Clash," 1.

17. Ibid., 1.

THE POLICE STATION

The apparent order not to harm unarmed IPTF officers and other foreign civilians did not apply to SFOR. At 4:30 A.M., SFOR troops were already manning observation posts and blocking positions in and around Brcko to prevent the movement of rifles into the city and to support the scheduled IPTF inspection of the local police station. A platoon of U.S. soldiers had fortified their position in front of the main police station with concertina wire as they confronted a hostile mob with women and children in the front ranks and men at the rear. The rioters were armed with brick-size stones and timbers taken from the rubble of war-damaged buildings. The mob threatened the soldiers with clubs and mimed how they would kill them with pistols and knives. They attacked the troops in waves, with women and children throwing stones and men and youths swinging clubs and fists. The struggle lasted until midmorning.[18]

The Americans at the police station, led by Sergeant First Class Phillip Burgess, were members of D Company, Second Battalion, Second Infantry Regiment, First Infantry Division. The mob quickly cut off Burgess and his troops from the U.S. soldiers guarding the Brcko Bridge. D Company held its position at the police station until about 10:00 A.M., when it was "pretty much overwhelmed."[19] Demonstrators used their bare hands to tear down the barbed wire protecting the troops. Burgess was hit by a club and suffered a cut that closed his left eye. Another soldier, Sergeant Matthew Martin, was more seriously injured when the three-man crew of his Bradley fighting vehicle was besieged by the mob, which put steel pipes in the treads to prevent it from moving. When Martin emerged in an attempt to reason with the crowd, he was struck in the face with a board and suffered a broken nose and damage to his eye. With his position becoming increasingly untenable and Martin needing medical attention, Sergeant Burgess led his platoon away from the police station to a position south of town, where Martin was picked up by vehicles from Camp McGovern for medical evacuation to Germany.[20]

During the confrontation, a seventeen-year-old Bosnian Serb high school student, Mladen Pajic, was shot in the thigh when a U.S. solider fired his sidearm into the pavement and the bullet ricocheted. The boy's brother said: "They didn't shoot right at the people. I guess that is not allowed."[21] The soldiers at the station had authority to use force to disperse the crowds but were unwilling to use their weapons against unarmed demonstrators. For

---

18. Telephone interview with Colonel James Greer, July 10, 2002.

19. Jerry Merideth, "They Got Me Good, GI Relates," *Stars and Stripes*, August 29, 1997, 1.

20. "Medals Given to Soldiers Who Braved Attack," *Stars and Stripes*, August 31, 1997, 1.

21. Clark, *Waging Modern War*, 86.

their restraint and discipline, eighteen soldiers received medals and other commendations.

EVACUATION OF THE IPTF

After midmorning, the remainder of Grady's day was spent in a running debate with IPTF Sarajevo on whether to evacuate IPTF officers and other internationals from their homes in Brcko. Grady believed people were safer in their homes. Sarajevo disagreed. Trapped by hostile crowds and afraid for their lives, IPTF officers were telephoning Sarajevo and demanding to be rescued. At 1:00 P.M., IPTF Sarajevo ordered an evacuation of all IPTF and other internationals to Camp McGovern. Grady could not reach people in the town, but he devised a plan to evacuate the thirty officers at the IPTF station.[22] One group of SFOR armored personnel carriers (APCs) under the command of Army Second Lieutenant William White of D Company created a diversion by driving away from the station with the crowd in pursuit, as another group of vehicles arrived at the front of the IPTF station from the opposite direction. As the IPTF officers ran to the APCs, the mob ran back to attack the vehicles with rocks. Several officers suffered bruises, but there were no serious injuries. Lt. White was decorated for bravery. Once the IPTF station was unoccupied, it was quickly overrun and completely trashed by the mob. Equipment and furnishings were looted or destroyed and offices were vandalized. The station was a total loss.[23]

After arriving at Camp McGovern, Grady began to work with SFOR to evacuate the eighty-five IPTF officers who remained trapped in Brcko. The rescue operation involved many acts of individual heroism by U.S. forces. Among the most daring was an action conducted by four members of a U.S. Army force protection team from Camp McGovern. The mission began when a German IPTF officer assigned to McGovern received a call for help from two British and four Indian IPTF officers whose residence in Brcko was besieged by a mob. In response, the team, all volunteers, donned civilian clothes and borrowed a van from a local merchant who ran a shop on the military base. The team removed the van's license plates and painted Cyrillic letters on the side to make it look like a local vehicle. With a chief warrant officer at the wheel, a U.S. soldier who spoke the local language along as an interpreter, and the German IPTF officer and his radio, the team, armed and "locked and loaded," left McGovern for Brcko. Their first challenge was to explain their way past an SFOR checkpoint outside the town. Their next en-

---

22. Interview with Grady.
23. Merideth, "International Police Had to Flee," 1.

counter was with a group of Serbs armed with pipes and clubs who blocked the road and ordered them out of the van. When the driver refused, one Serb swung a pipe at the windshield but missed as the vehicle lurched forward and sped away, traveling by back roads to reach the IPTF officers' residence.[24]

The team found the house surrounded by an angry crowd. The van drove on for a block and then made a U-turn in front of a large, walled compound before heading back up the street to the residence. At that point, the team became aware of a U.S. Army Apache helicopter gunship hovering above them. Having been told before leaving McGovern that U.S. forces in Brcko were alerted to their mission, the team assumed the gunship was there to protect them. They did not know the helicopter crew was unaware of the mission and was reporting that an unmarked van full of armed Serbs had just turned in front of an arms depot housing interned Serb heavy weapons and ammunition.

Back at the residence, the team first noticed a Serb woman standing on the porch, brandishing an AK-47. They initially thought she posed a threat to the IPTF officers, who were looking out the windows. In fact, the woman was the IPTF officers' landlady, protecting her rent-paying boarders. Using the German IPTF officer's radio, the team tried to get the IPTF officers to come out to the van. When this tactic failed, two members of the team left the vehicle and began waving and motioning the officers to leave the residence.[25]

At this point, the helicopter arrived overhead. Again the team assumed the gunship had moved in to protect them. Instead, the helicopter crew was in radio contact with Camp McGovern, requesting permission to fire on the van if its armed passengers endangered the IPTF officers in the house. Fortunately, the helicopter's noise and downward prop wash created a momentary diversion that enabled the IPTF officers to reach the van, which sped off. At this point, McGovern warned the helicopter to be on the lookout for a U.S. team in a blue van. The gunship answered that the van below them was gray and was heading toward the U.S. military base. Aboard the van, the U.S. team was joking with the rescued British and Indian policemen when they spotted a heavily armed, rapid reaction force from McGovern that had been sent to intercept them. Having left the base with their weapons but without identification, the team was disarmed and held under guard until their commanding officer was brought to the roadblock to identify them. Once back in uniform, the team received a hero's welcome at the base and military commendations for bravery.[26]

---

24. Interview with Sergeant Mike Agate, former member of the U.S. Army Force Protection Team, Camp McGovern, December 18, 2001.

25. Interview with Agate.

26. Interview with Agate.

However, seventy-five to eighty IPTF officers remained trapped in the town and at risk of assault by gangs of increasingly intoxicated Serb thugs. Under a plan devised by Chief Grady, the remaining IPTF officers were told to slip away from their residences after dark and make their way to a few designated roads, where they would be picked up by SFOR vehicles. The plan misfired when the evacuees were given the wrong time and began arriving at the pickup points before the rescue vehicles had left Camp McGovern. Eventually, the recovery effort went forward, concluding at 3:30 A.M. with the safe recovery of the last IPTF officer from Brcko—twenty-three hours after the rent-a-mob had arrived.[27]

THE BRCKO BRIDGE

As various SFOR platoons were attacked and overrun by crowds of up to eight hundred rioters, they fell back toward the SFOR fixed position guarding the bridge across the Sava River. The Brcko Bridge, SFOR's principal lifeline to Croatia and its supply base in Hungary, was regularly guarded by a company of American SFOR troops from the U.S. Army's First Mechanized Infantry Division. The troops were barricaded behind sandbags and supported by an Abrams M-1 tank and two Bradley fighting vehicles. They were armed with M-16 automatic rifles, grenades, and sidearms. Facing them was a hostile mob of civilians, including large numbers of women and children. For nearly twelve hours, Serbs armed with bricks, railroad ties, and Molotov cocktails assaulted the bridge's defenders. The mob made repeated advances, pelting the soldiers with rocks and bricks. Rioters attempted to penetrate the wire barrier and to climb onto and damage military vehicles. As the troops were under orders not to fire, they used their rifles to push back the crowd, but the fighting was often hand-to-hand. There were fistfights. Troops grabbed rioters and pushed them back into the crowd. Serb men used railroad ties to damage vehicles and to injure soldiers, who lost their footing and fell to the ground.[28]

As the day wore on, the U.S. commander, Captain Kevin Hendricks, began to rotate his men to the Croatian side, where they were able to rest, eat, and recuperate out of sight of the struggle to control the bridge. He also began to use a careful, graduated escalation of warning shots—from pistols to rifles to machine guns—in an attempt to deter the crowd. Specific soldiers were assigned this responsibility, ordered when to fire, and instructed to aim at targets that could be hit without endangering the rioters. This tactic had

---

27. Interview with Grady.
28. Interview with Greer.

no apparent effect until the soldiers fired a heavy machine gun that tore away the facade of an abandoned building. This dissuaded the crowd, which drew back and limited further attacks to stones and Molotov cocktails.[29] Finally, when a Molotov cocktail was thrown at a military vehicle, the troops lost patience and fired tear gas, the first time this chemical agent was used in Bosnia. Tear gas was also dropped from a hovering helicopter.[30]

At 7:30 P.M., Momčilo Krajišnik, the Serb member of the Bosnian presidency, and Dragan Kalinić, speaker of the RS People's Assembly, arrived in Brcko in an impressive motorcade of black limousines. They stopped at the mayor's office, which was located adjacent to the Brcko Bridge, and went inside for a meeting with local officials.[31] At the conclusion of the meeting, Krajišnik emerged and stood on a vehicle to address the crowd that had been attacking the bridge. Krajišnik praised the demonstrators for their actions and for their sacrifices in defense of the Serbian people. Almost as suddenly as the violence at the bridge started, it was over. Krajišnik's speech, exhaustion, and the coming of darkness quieted the rioters. A few hours later, General Grange convened a meeting at Camp McGovern attended by Farrand, Grady, the mayor of Brcko, the new acting police chief, the local SDS party boss, and Colonel James Greer, commander of the Steel Tigers, Task Force 1-77 Armor, to discuss restoring public order.[32]

In Sarajevo, August 28 was the first day in office for Richard D. Kauzlarich, the new U.S. ambassador to Bosnia. Having arrived in Sarajevo the previous afternoon, Kauzlarich was informed of the situation in Brcko as he prepared for his first meeting with the Bosnian foreign minister and the formal presentation of his credentials to the Bosnian and Croat members of the tripartite Bosnian presidency. Kauzlarich and his staff were getting ready for a previously scheduled visit on August 30 from the U.S. special Balkan envoy, Ambassador Robert Gelbard, and the NATO Supreme Allied Commander Europe (SACEUR), General Wesley Clark. The new ambassador's immediate concern was for the safety of Americans in Brcko, particularly U.S. military forces and members of the American contingent of the IPTF. Kauzlarich presented his credentials at 11 A.M. The Serb member of the

---

29. Colonel James K. Greer, "The Urban Area during Stability Missions Case Study: Bosnia-Herzegovina, Part 2," in Russell W. Glenn, ed., *Capital Preservation: Preparing for Urban Operations in the Twenty-First Century,* proceedings of the RAND Arroyo-TRADOC-MCWL-OSD Urban Operations Conference, March 22–23, 2000.

30. Clark, *Waging Modern War,* 87.

31. "Bosnian Serb Leaders Krajisnik, Kalinic Arrive in Brcko," *Pale SRNA,* August 28, 1997, translated in Foreign Broadcast Information Service, doc. FTS19970828001239.

32. Interview with Greer.

presidency, Krajišnik, did not attend the presentation, in keeping with his policy of visiting Sarajevo only for formal meetings of the joint presidency.[33]

In the afternoon, Kauzlarich received a telephone call from Farrand, who briefed the ambassador on the situation in Brcko. Farrand was also concerned about the safety of the Americans, particularly those in the IPTF. By the time of the call, however, Farrand seemed comfortable that most of the Americans had already arrived safely at Camp McGovern. Farrand told the ambassador he was certain the riot was orchestrated by Serb hard-liners in the RS. Kauzlarich's day concluded with a meeting with a U.S. congressional delegation composed of members of the House of Representatives and led by Missouri Democrat Ike Skelton. In their meeting, the congressional delegation made clear to the ambassador their opposition to continuing U.S. troop presence in Bosnia. They also made clear they did not want U.S. troops placed in dangerous situations, such as pursuing war criminals, or subjected to the kind of risks they were experiencing at that moment in Brcko.[34]

In Washington, the retiring chairman of the Joint Chiefs of Staff, General John Shalikashvili, held his farewell press conference on August 28. The general played down the Brcko incident, telling reporters the police chiefs in four Bosnian Serb towns had changed allegiance to Mrs. Plavšić, and the UN IPTF had gone there to begin the process of police reform. He noted that things had gone smoothly in all the towns but Brcko, "where some hard-liners had resisted, moving in busloads of supporters and agitating." Shalikashvili said that "some elements (peacekeepers) got caught up in the middle of a demonstration, which got pretty heated."[35] White House Deputy Press Secretary Joe Lockhart took a stronger line. Speaking from the president's vacation retreat on Martha's Vineyard, Lockhart said the United States "will hold the parties' leadership responsible for keeping their people under control."[36]

On August 30, Ambassador Gelbard, the U.S. special representative for implementation of the Dayton Accords, arrived in Sarajevo and delivered a blunt warning to Krajišnik and other hard-line Serbs during a visit to their headquarters in Pale. Speaking to a Krajišnik aide, Gelbard accused the hard-liners of instigating the violence in Brcko and of "incredible

---

33. Interview with Richard Kauzlarich, former U.S. ambassador to Bosnia, Washington, DC, January 3, 2002.

34. Interview with Kauzlarich.

35. Cody, "Bosnian Serb's Backers Stone American Troops."

36. "Tanjug Criticizes SFOR in Brcko," *Belgrade Tanjug,* August 28, 1997, translated in Foreign Broadcast Information Service, doc. FTS19970828001415.

cowardice in using women and children as shields" during the violence. Gelbard warned that continued opposition to implementing the Dayton Accords would not be tolerated, and any repetition of the events in Brcko would have "the most serious consequences imaginable."[37] Gelbard's tough message was reinforced by a warning from General Clark: Peacekeeping troops in Bosnia would use deadly force, if necessary, to deal with future mob violence and to protect U.S. forces.[38] Clark's statement was made in accordance with guidance received from U.S. Secretary of Defense William Cohen to not "let our troops be forced off the field of battle."[39] On September 3, Defense Department officials announced that an additional eighteen F-16 fighters based in Aviana, Italy, would patrol the skies over Bosnia to deter those who might foment violence or attempt to disrupt the September elections.[40]

On September 2 in Brcko, Farrand, Grange, and Ambassador Jacques Klein, the principal deputy high representative, appeared at a media conference to demonstrate the international community's support for Farrand and the Dayton process. Klein said it was clear that the August 28 riot was "orchestrated from elsewhere." The "conductors," Klein said, were the same leaders who had led the Serbs into "cul-de-sacs" that were not in their interest. He said the international community was evenhanded, but that it would help those who supported democracy and the Dayton process. Farrand echoed Klein's remarks, saying that the August 28 event was part of a deliberate plan to use violence to discredit the international community, particularly SFOR and the IPTF. As evidence that the violence had been orchestrated, Farrand cited the sirens that signaled the start of the riot and the fact that the mobs at every location made the same demands. Farrand said the citizens of Brcko were ashamed of the violence and embarrassed that Serbs were responsible for the disturbance. He said the international community knew who was responsible and would "keep the spotlight of accountability on those authorities."[41] General Grange condemned the local Brcko police for not attempting to control the riot and said that it appeared that the police, in conjunction with the local radio station, had incited it.

---

37. Alison Smale, "Tough and Sharp Words Exchanged," *Stars and Stripes*, August 31, 1997, 1.

38. Lee Hockstader, "U.S. Troops Pull Back from Bosnian Bridge, Stir Debate over Reasons and Results," *Washington Post*, September 4, 1997, A27.

39. Clark, *Waging Modern War*, 87.

40. Hockstader, "U.S. Troops Pull Back."

41. Office of the High Representative, "Press Conference by the Principal Deputy High Representative, Ambassador Jacques Klein, and Deputy High Representative/Supervisor for Brcko, Ambassador Robert Farrand," September 2, 1997.

Grange praised the performance of his soldiers, saying they had shown heroic restraint in the face of "insults and cowardice."[42]

On September 6, U.S. forces withdrew from the Brcko Bridge, believing they could do a better job of providing security for the town by active patrolling rather than guarding fixed positions. While tactically correct, the withdrawal was a political disaster. It created the impression that the Serb mob had achieved its objective of intimidating and driving away the U.S. soldiers. International civilian administrators in Bosnia and the media criticized SFOR for sending a message of weakness by abandoning its position in the face of Serb pressure just before September's municipal elections.[43]

STATUS OF BRCKO

Behind the bold facade of official statements, the Brcko incident left the Clinton administration and U.S. military leaders with a bad case of the jitters. The SFOR decision to help President Plavšić's supporters seize police stations and television transmitters was NATO's boldest move in the nineteen months since the beginning of the peace process. That pro-Karadžić forces could quickly organize a mob assault on American troops in Brcko sent a political message and raised the specter of U.S. casualties, with the attendant possible loss of U.S. congressional and public support. U.S. concerns focused on two principal issues. The first was Brcko.

Before the Bosnian conflict, Brcko was one of Yugoslavia's most prosperous communities. Its location near the Zagreb-Belgrade highway and its port on the Sava River, the largest river port in Bosnia, made it an important trading center. The town and its suburbs covered about a fifth of Brcko municipality. It had a multiethnic population of 41,000 people, 55 percent Muslim, 19 percent Serb, and 7 percent Croat. In April 1992 a Serb militia had occupied Brcko, killing or driving out the non-Serb inhabitants and destroying their homes. Hundreds of ethnic Croats and Muslims were herded into a bus company barn, where they were systematically tortured and executed. Following the ethnic cleansing, the town was inhabited entirely by Serbs.[44]

At Dayton the status of Brcko had not been resolved. Under the General Framework Agreement for Peace in Bosnia and Herzegovina (GFAP)—the Dayton Accords—the division of territory between the Croat-Muslim Federation and the RS made Brcko the geographic linchpin of the peace process. Brcko's location astride the five-kilometer-wide Posavina Corri-

42. Jerry Merideth, "Official Says SFOR Won't Leave," *Stars and Stripes,* August 30, 1997, 5.

43. Hockstader, "U.S. Troops Pull Back."

44. Bosco, "After Genocide."

dor connecting the eastern and western parts of Bosnian Serb territory threatened control over the road, rail, and river routes linking the RS capital of Banja Luka with the Serb hard-liner stronghold of Pale. Its position also gave it control of the north-south lines of communication linking the industrial city of Tuzla in the Bosnian Federation with the river port and bridge over the Sava River to Croatia and the rest of Europe. With all parties making a claim for this strategic location, a compromise was reached. Brcko would remain under the control of Serb authorities and its final status would be determined one year after the signing of the agreement—originally December 1996—by an arbitration tribunal composed of three members: an ethnic Serb, Dr. Vitomir Popovic; an ethnic Muslim, Professor Cazim Sadikovic; and the presiding arbitrator, American lawyer Roberts Owen.[45] The Dayton Accords stated that "the Parties agree to binding arbitration of the disputed portion of the Inter-Entity Boundary Line in the Brcko area indicated on the map attached at the Appendix." In an apparent oversight, the map was omitted. As a result, not only the status of Brcko needed to be determined, but also the extent of the area subject to arbitration.[46]

Throughout the first year after Dayton, the pressure on the arbitration tribunal mounted. The federation's argument was that Brcko should be returned to its original Muslim and Croat inhabitants. The Serbs responded that if Brcko were given to the federation, the RS would be divided and effectively destroyed. Brcko's proximity to the Arizona market, a flourishing free-trade zone located in the Zone of Separation between the RS and the Bosnian Federation, gave it additional postwar prominence. After Dayton, Serb authorities in Pale attempted to reinforce their claim on Brcko by relocating displaced persons to the town. In March 1996 the Serbs conducted a form of ethnic self-cleansing by removing ethnic Serbs from the Sarajevo suburbs before these areas transferred to control of the federation. Some 10,000 Serbs were brought to Brcko to join other Serbs relocated during the conflict.[47] Afterward, two-thirds of Brcko's Serb population was composed of displaced people from other areas. Against this background, the arbitration tribunal met in February 1997, but it was unable to reach a decision. It did, however, call to appoint an international supervisor for Brcko and deploy a UN IPTF contingent to monitor the local Serb police. As the Bosnian members of the arbitration tribunal continued to cancel each other's

---

45. Richard Holbrooke, *To End a War* (New York: Random House, 1998), 308.

46. International Crisis Group, "Brcko Arbitration: Proposal for Peace," ICG Bosnia Report no. 18, Washington, DC, January 20, 1997, 1.

47. Bosco, "After Genocide."

votes, it became clear that the decision rested with Owen and, in a larger sense, with the United States.

As the international supervisor for Brcko, Farrand was directly subordinate to the high representative, the senior civilian official responsible for peace implementation in Bosnia. His mandate was to restore the city's prewar multiethnic character by facilitating the return of former residents. During the conflict Brcko's suburbs had been reduced to bombed-out houses and mine fields. Starting in the summer of 1997, Farrand began the difficult task of rebuilding houses and encouraging the original residents to return. Farrand's actions generated high-level attention from the U.S. government. In June, Secretary of State Madeleine Albright visited Brcko to reopen the bridge over the Sava River. In a warning to the hard-line Serbs who still controlled the town's government, Albright said a price would be paid for the atrocities that had been committed. Brcko was a ward of the international community, but it had an American protector; located in the American sector of Bosnia with its American administrator and American arbitrator, Brcko was seen as an American problem. The Serb mob action in Brcko thus was a direct challenge to the United States.

The second issue of concern to U.S. policymakers was the U.S. military force structure in Bosnia. Designed to intimidate and, if necessary, quickly defeat Serb military forces, the U.S. contingents in the NATO-led Implementation Force (IFOR) and the follow-on SFOR were built around heavy armored divisions, supported by helicopter gunships and airpower. Following IFOR's entry into Bosnia in January 1996, the military tasks assigned in Annex I of the Dayton Accords were quickly accomplished. These tasks included supervising the separation of opposing military forces, cantonment of heavy weapons, monitoring the Zone of Separation between the entities, and assuring a safe and secure environment. To accommodate those who wanted a larger role for NATO, the Dayton Accords included a formula that gave IFOR the authority to assist with civilian implementation, but limited its obligations to the military requirements in the accords. Completion of the assigned military tasks did not lead to a military withdrawal. Instead, NATO was increasingly drawn into assisting with the implementation of the civilian aspects of the peace process.[48]

Under Dayton, the OHR was responsible for civilian implementation. Its authority, however, was limited to offering guidance to the various international organizations, non-governmental organizations (NGOs), and bilateral donors involved in postconflict state building. The OHR could coordinate

---

48. Ivo Daalder, *Getting to Dayton: The Making of America's Bosnia Policy* (Washington, DC: Brookings Institution Press, 2000), 140–150.

but not direct the reconstruction effort. There also was no requirement in the accords for cooperation between NATO and the high representative. NATO resisted pressure to become involved in civilian implementation, particularly police functions. In March 1996, during the transfer of Serbs from the Sarajevo suburbs, NATO troops did not intervene to prevent Serb militants from torching buildings, destroying property, and forcing the evacuation of Serb residents. It was also clearly understood that the primary task for U.S. elements in IFOR was force protection, or the use of all means necessary to avoid casualties. U.S. military forces generally remained within their fortified bases, venturing out only in armored convoys with troops swathed in Kevlar. This policy severely restricted U.S. troops' ability to interact with civilians and to engage in postconflict reconstruction.[49]

In the aftermath of the events of August 28, it was clear that the mob action in Brcko was an asymmetrical response by Serb hard-liners to SFOR's heavy armored forces. Serb leaders knew they could never challenge SFOR militarily. They also knew SFOR soldiers would not harm civilians. The Serbs had observed the progress of the intifada in Israel and noted the success of mob actions against conventional forces. The mob in Brcko was not a spontaneous gathering of people with a complaint; many people subsequently admitted they were paid one hundred deutsche marks to participate. The mob was armed with clubs, stones, and Molotov cocktails that were used to set vehicles on fire. They were highly disciplined and responded to instructions from demonstration organizers. A group of several hundred would mass and intensively attack a small group of soldiers, then fall back, rest, and eat before going back on the offensive in response to new instructions. By attacking in waves over a prolonged period, they wore down the troops and eventually forced them off their positions.[50]

The Brcko incident caught SFOR by surprise. No preplanning had been done to deal with such a challenge, and afterward, it was clear to the new SFOR commander, General Eric K. Shinseki, that the U.S. military had faced an enemy in Brcko that it was ill prepared to fight. Tanks, armored personnel carriers, and helicopter gunships were of little use against hostile mobs of women and children providing cover for club-wielding thugs who threw stones and Molotov cocktails. U.S. military attention focused on the confrontation on the bridge, where American soldiers were pinned down by a hail of rocks and bottles. Regular infantry guarding fixed positions with automatic weapons, fixed bayonets, and machine guns were at a disadvantage against crowds that rampaged at will. Fortunately, the

---

49. Holbrooke, *To End a War*, 216–217.
50. Greer, "The Urban Area during Stability Missions."

soldiers had performed admirably and had not lost their composure under extreme provocation—despite taking casualties—but they had not been ready to confront a violent mob. Unable to challenge the United States with conventional military forces, Serb hard-liners appeared to have found a way to turn American heavy weapons and respect for human rights into liabilities. In pursuit of their goal of obstructing Dayton implementation, they had found a means to embarrass the United States and the international community.[51]

THE U.S. REACTION

In response to the incident in Brcko, the Pentagon's first reaction was to look for a quick fix by using new technology. On September 3, the Pentagon announced that U.S. troops in Bosnia would be equipped with sponge grenades and dye-filled balloons to use against unruly Bosnians. The sponge grenades were 40-mm projectiles fired from grenade launchers that were designed to knock people down but not cause serious injury. The balloons were filled with latex paint and could be thrown by soldiers to mark ringleaders and violent militants for later arrest. Some balloons contained special ink visible only under a black light. According to a Pentagon spokesman, the nonlethal weapons were not intended to turn U.S. troops into international police but to give them a broader range of options.[52]

Simply equipping infantry and armored forces with a range of nonlethal weapons, however, was not the answer. Pentagon officials knew that technology, no matter how imaginative, was no substitute for international security forces with the proper training and equipment to handle civil disorder. Such forces would need to be highly mobile and have effective communications that would enable them to respond quickly to areas threatened by mob violence. They also would have to interact effectively with civilians, especially as they would be dealing with representatives of newly elected municipal governments following the September elections. To avoid exacerbating tensions, these security forces would need to be trained to use the minimum amount of force required to achieve their objectives. They would need experience in dealing with civil disorder, especially demonstrations organized by nationalistic, corrupt, political elites and their allies, the organized criminal enterprises that controlled many Bosnian communities. As such groups were supported by the remnants of former secret security

---

51. Interview with Kauzlarich.
52. Bill Gertz, "U.S. Peace Troops Get Non-Lethal Arms for Use in Bosnia: Commanders Order Sponge Grenades," *Washington Post*, September 3, 1997, A7.

services, international forces would also need to be able to defend themselves against armed groups if required.

Such highly capable forces existed, but not in the U.S. inventory, and not in Bosnia. Constabulary forces—mobile forces with the capacity to perform both police and military functions—were part of the force structure of many U.S. European allies. None had been deployed to Bosnia as part of the NATO military force, but individual gendarmes were serving as unarmed police monitors with the IPTF. Constabulary forces were, however, in short supply. In most European countries, they were assigned civilian police functions in peacetime and were fully engaged with domestic police duties. The challenge facing U.S. officials was to convince European members of NATO of the wisdom and necessity of assigning such forces to Bosnia, where they would face potentially dangerous confrontations. The United Nations Protection Force (UNPROFOR), which served in Bosnia from 1992 to 1995, included seven hundred UN civilian police monitors with significant contingents from European countries. Some of these European officers were taken hostage and used as human shields or otherwise humiliated by all factions.[53] European governments recalled these bitter experiences and did not want them repeated. To convince the Europeans to commit police constabulary units to deal with future mob actions like the incident in Brcko was going to be a hard sell. In the year ahead, NATO would have to decide whether to extend its presence in Bosnia beyond the June 1998 expiration date for SFOR's mandate. This decision depended on whether U.S. troops would remain in Bosnia despite President Clinton's promise that they would be out by the June deadline. It was unlikely European governments would volunteer their police forces for hazardous duty in Bosnia if it appeared the United States was preparing to withdraw.

---

53. Laura Silber and Allan Little, *The Death of Yugoslavia* (London: Penguin Books, 1995), 335–350.

2
Constabulary

I f constabulary forces were the solution to the problems international peacekeepers encountered in Brcko, there remained some obstacles to embracing the concept—first and foremost, finding a proper definition of the term. What exactly is a constabulary? A common definition is that it is a "body of peace officers organized on a military basis,"[1] but the converse is also true. There are constabularies that are military organizations with the characteristics and authority of police forces. Constabulary forces are found in both democratic and authoritarian countries, and the widespread belief that the United States has never had such forces is mistaken.

Among academics, there is a range of opinion on what constitutes a constabulary. Some scholars have sought to define constabulary by the nature of its organizational structure, while others have developed definitions based on the functions or the tasks it performs. In the former group, Erwin A. Schmidl defines constabulary as a force that is "organized along military lines, providing basic law enforcement and safety in a not yet fully stabilized environment. Such a force can provide the nucleus for a professional law enforcement or police force." He points to the Mexican Rurales and the Canadian Mounties as examples.[2] Morris Janowitz, an American sociologist on the military, takes a functional approach: "The military establishment becomes a constabulary force when it is continuously prepared to act, committed to the minimum use of force, and seeks viable international relations rather than victory because it has incorporated a protective military posture."[3] Charles Moskos, Jr.,

1. *Webster's Desk Dictionary*, s.v. "constabulary."

2. Erwin A. Schmidl, "Police Functions in Peace Operations: A Historical Overview," in Robert Oakley, Michael Dziedzic, and Eliot Goldberg, eds., *Policing the New World Disorder* (Washington, DC: National Defense University Press, 1998), 22.

3. Morris Janowitz, *The Professional Soldier: A Social and Political Portrait* (New York: Free Press of Glencoe, 1960), 418.

supports Janowitz's view, noting the emergence of a "constabulary ethic" among peacekeeping troops in Cyprus that was based on "behavioral adherence to the minimum-use-of-force concept." In contrast to regular armed forces, Moskos states, constabularies are concerned with attaining viable political compromises rather than resolving a conflict by force.[4] Other definitions focus on the tasks constabulary forces are expected to perform. Don Snider and Kimberly Field define a constabulary force as "one which provides for public security in a post-conflict area of operation after the combat-heavy units have redeployed and before peacebuilding efforts have succeeded in re-establishing local or federal law enforcement agencies."[5]

The search for a definition of constabulary forces is complicated by the common use of the term *paramilitary* to describe a wide range of armed groups that may resemble constabularies. British journalists first used the term to describe the Nazi-sponsored Brownshirts in the 1930s, but para-militaries are normally nonstate actors, illegitimate, poorly trained, lightly armed, highly fragmented, and politically motivated. The U.S. Defense De-partment defines paramilitary forces as "distinct from the armed forces of a country, but resembling them in organization, equipment, training, or mis-sion."[6] Lumped together as paramilitaries have been such diverse entities as the Yugoslav Interior Ministry's Special Police Units, Haiti's Tontons Ma-coutes, and the Irish Republican Army. The Yugoslav units, which perpe-trated ethnic cleansing in Bosnia, were comparable to mechanized infantry in Western armies. The Tontons Macoutes, which terrorized Haitians dur-ing the regime of François "Papa Doc" Duvalier, were neither military nor police, but had overlapping functions and common membership. The Irish Republican Army was a secretive terrorist organization that affected military dress and opposed British rule in Northern Ireland.[7]

Andrew Scobell and Brad Hammit very broadly define a paramili-tary as any uniformed group, usually armed, that is neither purely military nor police in form and function. Such a group may or may not serve as an agent of the state, perform national security functions, or have a wartime role as an adjunct of the regular armed forces. Alice Hills counters that "it

---

4. Charles Moskos, Jr., *Peace Soldiers: The Sociology of a United Nations Military Force* (Chicago: University of Chicago Press, 1976), 93, 130.

5. Don M. Snider and Kimberly Field, memorandum to the Strategic Studies Institute's Re-search and Publication Board on *A Constabulary Force: Impacts on Force Structure and Culture Project,* U.S. Military Academy, August 11, 2000.

6. Andrew Scobell and Brad Hammitt, "Goons, Gunmen, and Gendarmerie: Toward Reconceptualizing Paramilitary Formations," *Journal of Political and Military Sociology* 26, no. 2 (1998): 213–221.

7. Scobell and Hammitt, "Goons."

is impossible to suggest one definition to contain all so-called paramilitary forces, but it is reasonable to suggest that paramilitary forces are forces whose training, organization, equipment, and control suggest they may be used in support, or in lieu, of regular military forces." Hills warns that attempts to fit constabulary forces under an umbrella definition of paramilitary forces can erroneously link them to organizations that have historically operated outside of a specific mandate and have used coercion or violence to further political agendas.[8]

Robert Oakley, Michael Dziedzic, and Eliot Goldberg identify a specific role for constabulary forces in peace operations. In Dziedzic's conceptual introduction to the volume, "Policing the New World Disorder," international military forces intervening in failed states inevitably encounter an atmosphere of complete disorder brought about by the collapse or defeat of indigenous security forces during the conflict. The military's first responsibility is to restore order and create a stable and secure environment. Military forces are well suited to this task because they can deploy rapidly and employ overwhelming force. The military's role in the initial phase of a peace operation entails separating local armed groups, restricting them to assembly areas, impounding their weapons, and supervising demobilization. While this role is critical, Dziedzic points out that the military is a "blunt instrument" capable only of imposing a rigid form of internal order that normally does not extend to dealing with civil disturbances, acts of revenge, and ordinary crime. Military forces are reluctant to engage in confrontations with civilians and are neither trained nor equipped to control riots, negotiations, or deescalation of conflicts. For this reason, military officers do not seek these duties and are often unwilling to perform them.[9]

Normally, military forces rely on the local police to deal with civilians and problems related to domestic law enforcement. In postconflict environments, however, Dziedzic notes that local police forces are incapable of restoring public order and sometimes participate in the violence or threaten the international intervention force. At the same time, international civilian police forces have proven unable to deploy rapidly and are often precluded from helping to restore internal security, either because of their mandate or because they are unarmed. Dziedzic argues that a "security gap" is created by the absence of a force that can maintain public order and restore the rule of law. Those who oppose peace often take advantage of this gap to engage in politically motivated violence and promote civil unrest.

8. Alice Hills, "International Peace Support Operations and CIVPOL: Should There Be a Permanent Global Gendarmerie?," *International Peacekeeping* 5, no. 3 (Autumn 1998), 35–37.

9. Michael J. Dziedzic, "Introduction," in *Policing the New World Disorder*, 8–13.

While restoring absolute public security is impossible, Dziedzic argues that the security gap can be narrowed if international military forces are more willing to expand their scope of operations and if international constabulary forces are deployed to perform the functions required to restore internal stability. He and his coeditors point out that constabulary forces can restore public order and are better suited for law enforcement and interacting with local police and civilians than are military forces. In Panama in 1990, U.S. military police and military reservists, many of whom were police officers in civilian life, were assigned the task of restoring and maintaining public order. They were teamed with newly trained members of the Panamanian national police to jointly take on responsibility for providing police services and maintaining internal security.

Even after the military has established effective control and international and local civilian police are in place, Dziedzic notes that there is a continuing need for constabulary forces. Between the "outer shell" of security provided by the military and the "inner shell" of security provided by civilian police, courts, and prisons, an "enforcement gap" may arise. Typically this gap relates to the "basic maintenance of law and order or noncompliance with the peace agreement" and involves serious breakdowns in public order as well as challenges from spoilers who want to continue the conflict. Even in mature peace operations, Dziedzic points out, the international community can be acutely challenged because the capabilities of the international military and the international and local police may not overlap. Military forces may have only heavy armor units available, while the police may not have the weapons, equipment, or training to handle major confrontations—as has been the case where international civilian police have been deployed. The experience of international police in peace operations has demonstrated the need for specially trained and equipped constabulary forces to support the police and, if necessary, intervene directly to restore public order.

For the purpose of this study, the term constabulary force refers to armed forces of the state with both military capabilities and police powers. Such forces can serve in either a military or a civilian capacity and operate independently or in cooperation with other military or civilian police forces—as is the case for the constabulary forces of France, Italy, the Netherlands, and Spain. These forces are highly trained, flexible organizations with distinct histories of civilian and military service to their respective governments. They have a clear command structure and operate under specific guidelines laid out in their individual mandates. Their primary functions center on the protection and well-being of their respective countries and citizens and the fulfillment of the interests and international obligations of their governments.

But constabulary forces from France, Italy, the Netherlands, and Spain have also been involved in international efforts to keep the peace.

Existing constabulary forces in democratic countries are trained and tasked with performing police functions such as traffic control, criminal investigations, and public security. They also serve as border guards, customs officers, and riot squads. Beyond the specific functions outlined in their mandates, constabulary forces assist police forces in times of need, by patrolling, providing area security, staffing checkpoints, and intervening directly if events go beyond the competency of civil police.

A second characteristic of constabulary forces is their participation in the activities of the military organizations of their countries. Whether attached to a particular unit in times of war, assisting military planning, or providing military police services, constabulary forces are trained to function as part of the national armed forces in times of war. In many cases, they are trained to operate as mobile light infantry and to perform military police duties such as handling prisoners, directing vehicle traffic, and policing the battlefield.

Third, deployed as members of an international peacekeeping force, constabularies perform both military and police functions and can be assigned in either a military or a civilian capacity. Constabulary units served with NATO military forces in Bosnia, in both NATO military and UN civilian police forces in Kosovo, and as UN civilian police in East Timor. The combined training and experience of these units make them ideal for service in complex contingency operations, where flexibility and adaptability are critical requirements.

CONSTABULARY FORCES IN EUROPE

The French Gendarmerie

Most of the world's constabulary forces are modeled on France's Gendarmerie Nationale. This national police force is military in character and answers to the ministry of defense. The Gendarmerie is divided into two subdivisions: the Departmental Gendarmerie (Gendarmerie Départementale) and the Mobile Gendarmerie (Gendarmerie Mobile).[10] Additionally, there are special formations with about 4,500 personnel, including the Republican Guard, and squads to protect commercial aviation. The Departmental Gendarmerie is responsible for law enforcement in towns with fewer than 10,000 inhabitants and in rural areas, and for fulfilling the duties of a military police. Special units of the Departmental Gendarmerie handle

10. See "La Gendarmerie," Gendarmerie Nationale website, available at http://www.defense.gouv.fr/gendarmerie/ (accessed October 16, 2012).

investigations for the judicial police, undertake surveillance duties, prevent and research traffic law violations, and protect mountain regions and trails. The Mobile Gendarmerie's personnel constitute a reserve force that can be used to maintain public order. It is sent into action on the orders of the municipal authorities of any of France's territorial-administrative départements to deal with emergencies or serious civil disturbances.[11] Recruits must have completed military service and meet other standards. Additionally, they must complete basic and specialized training courses. Officer candidates are usually recruited from the army officer corps; they also must complete a training course at the Gendarmerie officers' school.

In peacetime, much of the Gendarmerie is engaged in routine domestic police work. Some 53 percent of its missions involved administrative policing, traffic control, and public security.[12] Specialized Maritime Gendarmerie and Air Transport Gendarmerie units are responsible for the security of installations and for investigating accidents.[13] An additional 35 percent of the organization's work was in judicial investigation. In times of war, the Gendarmerie comes under the Ministry of Defense and is considered part of the French army. Its duties include protection of domestic territory and military police functions.

The Italian Carabinieri

Formed in 1814 as part of the Army of the States of Savoy, the Carabinieri's authority was extended to all of Italy after reunification in 1861. The Carabinieri are an arm of the Italian armed forces and report to the Ministry of Defense in matters of military pertinence. In matters of domestic public order, including crime and natural disasters, they are subordinate to the Ministry of the Interior. Specialized units answer to other government ministries, including Health, Culture, Labor, Agriculture, and Foreign Affairs.

The Carabinieri are both military police and an internal security force. Duties range from criminal investigation to riot control to border patrol, often in tandem with regular army units. Like the Gendarmerie, the Carabinieri are organized along military lines, composed of 5 divisions, 18 regional commands (*comandi di regione*), 102 provincial commands (*comandi provinciali*), 11 groups (*gruppi*), 526 companies (*compagnie*), and 4,663 stations (*stazioni*); the divisions have interregional competence.[14]

---

11. John Andrade, *World Police and Paramilitary Forces* (New York: Stockton Press, 1985), 67–71.

12. "Les missions," Gendarmerie Nationale website.

13. "Les différentes composantes de la gendarmeries," Gendarmerie Nationale website.

14. "I Reparti," Carabinieri website, available at www.carabinieri.it/ (accessed October 17, 2012).

Members are recruited mainly from military personnel leaving the service, so most of the Carabinieri have military experience. Some lower rank-ing positions may be filled with personnel with no military experience on a contract basis, but candidates for officer and noncommissioned officer (NCO) positions are always military veterans. Recruits complete a nine-month course at one of the Carabinieri academies and then serve nine months in a training unit. NCO and officer candidates receive additional training at specialized schools.[15]

The Netherlands' Royal Marechaussee

The Royal Constabulary (Marechaussee) is one of three police forces in the Netherlands. It was first established in 1814 by King Wilhelm I as a gendar-merie force with the dual task of maintaining law and order and monitoring borders and highways. During World War I and World War II, the compo-sition and status of the Marechaussee changed frequently, particularly under the orders of occupying forces. After liberation in 1945, the Marechaussee once again returned to its original mandate and duties.[16]

A military police corps, the Marechaussee is subordinate to the Minis-try of Defense, but other ministries are closely involved with its duties. Its personnel are assigned to the ministry of defense and the navy, army, and air force as a police force. The riot squad unit assists the state police (*Rijkspolitie*) and the municipal police (*Gemeentepolitie*).[17] The Marechaussee command is divided into districts, one for each of the Dutch provinces. Each district commands a number of brigades. More important municipalities, such as Amsterdam, and the international airport are assigned a brigade.[18]

The Marechaussee training center in Apeldoorn provides instruction for all ranks from sergeants to officers. Personnel receive general military training and are initially offered a short-term contract of service. Upon completion of the contract, candidates are reevaluated and potentially offered a fixed-term or indefinite contract of service with the corps. Officers appointed to the Marechaussee are required to have served at least three to four years in the military before entering the force. Officers can choose to continue their specialization training in law or military studies at the university level. All attendees at the training center receive instruction on security and service

15. Andrade, *World Police*, 101–103.

16. See the English-language brochure on the Marechaussee published by the Netherlands Ministry of Defense, *The Royal Marechaussee* (Amsterdam: Ministry of Defense, January 1977), 3–4.

17. *The Royal Marechaussee*, 9–13.

18. Andrade, *World Police*, 124–143.

procedures, ethical issues surrounding the use of force, social development, social skills, and marksmanship. NCOs who are offered fixed-term contracts also undergo extensive legal and managerial training.[19]

The Spanish Guardia Civil

One of three main police forces in Spain, the Guardia Civil was formed in 1940 from a merger of the original Guardia Civil and the Carabineros. The Guardia Civil is an organ of the Ministry of Internal Affairs and is directly under the State Security Secretariat. It is a constabulary force with both civilian and military capabilities. In times of war, it comes under the authority of the Ministry of Defense.[20] The Guardia is organized into seventeen zones that correspond with Spain's provincial boundaries. Each zone is policed by mobile patrols, typically consisting of three or more officers, with a separate traffic division responsible for patrolling main roads. Other units include four companies of the Rural Antiterrorist Group, stationed in the Basque country and Navarre to handle extremist activities by Basque separatists; helicopter and special intervention units can supplement this force, if necessary. Mountain units are stationed along the Pyrenees frontier to deter smugglers and terrorists, as well as to provide routine police and rescue services.[21]

Recruitment, training, and deployment are matters of joint responsibility for the two ministries. The sharing arrangement came as a result of the 1986 Organic Law on the Security Corps and Forces, passed to unify different elements of the national police corps and introduce a common ethics code for police practices. Although the Guardia Civil remained separate from the national police corps, the new law provided for the appointment of the first civilian director-general of the force.[22] Before 1986, the director-general was always an army lieutenant general.[23]

The Guardia Civil has a long tradition of family service, and the majority of its recruits are the sons of former or current guardsmen. The 1986 reform laws stipulated that the two-year compulsory military service requirement for men could be performed in the Guardia instead of the army. Recruits entering at the age of sixteen or seventeen undergo a two-year course at one

---

19. *The Royal Marechaussee,* 17–19.

20. Information on Spain's Guardia Civil can be found on the Federation of American Scientists' Intelligence Resource Program website of world intelligence and security agencies, available at http://www.fas.org/irp (accessed November 26, 2012).

21. Federation of American Scientists.

22. Ibid.

23. Andrade, *World Police,* 142–143.

of the Guardia's training colleges prior to service. Entrants that have served the required two-year period in the army can join the force after an eleven-month training course at one of the colleges. After fourteen years of service, guardsmen can be promoted to officer rank. Direct commissions are possible for graduates of the General Military Academy in Zaragoza. Cadets enter the Guardia as lieutenants following an additional three years of training at the Special Academy of the Civil Guard at Aranjuez.[24]

HISTORY OF CONSTABULARY FORCES IN THE UNITED STATES

Contrary to popular opinion, constabulary forces have a history in the United States. They have formal roots in the Second Amendment of the U.S. Constitution, which states: "a well regulated Militia, being necessary to the security of a free State, the right of the people to keep and bear Arms, shall not be infringed." This amendment ensured that the states would have forces to uphold laws and repel invasion.[25]

The Texas Rangers

The best-known historical example of a U.S. constabulary force is the Texas Rangers. During their storied past, the Rangers served as a volunteer frontier defense force, a military unit within the Confederate army during the Civil War, and as a Texas state constabulary with responsibilities for border control, frontier defense, and law enforcement. The origin of the Texas Rangers is found in the tradition of frontier self-defense forces organized in the original American colonies. Local militias, called rangers, protected the frontiers of Virginia, the Carolinas, and Georgia.[26] Beginning in the 1820s, when Texas was under Spanish rule, English-speaking settlers from the southern United States requested permission from the Spanish authorities to form militias to preserve local order. The Spanish governor, Colonel José Félix Trespalacios, responded by organizing a volunteer force based on the Spanish militia system that had been transplanted to Mexico. The earliest defenders of Texas were a "hybrid of Hispanic-Mexican traditions" with the Anglo-Saxon concepts brought to Texas from the United States.[27]

---

24. Federation of American Scientists.

25. William Rosenau, "Peace Operations, Emergency Law Enforcement, and Constabulary Forces," in Antonia Chayes and George T. Raach, eds., *Peace Operations: Developing an American Strategy* (Washington, DC: National Defense University Press, 1995).

26. Charles M. Robinson III, *The Men Who Wear the Star: The Story of the Texas Rangers* (New York: Random House, 2000), 7.

27. Robinson, *Men Who Wear the Star*, 14.

Stephen F. Austin, considered the father of Texas, first referred to the citizen militias as rangers in 1823 "because their duties compelled them to 'range' over the entire territory of Texas." The Rangers were citizen-soldiers who assembled when necessary and returned to their homes when no longer needed. Their primary role was to protect frontier settlers against attacks by Native American tribes.[28] In 1835, at the outbreak of the Texas war for independence, the permanent council of the new Texas Republic created a corps of Rangers with three companies, each with fifty-six men. The Texans' principal adversary was the Mexican army, led by General Antonio López de Santa Anna. The conflict was, however, a two-front war, which also involved fighting against Native American tribes along Texas's northwestern frontier. Ranger companies were assigned the latter mission, while the Texas militia faced the Mexicans. A Ranger company, however, did manage to reach the besieged Alamo before the famous battle, and its members died with the other defenders.[29]

After winning freedom from Mexico, Texas became the twenty-eighth U.S. state in 1845. In 1846 the United States declared war on Mexico. Texas Ranger companies were mustered into the U.S. Army and served as scouts. This situation was repeated when Texas seceded from the Union and joined the Confederacy during the American Civil War. A Ranger regiment was formed as part of the Confederate army to protect frontier settlements against marauding Plains tribes and Mexican bandits, while thousands of individual Texans went east to join regular military units.[30] Little fighting related to the Civil War took place on Texas soil, but there were serious clashes with various Native American tribes. During the conflict, the western edge of the frontier retreated nearly 150 miles as outlying settlements were attacked and survivors moved back to more established communities for protection. In the words of one Texan, "It looked as if all the Indians on the Plains had found out there was a good place in Texas for their business and had gathered there."[31]

After the Civil War, the full force of Reconstruction fell on Texas. The state was left in economic and social chaos. Conditions were not unlike those in contemporary failed states that have experienced civil war resulting from political, ethnic, or religious conflicts. The justice system in post–Civil War Texas was in shambles. Most counties did not have the money

---

28. Texas Department of Public Safety, "Historical Development," available at http://www.txdps.state.tx.us/TexasRangers/HistoricalDevelopment.htm (accessed November 26, 2012).

29. Robinson, *Men Who Wear the Star*, 31–38.

30. Texas Department of Public Safety, "Historical Development."

31. Robinson, *Men Who Wear the Star*, 159.

for sheriff's deputies, courthouses, or jails. The security at the jails that did exist was so flimsy that prisoners could simply walk out. Judges rarely leveled fines because the defendants usually could not afford to pay them, and juries often could not be formed because the few qualified males had taken the loyalty oath required of former Confederate citizens. In some areas, outlaws made up such a large percentage of the population that they could operate with impunity.[32] Frontier communities and citizens' groups repeatedly called upon the Radical Republican governor, Edmund Davis, to raise Ranger companies for their defense against Native American tribes and bandits. On September 21, 1866, the Texas legislature passed the first law that explicitly referred to Texas Rangers, but the frontier defense force authorized in the bill was never funded.[33] For the next ten years, the Texas Rangers ceased to exist; law enforcement was the responsibility of a highly politicized and widely hated Texas State Police Force, which was eventually disbanded. This force did, however, demonstrate the value of a "permanent constabulary."[34]

In April 1874 the state legislature created the Frontier Battalion, or Texas Rangers, as a "permanent, professional, statewide gendarmerie," ending the era of the citizen ranger. In addition to their traditional duties of fighting Native American tribes and patrolling the Mexican border, the Rangers would have civil police powers. In the words of an early historian, "this did not lessen their duties as soldiers, but greatly widened their field of usefulness and brought them into closer touch with law-abiding people by giving them authority to act as peace officers statewide." Although Ranger companies spent much of the early 1870s fighting Apaches on the state's western borders, civil police authority was also needed, as the closing of the frontier coincided with an outbreak of lawlessness from highwaymen, rustlers, and bank robbers: "When a Ranger was going to meet an outside enemy, for example, the Indians or the Mexicans, he was very close to being a soldier; however, when he had to turn to the enemies within his own society—outlaws, train robbers, and highwaymen, he was a detective and policeman."[35] In the aftermath of the bitter Civil War, the Rangers also had to deal with revenge killings, blood feuds, and range wars, which were fought between rival bands and resulted in hundreds of casualties. One classic feud

---

32. Robinson, *Men Who Wear the Star,* 155.

33. An Act to Provide for the Protection of the Frontier of the State of Texas, September 21, 1866, Texas Legislature, General Laws of the State of Texas—1866, 10–12, cited in Robinson, *Men Who Wear the Star,* 157.

34. Texas Department of Public Safety, "Historical Development."

35. Robinson, *Men Who Wear the Star,* 168.

erupted in 1875 between German cattle ranchers who had supported the Union and Anglo-Saxon farmers who had fought with the Confederacy.

During the 1870s, the Texas Rangers were involved in some shootouts with the most celebrated outlaws in the history of the Old West. Ranger John B. Armstrong confronted John Wesley Hardin, an outlaw who reputedly had killed thirty-one men, and three companions on a train. When the smoke from Armstrong's Colt .45 Peacemaker cleared, Hardin had been knocked unconscious, one of the desperadoes was dead, and the other two were in custody. This incident helped establish the Rangers' reputation for personal bravery in the face of daunting odds. A similar fate befell notorious train robber Sam Bass, who was wounded and later died after his gang engaged in a shootout with four Rangers. The Rangers' legendary prowess in surmounting overwhelming odds was summed up in the oft-used phrase, "One riot, One Ranger."[36]

Between 1874 and the early part of the twentieth century, the mythology of the Texas Rangers grew in dime novels and pulp magazines. During the Woodrow Wilson administration, the Rangers' reputation received a boost when they were drawn into the U.S. campaign against the Mexican revolutionary Francisco "Pancho" Villa in 1916. Wilson federalized the National Guard, turning the Big Bend area of Rio Grande river country into a virtual war zone. The governor of Texas, James Edward Ferguson, created special units of the Texas Rangers to defend the border. After Villa conducted raids into the United States, Ranger units patrolled the Rio Grande, ensuring that the Mexican combatants stayed on their side.[37]

At the end of the border disturbances in 1917, the Rangers became concerned with routine law enforcement, and during the 1920s and 1930s, the popular legend of the Texas Rangers virtually replaced the reality. The fictional portrayal of the Rangers took on added dimensions through novels, mass marketing, and the new medium of radio. On January 30, 1933, the "most famous Texas Ranger of all"—the Lone Ranger—made his debut on station WXYZ in Detroit. According to the fictional story line, a young Texas Ranger was the sole survivor of an ambush of his Ranger company by outlaws. Nursed back to health by his "faithful Indian companion," Tonto, he became the Lone Ranger, wearing a black mask to conceal his identity. The Lone Ranger rode his white horse, Silver, through decades of radio shows, television programs, and motion pictures.[38] The theme of all of the Lone Ranger episodes was the same: Someone was in trouble, and the Masked Rider of the Plains came to the rescue.

36. Texas Department of Public Safety, "Historical Development."

37. Robinson, *Men Who Wear the Star*, 273.

38. Ibid, 285.

U.S. EXPERIENCE WITH CONSTABULARY FORCES ABROAD

The U.S. experience with constabulary forces in foreign interventions dates from the era of gunboat diplomacy at the turn of the twentieth century. U.S. Marines occupied several Caribbean and Central American countries to protect U.S. investments, enforce internal stability, and foreclose the possibility of foreign encroachments in a region seen as vital to U.S. security. U.S. military authorities sought to restore internal stability by creating native constabularies with U.S. Marine officers to shore up local regimes and safeguard American interests. The first of these constabularies, the Cuban Rural Guard, was created in 1898. Within the next two decades, the United States established the Policia Nacional in Panama (1904), the Guardia Nacional de Nicaragua in Nicaragua (1912), the Garde d'Haiti in Haiti (1915), and the Guardia Nacional Dominicana in the Dominican Republic (1916), following military interventions.[39] These forces were military in organization but were vested with police powers and performed police functions. In every case except Cuba, the indigenous constabularies evolved into antidemocratic armies, providing a vehicle for local dictators to gain power.

Cuba

In 1898, immediately after the Spanish-American War, the U.S. army's occupation force of 45,000 soldiers was inadequate to both conduct military patrols and handle local law enforcement. Maintaining internal stability in Cuba was particularly challenging given the breakdown in public order, environmental and health threats to U.S. soldiers, and demands from Congress and the public to bring the troops home after the U.S. victory. In time, this issue took on additional importance as the United States faced a growing insurgency in the Philippines. After the Spanish surrendered in Manila, indigenous rebel groups refused to accept the U.S. occupation and continued their fight for independence. With nearly 30,000 former members of the Cuban Liberation Army unemployed, the risk of a similar uprising in Cuba was too great to ignore.[40]

The U.S. military governor of Santiago Province, Brigadier General Leonard Wood, formed a Cuban rural constabulary to restore public order in the chaotic region that had been the principal battlefield of the war. The force, modeled on Spain's Guardia Civil, was led by U.S. officers and

---

39. Ethan Nadelmann, *Cops across Borders: The Internationalization of U.S. Criminal Law Enforcement* (University Park: Pennsylvania State University Press, 1993), 111–112.

40. Ivan Musicant, *The Banana Wars: A History of United States Military Intervention in Latin America from the Spanish-American War to the Invasion of Panama* (New York: Macmillan, 1990), 46.

numbered 1,600 constables. It was dressed and equipped to resemble the U.S. cavalry, but its duties ranged from suppressing banditry to executing court orders and investigating crimes, accidents, and arson. In 1899 General Wood became the military governor of Cuba, and in April 1901 the constabulary formally became the Cuban Rural Guard. Under close U.S. supervision, the Rural Guard became, for a time, the most important police force in Cuba.[41]

The War Department liked Wood's experiment because it enabled the Wilson administration to respond to public and congressional pressure to bring home U.S. forces who were in danger from tropical diseases and armed brigands. The Cuban Rural Guard initially was so successful that Secretary of War Russell Alger recommended forming a similar constabulary "sworn in the service of the United States for police duty" for Puerto Rico and the Philippines. His successor, Elihu Root, also endorsed the idea, noting that creating such a force would absorb potential bandits, "educating them into Americans and making an effective fighting force."[42]

Panama

In November 1903 a group of Panamanian revolutionaries successfully rose up against the Colombian government with the assistance of U.S. naval and marine forces, who prevented the Colombians from suppressing the insurrection. On November 6, President Theodore Roosevelt recognized the new Republic of Panama. On November 18, 1904, Secretary of State John Hay and Panama's new ambassador to the United States signed the Hay–Bunau-Varilla Treaty, granting to the United States "in perpetuity the use, occupation, and control of a zone of land . . . for the construction, maintenance, operation, sanitation, and protection" of a canal that would be constructed by the United States linking the Atlantic and Pacific Oceans. Panama became a de facto protectorate of the United States through other treaty provisions that guaranteed Panamanian independence in return for the U.S. right to intervene in Panama's domestic affairs.[43]

In 1904 the small Panamanian army was disbanded at the request of the U.S. diplomatic mission and replaced by a constabulary force with police powers. The new Corps of National Police was composed of seven hundred Panamanians with Americans in charge. For the next forty-nine years the National Police, which increased in strength to about one thousand men, was the country's only armed force. Panama did not need a national army

---

41. Allan Millett, "The Rise and Fall of the Cuban Rural Guard," *The Americas* (October 1972), 191–194.

42. Millett, "Rise and Fall of the Cuban Rural Guard."

43. Musicant, *Banana Wars*, 132–136.

because the United States guaranteed its independence. U.S. leadership of the police was intended to impart democratic ideals to and ensure American control of Panamanian affairs, an arrangement that would also result in substantial savings compared to the cost of stationing U.S. troops in Panama. The force received extensive U.S. material assistance and training, increasing its influence. The United States hoped that the presence of a professional constabulary would help shape Panamanian political opinion in favor of continued U.S. presence in the Canal Zone. Unfortunately, the police's monopoly of armed force within the country made it an ideal vehicle for a commander with political ambitions and a disregard for democratic principles.[44]

By 1948 the National Police and its commander, José Antonio Remón, could install and remove presidents at will. In 1953 Remon transformed the police into a military force with a new name, the National Guard. In the 1970s President Jimmy Carter negotiated the full transfer of the Panama Canal and the Canal Zone to Panama beginning in the year 2000. The negotiations succeeded in large part because of the cooperation of the head of the National Guard, Panamanian strongman General Omar Torrijos. In 1983 a new law created the Panama Defense Force (PDF) as the successor to the National Guard. Critics of the law claimed it "implied the militarization of national life, converted Panama into a police state, made the members of the armed forces privileged citizens, and gave the force commander authoritarian and totalitarian power." Five years later the PDF and its new commander, General Manuel Noriega Moreno, were targets of a U.S. military invasion of Panama, Operation Just Cause.[45]

Nicaragua

U.S. Marines occupied Nicaragua from 1912 to 1933. Until 1925, internal order was assured by the presence of a one-hundred-member Marine guard at the U.S. legation in Managua. In 1925, public complaints about the Marines' arrogant and abusive behavior led the State Department to submit a detailed plan to the Nicaraguan government for establishing a U.S.-trained constabulary, the Guardia Nacional, with U.S. Marine officers and Nicaraguan personnel.[46] Under the plan, the force eventually was to replace Nicaragua's existing national police, navy, and army. The force would be divided

44. Robert Harding, *Military Foundations of Panamanian Politics* (New Brunswick, NJ: Transaction Publishers, 2001), 29–31.

45. Sandra Meditz and Dennis Hanratty, eds., *Panama: A Country Study* (Washington, DC: Federal Research Division, 1989), 22, 28, 34, 224.

46. Thomas Walker, *Nicaragua without Illusions: Regime Transition and Structural Adjustment in the 1990s* (Wilmington, DE: Scholarly Resources, 1997), 3.

into a constabulary proper and a training branch, with U.S. officers holding the primary positions in both parts. To head the force, the State Department appointed Marine Major Calvin Carter, who had served in the Philippine constabulary.[47]

Initial efforts to organize the Guardia were overtaken by the country's rapid descent into civil war. In 1927, U.S. Marines intervened in force to end the conflict. President Calvin Coolidge sent former secretary of war Henry Stimson to Nicaragua to dictate the peace. Stimson's terms included a ceasefire and general amnesty, inclusion of the opposition Liberal Party in President Adolfo Diaz's cabinet, general disarmament, and creation of a new Guardia, under the command of U.S. Marine officers, accompanied by a drawdown of U.S. military forces. When the rebel commander, General José Maria Moncada, and his subordinates presented Stimson with a signed agreement to his terms, one rebel leader refused to go along. His name was Augusto César Sandino, and his followers became known as Sandinistas.[48]

To implement Stimson's proposal, President Diaz issued an emergency decree on July 30, 1927, authorizing a new Guardia, with U.S. Marine Lieutenant Colonel Elias Beadle—promoted to the Nicaraguan rank of brigadier general—as its commanding officer. An initial complement of 93 officers and 1,136 men was recruited, but the force eventually grew to 2,500. The new constabulary would take over "police functions, control the movement of arms, and manage all buildings and material connected with such functions." Technically the Guardia reported to the president of Nicaragua, but its U.S. officers were responsible for recruitment, training, promotion, discipline, and operations. The United States insisted that the Guardia be the country's sole security force under centralized authority, resisting local demands to create a municipal police force in Managua until 1931, when such a force was authorized as an integral part of the Guardia. Beadle prioritized indoctrinating the U.S. norms of political neutrality and national patriotism in new recruits. The Guardia's first assignments were disarming rival factions and providing security for presidential elections in 1928 and congressional elections in 1930. In both elections, the Guardia performed with notable impartiality.[49]

The Guardia's primary preoccupation, however, was the threat posed by Sandino's growing insurgency. By the fall of 1932 there was almost continuous fighting in all parts of the country. The Sandinistas' rebellion marked the

---

47. Musicant, *Banana Wars*, 287.

48. Musicant, *Banana Wars*, 298.

49. Marvin Goldwert, *The Constabulary in the Dominican Republic and Nicaragua: Progeny and Legacy of United States Intervention* (Gainesville: University of Florida Press, 1962), 32–36.

first time U.S. Marines, supported by local forces, encountered a national liberation movement led by a modern and charismatic leader with an international reputation.[50] The Marines and the Guardia fought bravely and won most of their battles, but Sandino embodied an appeal to nationalism that could not be defeated militarily. The Sandinista cause received strong support from the U.S. left and broad support from governments in Latin America. Fundraisers were held in New York and Washington, where police arrested hundreds of pro-Sandino demonstrators.

Mired in the Great Depression, President Herbert Hoover made U.S. withdrawal from Nicaragua a priority. On November 6 a Liberal, Dr. Juan Sacasa, was elected president there. He appointed a former provincial governor, Anastasio Somoza, head of the Guardia, which had assumed full responsibility for the war against Sandino. On January 1, 1933, the day of Sacasa's inauguration, U.S. forces completed their withdrawal. The Marines had suffered 135 killed and 66 wounded in fighting against Sandinistas. President Sacasa negotiated a truce with Sandino, who joined him for dinner at the presidential palace on February 21, 1934. After dinner, Sandino was kidnapped on Somoza's orders and killed by a Guardia firing squad.[51] In 1936, Somoza staged a coup d'état, establishing a family dictatorship that ruled Nicaragua until a new generation of Sandinistas overthrew it in 1979. By then the Guardia had become a "Mafia in uniform" that controlled prostitution and gambling, engaged in smuggling, ran protection rackets, took bribes and kickbacks, and was thoroughly hated by all Nicaraguans.[52]

Dominican Republic

By 1916 the Dominican Republic had established a tradition of politics through revolt and military rule. Civil war had replaced elections as the mechanism to transfer power from one member of the country's landowning, military elite to another. Faced with this continuous instability, U.S. secretary of state William Jennings Bryan proposed that the United States assist in organizing a nonpartisan constabulary to maintain public order. Dominican president Juan Isidro Jiménez Pereyra resisted this suggestion until a major insurrection against his government prompted the landing of U.S. Marines. On November 29, 1916, Rear Admiral H. S. Knapp issued a proclamation declaring the Dominican Republic subject to U.S. military administration. In Nicaragua, the U.S. intervention had limited objectives, and national

50. Goldwert, *Constabulary*, 340–361.

51. Ibid., 42–47.

52. Walker, *Nicaragua without Illusions*, 4–5.

institutions such as the presidency, congress, and courts continued to function. In the Dominican Republic, the United States established a virtual dictatorship with U.S. military officers in charge of the country's institutions. Admiral Knapp became military governor and ruled by decree.[53]

The primary result of the U.S. military intervention was the replacement of the traditional warring militias with a modern, unified constabulary, the Guardia Nacional Dominicana. The Guardia was to be commanded by U.S. Marines until local officers could be trained to replace them.[54] But the intervention alienated the Dominican upper class, which refused to serve as officers in the constabulary. Since the United States could not attract educated Dominicans to take positions of command, these senior positions went by default to members of the lower classes and opportunists who saw Guardia service as the road to social and political advancement. The Guardia's enlisted ranks were also drawn largely from the illiterate lower strata of society, including former criminals and men of questionable character. Dominicans despised and considered traitors those who cooperated with the Americans by joining the Guardia. When the United States entered World War I, there was also a problem providing competent U.S. military officers. Not surprisingly, the constabulary developed a reputation for uncivil and abusive behavior.[55]

With an initial strength of fewer than one thousand officers and enlisted men, the Guardia's first task was to pacify the northern and eastern provinces, a rural area with a long tradition of banditry. In 1922 Brigadier General Harry Lee assumed command of the Marine brigade in the Dominican Republic. Lee organized a special Guardia force of Marine officers and enlisted men that had suffered at the hands of the bandits and wanted revenge. In cooperation with the Marine brigade and with the assistance of these special constabulary units, the Guardia pacified the region at a heavy cost to local civilians. The Guardia's focus then shifted to the south, and its mission changed from military duties to policing. An academy was also founded to improve the quality of the local officers.[56]

Among those who took advantage of the possibility for advancement in the Guardia was a small-town, petty criminal named Rafael Leónidas Trujillo Molina. Trujillo graduated from the military academy and in five years rose to the highest echelons of the constabulary. On June 14, 1921, the

---

53. Goldwert, *Constabulary*, 5–7.

54. Martha Huggins, *Political Policing: The United States and Latin America* (Durham, NC: Duke University Press, 1998), 27.

55. Musicant, *Banana Wars*, 235–237, 274–275.

56. Musicant, *Banana Wars*, 275–284.

U.S. government issued a proclamation to withdraw its forces and dispatch a U.S. military mission to the Dominican Republic to maintain the Guardia's political neutrality. The Dominicans resisted this plan, but the constabulary was transferred to civilian control and its title changed to the Dominican National Police. This change was in keeping with the U.S. conception of the future function of the force. A subsequent U.S. decree aimed at ensuring the force's political neutrality by transferring authority for appointments and promotions from the president to the police commander. This effort backfired. Following the U.S. military withdrawal, Trujillo became commander of the National Police and used his authority over appointments to turn the force into his private army. In 1928 Trujillo was appointed chief of staff of the renamed National Army. In May 1930 an election was held in which Trujillo ran unopposed and became president, beginning the longest period of dictatorial rule in the history of the Dominican Republic.[57]

Haiti

On July 28, 1915, U.S. Marines landed in Port-au-Prince to restore order after a mob broke into the French legation, seized Haitian president Jean Vilbrun Guillaume Sam, tore his body to pieces, and ran through the streets carrying the parts. The Marines departed on August 15, 1934, following a "cordial and dignified ceremony" at which a crowd of ten thousand Haitians applauded the lowering of the American flag.[58] In the intervening nineteen years, Marine Corps officers served as Haiti's effective chief executive, commanded its security forces, disbanded its parliament, managed its elections, ran its civil administration and judiciary, developed its transportation, communication, and education systems, controlled its media, and conducted its international relations. Authority for these actions rested on the presence of a Marine brigade and the U.S. Marine-led Haitian constabulary, the Garde d'Haiti, which repeatedly crushed internal dissent.[59] In 1925 a visiting delegation of the Women's International League for Peace and Freedom concluded that Haiti's problems did not result from "individual instances of misused power, but in the fundamental fact of the armed occupation of the country."[60]

A major goal of the U.S. occupation was to develop an indigenous security force that would end Haiti's history of repeated military insurrections. The

---

57. Goldwert, *Constabulary*, 15–21.
58. Hans Schmidt, *The United States Occupation of Haiti, 1915–1934* (New Brunswick, NJ: Rutgers University Press, 1995), 230.
59. Schmidt, *United States Occupation of Haiti*.
60. Emily Balch, *Occupied Haiti* (New York: Writers Publishing, 1927), vii.

history of the Haitian police constabulary is divided into three stages that roughly coincided with outbreaks of rebellion against the U.S. occupation. Haitian dissatisfaction grew out of the revival of a corvée law permitting the use of forced labor in road construction. The Garde d'Haiti forced peasants to report to work sites and to donate their labor. This road-building program led to a dramatic increase in anti-Americanism and generated a guerrilla resistance movement that engaged in periodic insurrections. In 1915 a Haitian constabulary was established with Marine Corps officers to perform police duties. From 1922 to 1928, with the consolidation of authority in the hands of a U.S. Marine general who served as high commissioner, the constabulary became both a military and a police force. From 1928 to 1934, following the Haitianization of the officer corps, the Garde became a military force, but continued to perform police functions, particularly in Port-au-Prince.[61]

The Marines divided Haiti into four military departments, with regional headquarters linked to a central command in the capital by a network of newly built roads and a telegraph system. This created a hierarchical military organization for the country, to which the Marines added an effective system for intelligence collection and a rural police force. In 1925 the Marines appointed chefs de section aided by gardes champêtres, who were provided with "blue denim uniforms and rifles and ammunition," to maintain order in the countryside.[62] The Marine-led Garde d'Haiti created a model in which U.S. military officers provided guidance to Haitian political leaders. When the Americans left, Haitian military officers continued their dominance over civil authorities.[63] The Garde evolved into the Forces Armées d'Haiti and the gardes champêtres into the attachés that were the primary targets of Operation Uphold Democracy, the U.S.-led multinational force intervention in Haiti in 1994.

POST–WORLD WAR II EXPERIENCE

The U.S. Constabulary in Germany

The U.S. Army has performed constabulary functions throughout most of its history, and on several occasions it has organized forces that it formally characterized as constabularies. In the very early years of its history, the army was frequently called upon to enforce the authority of the new central government. As the need to protect the federal government's authority became

---

61. Michel Laguerre, *The Military and Society in Haiti* (Knoxville: University of Tennessee Press, 1993), 63.

62. Balch, *Occupied Haiti*, 130.

63. Laguerre, *Military and Society*, 79–80.

paramount during the Civil War, the army's internal policing activity increased to dealing with strikes and other manifestations of civil unrest. Following the Civil War, the army protected settlements and was often the only source of law and order on the U.S. frontier. In the opening decades of the twentieth century, the army was called out on numerous occasions to control large-scale civil disturbances. According to the U.S Army's chief historian, General John S. Brown, the army's most successful effort to create a constabulary force was in the Philippines from 1902 to 1935. The army's largest effort occurred immediately after World War II, when several constabulary regiments were formed to police the U.S. zone of occupation in Germany.[64]

At the end of World War II in Europe, the United States had to provide a permanent occupation force in Germany at the same time it was redeploying forces to the Pacific and demobilizing excess forces on the continent. When Japan surrendered four months later, redeployment ended, and general demobilization began in earnest. The wartime Allies divided Germany into zones with an occupying power responsible in each zone for civil administration, including law enforcement. Germany had no government. Its economy and infrastructure were in ruins. People were hungry. The country was spotted with camps for displaced persons and refugees. Amid the deprivation and disorder, the U.S. Army began considering plans for the most efficient use of the relatively small forces that would be available, given the public demand to return U.S. troops to the United States. In 1945 General George C. Marshall asked General Dwight D. Eisenhower to comment on a plan of occupation for Japan and Korea that envisioned a military police organization composed of local personnel with U.S. officers. Eisenhower thought the plan could also be applied in Europe, but it required modification: The organization should be composed entirely of U.S. military personnel. He believed the "police-type method of occupation offered the most logical, long-range solution to the problem of security coverage in Germany."[65]

In October 1945, the War Department asked the European Theater Headquarters to consider organizing the majority of the U.S. occupation force into an efficient military police force modeled on state police forces in the United States. By the end of 1945, the theater headquarters had provided Washington with a plan for an elite, highly mobile force, composed of the best soldiers available from the voluntary reenlistment program and

---

64. John Brown, "Combat Cops?," *Armed Forces Journal* (September 2000), available at http://www.afji.com/AFJI.Mags/2000/September/combat_2.html (accessed October 17, 2012).

65. Major James Snyder, "The Establishment and Operations of the United States Constabulary, October 3, 1945–June 30, 1947," Historical Sub-Section C-3.

equipped with the most modern weapons, communications, vehicles, and aircraft. It would be organized to coincide with the geographic divisions of German civil administration to facilitate liaison with the German police and the U.S. Office of Military Government. The force would include 3 brigades, 9 regiments, 27 squadrons, and 135 troops—the organization's primary unit—plus headquarters units. Troops would be organized on the pattern of mechanized ("mecz") cavalry units used during the war. Each troop would have three Jeeps and one armored car to serve as a command vehicle. Each regiment would have a mobile reserve of one company equipped with light tanks. Horses would be provided for patrolling in mountainous terrain and motorcycles for controlling traffic on the autobahn. Members of the new force would wear U.S. military uniforms but would be distinguished by a lightning bolt shoulder patch, bright yellow scarves, and helmet covers with insignia and yellow and blue stripes. The new force, which would have an authorized strength of 32,750 personnel, would be called the United States Constabulary.[66]

To train the new force, a constabulary school was established at a former Nazi youth training academy in Sonthofen, Germany, which was located in a winter sports area at the foot of the Allgau Alps. Its curriculum included courses in German geography, history, and politics, plus basic police skills such as criminal investigation, report writing, arrest procedures, self-defense, patrolling, and the role, mission, and authority of the constabulary. The school received professional guidance from Colonel J. H. Harwood, a former state police commissioner of Rhode Island, who also developed a trooper's handbook. The constabulary drew its personnel from armored cavalry divisions with some of the most distinguished combat records in the European theater. Unfortunately, redeployment and demobilization had reduced these units to only 25 percent of their wartime strength, and most combat veterans had returned to the United States. The army's goal was to have the organizational structure of the new force in place and 20,000 personnel trained and ready for duty the following summer.

On July 1, 1946, the U.S. Constabulary in Germany became operational on schedule. Its mission was to maintain general military and civil security within and to control the borders of the U.S. zone of occupation, an area of more than 40,000 square miles of territory—nearly the size of Pennsylvania—and nearly 1,400 miles of international borders and zone boundaries.

---

66. Historical Division, Headquarters European Command, "History of the U.S. Constabulary January 10, 1946 to December 31, 1946," Historical Manuscripts Collection, file no. 8-3.1 CA 37, available at http://www.army.mil/cmh-pg/reference/cstb46.htm (accessed November 26, 2012).

This area was inhabited by 16 million Germans and more than 500,000 refugees of many nationalities. It included numerous large cities, most of which had suffered extensive war damage.[67]

Almost before it could begin work, the constabulary was nearly decimated by a sudden speed-up in demobilization that resulted in the loss of 14,000 personnel, nearly 43 percent of its strength, in the first two months of operation. The task of finding and training replacements for those who had just graduated from the constabulary school was staggering. There was also a serious shortage of NCOs and junior officers. During the first year of operation, a soldier stayed in the constabulary about eight months, on average. While other army occupation units experienced difficulties in maintaining sufficient personnel, the problem was more acute for the constabulary, given its unique mission. Constabulary officers were required to operate in small groups with limited supervision. They also had to prepare detailed incident and crime reports, interpret military government regulations and U.S. military laws, apply the rules of evidence, and use discerning judgment. Operating in a country where black markets provided the majority of economic activity, personnel also needed strength of character, discipline, and dedication to duty. Constabulary members were subjected to a broad variety of temptations offered by people in desperate circumstances.

There was no shortage of challenging assignments for the new force. The largest and most widely publicized operations were conducted by troop or larger-size units against black marketing and illicit trafficking of contraband goods across international borders and between zones of occupation. These operations took the form of search-and-check operations, shows of force, zonewide checks, and operations conducted in conjunction with Allied forces against Germans, refugee camps, and, in some cases, U.S. forces. One such effort, Operation Scotch, was conducted on November 22, 1946. It combined a light tank troop, a motorcycle platoon, a horse platoon, and light aircraft, which were used to establish road blocks, inspect traffic, and search eighteen square miles of mountainous terrain, coordinated with a parallel French operation along the border between the respective zones of occupation. Operation Scotch netted a number of illegal border crossers, large quantities of cigarettes, cloth, weapons, and liquor, and a number of "suspicious characters." Operation Camel, a raid on a refugee camp, occurred seven days later on November 29. A constabulary force of 676 officers and troops searched persons and buildings in a camp housing Polish refugees where black marketing and other types of nefarious activities were taking place.

---

67. Historical Division, "History of the U.S. Constabulary."

The following spring, a large operation, code-named Traveler, was conducted around U.S. military bases to snare AWOL soldiers and military and civilian personnel engaged in illegal activities.

Within the U.S. zone, the U.S. constabulary's responsibility for law enforcement and civil security was exercised through extensive patrolling and through close liaison with the U.S. military government, U.S. military police, the U.S. Counter Intelligence Corps, the Criminal Investigation Division, and the German police. Liaison was conducted with counterpart agencies in the British and French zones and, with frustrating delays and other difficulties, Soviet authorities. The constabulary operated in a postconflict environment of ruined cities, camps of displaced persons and refugees, political agitation by parties of conflicting ideologies, and a suspicious, disillusioned, needy, and often nearly starving population. All goods, including food and daily necessities, were in extremely short supply, and black marketing and petty crime flourished. Refugees posed a particular problem, accounting for a disproportionate percentage of violent crimes involving the use of firearms. Camps containing displaced Jews presented special problems, as they could not be resettled and most agitated to leave Germany. During the first six months of their operations, constabulary forces conducted 168,000 patrols in Jeeps, tanks, and armored cars. Over time, an analysis of crime statistics resulted in more patrols in high-crime areas. Constabulary patrols normally included an English-speaking German police officer, who made arrests in cases involving local citizens. U.S. constabulary forces handled arrests of Americans or foreign nationals.

In addition to controlling crime, the constabulary was responsible for managing civil disorder among the German population and border security. Civil disturbances involving German citizens were few and generally resulted from food shortages, the general scarcity of goods and living quarters, and competition from an influx of refugees. At times, the food situation became so serious that farms were attacked for their crops and U.S. Army facilities were robbed to obtain something to eat. In response, the constabulary was deployed in an antipilfering program to provide protection. On the boundary with the Soviet zone and on the Austrian frontier, teams of seven or eight constabulary soldiers manned border-crossing points. Constabulary forces and unarmed German police also patrolled on horseback, on foot, in vehicles, and by air at a depth of ten miles along the borders, turning back 26,000 undocumented travelers and intercepting 22,000 illegal border crossers during one six-month period in 1946.[68]

---

68. Snyder, "Establishment and Operations of the United States Constabulary."

As Germany recovered and assumed its place in a revitalized Europe, the need for the U.S. constabulary gradually disappeared. By 1948, West German police had assumed responsibility for the constabulary's civilian police and border control missions. At the same time, the pressing security needs of the Cold War caused the U.S. Army to strengthen its constabulary regiments for possible combat missions, adding reconnaissance, rifle, and heavy weapons platoons. Eventually the army deactivated the Fifteenth Constabulary Regiment and reorganized three other regiments into armored cavalry units. On November 24, 1950, the headquarters of the U.S. constabulary was deactivated, and its remaining elements were transferred to the Seventh Army. The last units of the U.S. constabulary were removed from active service in December 1952.[69]

U.S. Constabulary in Japan and Korea

In Germany, the United States shared responsibility for administering the country with three other occupying powers: After removing the Nazi regime, the Allies governed Germany directly, and in the American zone, General Lucius Clay was in charge of a military government that governed German citizens living within its borders. In Japan, the United States, for all practical purposes, acted alone in establishing a military government. Since Japan surrendered before the entry of U.S. forces, the United States established a military administration but left the emperor and the Japanese government in place. As the Supreme Commander for Allied Powers (SCAP), General Douglas MacArthur ruled Japan but did so indirectly through existing Japanese institutions. At its peak, MacArthur's headquarters consisted of some three thousand Americans and was organized in sections corresponding to the Japanese administration. Edicts were issued in the name of the emperor and carried out by Japanese government departments. More than two thousand Japanese civil servants were purged from public life for participation in war crimes. Most of these positions were in the Internal Affairs Ministry; technical ministries, such as the Ministry of Finance, were hardly affected by the vetting process.[70]

In Japan, General MacArthur initially commanded the U.S. Sixth and Eighth Armies, with a total of 230,000 men. In the first two months of occupation, these forces oversaw the disarmament and demobilization of

---

69. U.S. Army Center of Military History, "The U.S. Constabulary in Post-War Germany (1946–52)," Historical Manuscripts Collection, available at http://www.history.army.mil/html/forcestruc/constab-ip.html (accessed November 26, 2012).

70. Roy Licklider, "The American Way of State Building: Germany, Japan, Somalia, and Panama," *Small Wars and Insurgencies*, vol. 10, no. 3 (Winter 1999), 85–86.

the Japanese military, which was accomplished with Japanese cooperation and without resistance. At the end of the first year, the Sixth Army was disbanded, and by the end of 1948, U.S. military forces in Japan were reduced to 117,580 personnel. These troops were configured as constabulary and assigned to occupational duties. In contrast to Germany, the Japanese civil police remained in place and were responsible for law enforcement. The police enjoyed a positive reputation among the Japanese public, despite their broad and authoritarian powers. How to institute police reform thus became a sensitive issue within SCAP and with the Japanese government.[71]

During the occupation, SCAP removed senior police leaders, completely separated the police from the military, and reduced the former's function to law enforcement. Other institutions were created to take on firefighting, customs, intelligence gathering, and other functions. In 1948 SCAP created a Japanese police force of 125,000 personnel divided into two parts: a 30,000-member national rural police that operated in rural areas and small towns, and a 95,000-member force divided into 1,600 independent municipal police departments on the American model. In 1954, two years after the occupation ended, the Japanese government returned the police to central control under a national commission of public safety and a national police agency.[72]

As in Germany, U.S. military units in Japan were downsized and their personnel trained to perform constabulary functions. Unlike in Germany, however, the U.S. Army in Japan did not have time to reorganize, retrain, and reequip these units to face the new threats of the Cold War. Untrained for combat and equipped with World War II leftovers, U.S. military forces in Japan were rushed to Korea, where they heroically attempted to blunt the assault by the North Korean Army at the beginning of the Korean War.[73]

On June 25, 1950, North Korean forces crossed the thirty-eighth parallel, swept through Seoul, and were headed toward the southern coastal city of Pusan and total victory. To stop the advance, President Harry Truman ordered General MacArthur to send U.S. forces from Japan to halt the invasion and make clear that the United States would assist South Korea in resisting aggression. In response, MacArthur ordered the U.S. Army's 24th Infantry Division to move immediately from Japan to Korea. In terms of readiness for combat, MacArthur had little choice from among the four U.S. divisions under his command. On May 30, the 24th Division was reported to have the lowest combat

71. Richard Finn, *Winners in Peace: MacArthur, Yoshida, and Postwar Japan* (Berkeley: University of California Press, 1992), 35, 165.

72. Licklider, "American Way," 87.

73. Brown, "Combat Cops?"

effectiveness, but it was stationed closest to Korea and could arrive quickly. To engage the North Koreans as soon as possible, U.S. military authorities decided to send a small task force under the command of Lieutenant Colonel Charles Smith ahead by air. On July 1, Task Force Smith, made up of elements from the 1st Battalion, 21st Regiment, 24th Infantry Division, landed at Pusan's airfield. The task force comprised part of the battalion headquarters' company, two understrength rifle companies, a recoilless rifle platoon, two mortar platoons, and a medical company—a total of 406 officers and men. In Korea, the task force was joined by part of the 52nd Field Artillery Battalion, armed with 105 mm howitzers and 108 additional personnel. Smith immediately moved his force of 514 men north through hordes of fleeing refugees and retreating South Korean army units to Osan, where they engaged the enemy at dawn on July 5. The Americans were vulnerable to flanking attacks and had no reserves, and a steady rain precluded air support.[74]

The North Korean force of two regiments of six thousand men and thirty-three of the latest Soviet-made T-34 tanks rolled over the Americans. Outnumbered fifteen to one, Smith's men watched helplessly as the shells from their antiquated, World War II antitank weapons bounced off the North Korean armor. The Americans held their ground until they expended their ammunition and then fell back in disarray, suffering 181 casualties. Describing the engagement years later, Smith said, "After the tanks went through, what I saw was three tanks coming down and then about twenty-five vehicles, loaded, and behind them, North Korean soldiers walking four abreast as far as I could see." Smith said he was "very proud of the fact than not a man left his position until ordered," although everyone knew the odds against them. The enemy advance was delayed by seven hours.[75]

The pattern of the first engagement was repeated in the following days as the rest of the 24th Division arrived by boat and engaged the North Koreans. The Americans fought bravely, but superior North Korean weaponry and greater numbers overwhelmed U.S. units at every stand. The 34th Infantry was "thrown into a fight for which it was unprepared and was cut to pieces. Weak in numbers, completely out-gunned, unable to protect its flanks, and short of ammunition, it retreated in disorder, suffering extremely heavy casualties." In every case the Americans were ill-equipped, untrained, and had never been in combat.[76] So searing was this experience that

---

74. James Schnabel, *The United States Army in the Korean War, Policy and Direction: The First Year* (Washington, DC: Center of Military History, United States Army, 1972).

75. Jack Siemieniec, "Task Force Smith Recalls Historic Days," *Army News Service*, June 29, 2000.

76. Schnabel, *The United States Army in the Korean War.*

U.S. military leaders swore that "never again" would U.S. military forces be converted to other purposes that would result in their losing their "readiness" and combat effectiveness.[77] This attitude affected the pace of the drawdown of U.S. military forces after the Gulf War. It also heavily influenced thinking in the U.S. Army concerning the use of military forces in peace operations. Military officials were extremely wary of committing forces to peacekeeping roles that would blunt their warfighting effectiveness. They also strongly resisted suggestions that the United States create special constabulary-type military units designed specifically for peace operations. The underlying fear was that in a future conflict, such forces might suffer the same fate as Task Force Smith.[78]

THE CONTEMPORARY U.S. EXPERIENCE

U.S. National Guard

The U.S. National Guard is the modern descendent of the colonial tradition of citizen militias. A uniquely American institution, the Guard is the oldest component of the U.S. armed forces; it celebrated its 376th birthday on December 13, 2012. Under the U.S. constitution, Congress was empowered to raise a militia, but appointing officers and training members was reserved to the states. The National Guard continues this historical tradition. It is composed primarily of civilians who serve their country and state on a part-time basis, reporting for one weekend each month and two weeks during the summer.[79] The Guard is unique in that it can serve under the authority of both federal and state governments. Normally, units are responsible to state governors, who can call the Guard into action during local emergencies, such as natural disasters or civil disturbances. In addition, the president can federalize the National Guard for domestic emergencies or service abroad. When federalized units are sent abroad, they are led by the commander of the theater in which they operate. National Guard divisions fought in both world wars, Korea, Vietnam, and Iraq. Guard units also saw extensive service with NATO forces in Bosnia, Kosovo, and Afghanistan.[80]

---

77. Brown, "Combat Cops?"

78. Interview with Scott Feil, executive director of the Role of American Military Power Program, Association of the U.S. Army, Washington, DC, August 12, 2002.

79. National Guard, "About the National Guard," available at http://www.ng.mil/About/default.aspx (accessed November 26, 2012).

80. Army National Guard, "History," available at http://www.arng.army.mil/history (accessed October 17, 2012).

In the United States, responsibility for civil disorder management, including riot control, rests with civilian law enforcement. When civil disturbances occur in U.S. cities, specially trained and equipped units of police are the first to respond, and normally this is all that is required. The National Park Police, which provides security for major demonstrations in Washington, DC, and urban police departments across the country have become expert in deterring potential violence and maintaining public order. In exceptional cases, however, when a disturbance is too great for civilian police forces to control, the National Guard is backup, operating under the authority of the state governor. Historically, federal authorities have been extremely reluctant to allow regular military troops to become involved in confrontations with Americans, as it is seen as blurring the distinction between military and civilian roles in a democracy, undermining the principle of civilian control of the military, and reducing military readiness. Federal authorities have preferred to have the National Guard's more politically acceptable citizen-soldiers handle domestic assignments, and units in all states are specially trained and equipped to deal with major civil disturbances. That said, the Guard has been called out infrequently, and most Americans can enumerate times when the National Guard has been used in this capacity.[81]

Between the start of the civil rights movement and the end of the Vietnam War, the National Guard was repeatedly forced into service as the country was torn by protests in U.S. cities. Washington, DC, and other places saw violent confrontations between demonstrators and police and National Guard troops. The president was also forced to deploy federal troops in several cities and to federalize the National Guard to quell civil disturbances. The Department of the Army's civil disturbance plan, nicknamed Garden Plot, was frequently utilized. During this period, a "landmark tragedy" in the history of the National Guard occurred on the campus of Kent State University: In May 1970 a small unit of the Ohio National Guard panicked when confronted by a group of college students during an antiwar protest. Isolated and fearing their lives were in danger, the guardsmen fired into the crowd, killing four students and wounding many others. The guardsmen were officially absolved of primary responsibility, but the incident had a major effect on the national psyche.[82]

In April 1992 large areas of southeast and south central Los Angeles were burned and badly damaged during six days of racial violence following the acquittal of four white Los Angeles Police Department (LAPD) of-

---

81. Rex Applegate, "Riot Control: Army and National Guard Unprepared to Rule the Mob," *Soldier of Fortune* (December 1992), 43–44.

82. Applegate, "Riot Control," 45.

ficers accused of beating an African American, Rodney King. The riots, the most destructive in U.S. history, resulted in the deaths of fifty-four people and more than $800 million in property damage. The rampage of violence, arson, looting, and other acts of criminal behavior quickly overwhelmed the LAPD. In response, California governor Pete Wilson activated 4,000 members of the California National Guard. Of those mobilized, the initial 2,000 were members of the 3rd Battalion, 160th Infantry (Mechanized), 40th Infantry Division of the California National Guard. This unit was especially well suited for the task, as most of its soldiers lived in the neighborhoods affected by the riots and many of them were police officers or had jobs related to law enforcement in private life. The California Guard had extensive experience in supporting police during natural disasters and some older members had been deployed during the Watts neighborhood riots in Los Angeles in 1965. The guardsmen were armed with M-16 rifles and sidearms, but they were used only to support the police in performing their duties. Guardsmen operated traffic control checkpoints, escorted fire trucks, protected buildings, and maintained security in areas that police had cleared. When the violence continued, President George H. W. Bush sent 2,000 regular army troops and 1,500 Marines with orders to "return fire if fired upon." The president also federalized the National Guard and sent 1,000 federal law enforcement officers into the city. A dusk-to-dawn curfew, exhausted rioters, and the presence of 3,500 federal troops, 4,000 guardsmen, 5,000 LAPD officers, and 4,000 other California police officers ended the disturbance.[83]

From December 1 to 3, 1999, some 425 members of the Washington State National Guard were activated to assist Seattle police in controlling violent demonstrations that erupted during the meeting of the World Trade Organization (WTO). Thousands of demonstrators from around the world gathered to peacefully protest the WTO's policies toward developing nations. Several hundred self-styled anarchists resorted to violence, rioting, looting, and arson in an attempt to disrupt the meeting. The National Guard's mission was to support the police, who used tear gas, flash bombs, and pepper spray and arrested hundreds of protesters. Guard soldiers who supported the police wore flak jackets and Kevlar helmets with face shields. They carried wooden batons but not firearms. Guardsmen did not engage demonstrators; they were used primarily to patrol sidewalks and keep demonstrators out of a fifty-square-block no-

---

83. Clark Staten, "Three Days of Hell in Los Angeles," *Emergencynet News Service*, April 29–May 1, 1992; Christopher Schnaubelt, "Lessons in Command and Control for the Los Angeles Riots," *Parameters* (Summer 1997), 88–109.

protest zone. In one instance, the Guard closed roads to protect protesters from auto traffic. Guardsmen also checked identification and performed security duties inside hotels housing WTO delegates and in the Seattle Convention Center. They reinforced the security detail at President Bill Clinton's hotel and provided a fifty-soldier reaction force for a precinct where police were forced to disperse demonstrators. The Wyoming Air National Guard contributed by flying in 3,300 pounds of civilian riot control munitions. Some Guardsmen encountered angry demonstrators, but suffered no injuries. It was the first time in eighty years—since the labor riots of 1919—that the National Guard had been called out to deal with civil disorder in Seattle.[84]

Following the terrorist attacks on September 11, 2001, the National Guard was activated in response to a request from President George W. Bush to upgrade security at airports and other sensitive locations. National Guard troops carrying M-16 rifles and wearing camouflage fatigues were highly visible at airports around the country, assisting local security agents in a variety of tasks. In addition to conducting armed patrols and providing area security, guardsmen watched over passenger screening points as private security employees checked baggage and assisted passengers through metal detectors. They also assisted with controlling traffic outside terminals at passenger drop-off points and in parking lots. Beyond providing a security presence, National Guard personnel did not, however, engage in law enforcement or replace local police and airport security officers.[85]

In the United States, the Posse Comitatus Act of 1878 generally prohibits federal armed forces from engaging in law enforcement activities. Congress adopted the law in response to abuses that federal military forces committed in the South during Reconstruction. The statute, as amended, states, "Whoever, except in cases and under instances expressly authorized by the Constitution or Act of Congress, willfully uses any part of the Army or Air Force as a posse comitatus or otherwise to execute the laws shall be fined under this title or imprisoned not more than two years, or both."[86] The law embodied the historic tradition of military subordination to strong civilian authority and the separation of military and law enforcement functions within the United States. It applied only to forces in federal service, however,

84. Bob Haskell, "Seattle Civil Disturbance Puts Guard on Duty," *Air Force News*, December 3, 1999; Ed Offley, "Guardsmen Protect WTO Delegates and Protesters Alike," *Seattle Post-Intelligencer*, December 2, 1999.

85. Cable News Network, "National Guard Protecting Nation's Airports," September 29, 2001.

86. 18 United States Code, Section 1385 (1994). Currently the fine is up to $250,000 for individuals.

not to state militias—and thus, not to the Guard in its normal status of state service. The provisions of the act do apply to the National Guard, however, when the president authorizes it to perform federal service.[87]

Even with the Posse Comitatus Act, the line between military and police functions has blurred, and the 1878 law is no longer the last word. Congress has enacted laws that provide a number of exemptions to the principle of posse comitatus—literally, the power or authority of the county—in dealing with civil disturbances and insurrections. These statutes authorize the president to provide military assistance to state governments upon request (section 331) or upon his own initiative to use the armed forces or federalized militia to suppress any rebellion that makes it impracticable to enforce U.S. laws through ordinary judicial proceedings (section 332). Section 333 also permits military intervention when the constitutional rights of any state's citizens are threatened by insurrection, domestic violence, unlawful combination, or conspiracy. Under section 332, before the militia can be called out, the president must by proclamation immediately order the insurgents to disperse—that is, to read them the riot act.[88]

Most of the congressional exemptions to the principle of excluding the armed forces from law enforcement functions have come in the context of the war on drugs, which George H. W. Bush declared in 1989. In response, Congress designated the Department of Defense as the lead agency for detecting and monitoring air and marine transport of illegal drugs to the United States. Congress also provided for the integration of U.S. command, control, and intelligence assets for drug interdiction. Finally, it approved funding for state governors to expand the use of the National Guard in drug control at state borders.[89] This meant further amending Title 10 of the United States Code to provide exceptions to the Posse Comitatus Act that authorized the secretary of defense to provide equipment and personnel to assist civilian agencies in the enforcement of drug, immigration, and tariff laws. The statute expressly forbids members of the U.S. Army, Navy, Air Force, or Marine Corps to participate directly in search, seizure, arrest, or other similar activity (section 375). Nevertheless, military personnel can operate equipment to intercept vessels or aircraft outside the land areas

---

87. Matthew Carlton Hammond, "The Posse Comitatus Act: A Principle in Need of Renewal," *Washington University Law Quarterly*, vol. 75, no. 2 (Summer 1997).

88. The legal interpretation of 10 United States Code, Sections 331–335, is from Sean Byrne, "Defending Sovereignty: Domestic Operations and Legal Precedents," *Military Review*, vol. 79, no. 1 (March/April 1999).

89. See United States Army, *Field Manual 100-19, Domestic Support Operations* (Washington, DC: Department of the Army, July 1993), particularly chapter 7, "Missions in Support of Law Enforcement."

of the United States or follow in hot pursuit of such craft inland (section 374b).[90]

National Guard participation in counternarcotics operations is provided for under U.S. Code Title 32, which states that the Guard may only perform counternarcotics duties that are consistent with state law. The National Guard Bureau has adopted policy guidelines that restrict the Guard's narcotics-related law enforcement activities to strictly controlled, secondary inspections or search of unattended vehicles or cargo. National Guard forces actively inspect cargo at U.S. entry points, but a civilian law enforcement agent always accompanies them. If guardsmen observe drug-related criminal activity, they report it to relevant civilian authorities for appropriate action.[91]

In the spring of 2002, President George W. Bush directed lawyers in the Defense and Justice Departments to review the Posse Comitatus Act and all other laws that restrict the military's ability to participate in domestic law enforcement. White House officials said the review was requested to determine whether domestic preparedness and responsiveness against terrorism would benefit from increased military participation. Officials noted that after September 11, the law prevented President Bush from ordering the National Guard to protect the nation's airports. Instead, the president had to request fifty individual state governors to use their authority to perform the same task. The president's call for a review of the law received an immediate endorsement from General Ralph Eberhart, chief of the new Northern Command, which is responsible for defense of the continental United States. Senator Joseph Biden (D-Delaware), chairman of the Senate Foreign Relations Committee at the time, also endorsed it, saying the law should be reexamined and updated.[92] The National Guard was not, however, included in President Bush's plan for the new Department of Homeland Security. Homeland Security Secretary Tom Ridge said the military's Northern Command would work with state governors to define suitable missions. Nearly a year after the September terrorist attacks, the National Guard still had 1,100 troops assisting the Customs and Immigration Service around the nation's borders and 80 troops guarding LaGuardia Airport in New York. There were also 500 Guardsmen stationed at nuclear power plants, reservoirs, landmarks, bridges, tunnels, and other possibly vulnerable sites.[93]

---

90. Byrne, "Defending Sovereignty."

91. Jay D. Wells and Thomas P. Baltazar, "Counter-Drug (CD) Operations," *Center for Army Lessons Learned Newsletter*, no. 91-4 (November 1991).

92. Eric Schmitt, "Military Role in U.S. Gains Favor," *New York Times*, July 22, 2002.

93. Bill Miller, "National Guard Awaits Niche in Homeland Security Plan," *Washington Post*, August 11, 2002, A1.

While the National Guard has a number of relevant characteristics, it does not qualify as a constabulary under the definition used in this study. The Guard has the capacity to deal with civil disturbances and perform a number of functions related to restoring and maintaining public order. It does not, however, have police powers, and by directive from the National Guard Bureau, it operates only in support of civilian law enforcement. Guardsmen are not trained and do not have executive authority to perform police functions, such as conducting criminal investigations and arresting (as opposed to detaining) offenders. In addition, when National Guard divisions are federalized for service abroad, they become subject to the limitations of the Posse Comitatus Act, as has occurred in peacekeeping operations in the Balkans. There is, however, a modern-day U.S. organization that has both military capabilities and police powers and that does fit this study's definition of a constabulary. That organization is the U.S. Army Military Police.

U.S. Army Military Police

At the end of the Cold War, the U.S. Army Military Police Corps reviewed its doctrine to determine if it "was properly articulating its multiple performance capabilities in support of U.S. forces deployed worldwide." The result of this review was a revision shaped by recognition that the following factors would influence future operations:

- The need to participate in "stability" and peace support operations in which "joint military, multinational, and interagency" cooperation would be common.
- The effect of asymmetrical threats, such as narcotics trafficking, organized crime, and terrorism, and the need to deal with humanitarian emergencies and natural disasters.
- Advances in information and communication technologies and the threats they may pose.
- The probable disappearance of traditional linear battlefields and subsequent requirements for forces that can perform specialized functions to accomplish operational requirements.[94]
- The new doctrine that emerged from this review increased the four traditional military police (MP) battlefield missions to five and modified several of the missions to include tasks commonly performed in peace operations. Under the revised doctrine, which continues in force, the U.S. Army MP has the following responsibilities:

---

94. United States Army, *Field Manual 3-19.1, Military Police Operations* (Washington, DC: Department of the Army, March 22, 2001).

- Area security: MP companies are equipped to conduct mobile patrols and to provide security to sensitive locations, such as ports, airports, bridges, and border control points.
- Maneuver and mobility support: On the battlefield, this involves conducting reconnaissance, keeping supply lines open, and regulating the flow of vehicles and units. In both war and peace operations, it also involves directing refugees and displaced persons and providing protection and humanitarian assistance.
- Internment and resettlement: On the battlefield, this involves taking custody of prisoners of war and civilians displaced by the conflict. It can also involve arresting military criminals and detaining civilians who commit crimes.
- Law enforcement: On U.S. military installations, MP units are responsible for the full spectrum of police functions, from traffic control to criminal investigations. In peace operations, they can perform public order and law enforcement functions, ranging from managing civil disorder to detaining lawbreakers.
- Information gathering: Like military scouts, military police conduct mounted reconnaissance patrols and are trained to find and fix the positions of enemy forces. Like civilian police, military police collect information related to civil disorder and criminal activity.[95]

U.S. Army MPs undergo the same basic training that the army gives to light infantry. MP companies are trained to operate much like military scouts, conducting reconnaissance and finding and engaging enemy forces. After completing basic training, MPs receive ten weeks of advanced individual training at the U.S. Army Military Police School at Fort Leonard Wood, Missouri, where they are introduced to basic police skills and law enforcement. MP recruits receive instruction in patrol, traffic control, crime scene protection, criminal investigation, community policing, use of force, nonviolent dispute resolution, relevant laws and codes of criminal procedures, first aid, and driver education. Once assigned to their units, MPs are trained to operate in three-man teams. The basic MP unit is a Humvee vehicle with a three-person crew under the command of an NCO. The vehicle is mounted with a crew-served weapon—an integrated machine gun system—and individual soldiers have automatic weapons, a grenade launcher, and sidearms. The units are trained to operate independently, as when controlling a checkpoint, and to coordinate with other units or quickly combine into a larger force when needed. Two three-person teams

---

95. U.S. Army, *Field Manual 3-19.1*.

make a squad; ten make a platoon. As a result of its training, armaments, and mobility, an MP company has greater versatility and more firepower than a regular light infantry company.[96]

What sets the MP apart from other soldiers is that police are trained to interact with civilians. MP recruits are generally selected from inductees who score above average on army intelligence tests. In their law enforcement training, MPs are taught interpersonal skills, how to establish trust, and how to use mediation and other conflict resolution techniques to resolve disputes. They are trained to make individual decisions and be comfortable in ambiguous situations. MPs are trained to use only the minimum amount of force necessary to control the situation. They are also trained to handle victims. This is important in peace operations, particularly in dealing with victims of sexual assault and people with medical problems.[97]

The ability to deal with civilians was evident in the performance of the 500 U.S. MPs who were part of the 5,600-member U.S. military contingent of NATO's Kosovo Force. The MPs were at the center of efforts to maintain public order in the U.S. area of responsibility. While regular troops chafed under the requirement to handle unruly crowds and resolve interpersonal disputes, the MPs took these aspects of daily operations in stride; trained as police and soldiers, they proved adept at interacting with civilians. Of particular importance was that MPs, like civilian police officers, operated on a force continuum, using only the minimum amount of force necessary. For the MPs in Kosovo, this approach to dealing with unruly citizens came down to five S's: shout, show your weapon, shoot to wound, shoot to kill, but shoot only at the instigator. Overall, MPs were more comfortable with a military mission where the goal was not victory but stability.[98]

---

96. Interview with Colonel Larry Forester, former director of the U.S. Army Peacekeeping Institute, U.S. Army War College, Carlisle Barracks, Pennsylvania, February 27, 2002.

97. Interview with Forester.

98. Thomas Ricks, "U.S. Military Police Embrace Kosovo Role," *Washington Post*, March 25, 2001, A21.

3

Test Case: Creating Postconflict Security in Bosnia

On November 21, 1995, after three weeks of negotiations at Wright-Patterson Air Force Base in Dayton, Ohio, the Bosnian war ended with the initialing of the General Framework Agreement for Peace in Bosnia and Herzegovina. Annex 11, titled "International Police Task Force," addressed the role of police. The Dayton Accords stipulated that the Bosnian entities would be responsible for creating a safe and secure environment for all persons in their jurisdictions by maintaining civilian law enforcement agencies, which would operate in accordance with human rights standards and fundamental freedoms. The parties to the agreement requested that the UN Security Council establish a UN international police task force to assist Bosnian law enforcement agencies in this effort.[1]

The mandate and organization of the International Police Task Force (IPTF) was the result of a compromise between U.S. and European diplomats and not the product of negotiations with the parties to the peace agreement. It also was not the work of police experts, as there were no police officers or law enforcement specialists at Dayton. The most important negotiations concerning the creation of the IPTF took place in Washington on the weekend before the final negotiations convened in Ohio. In a Saturday meeting at the State Department, representatives of the Contact Group—the United Kingdom, France, Russia, Germany, and the United States—met to work out differences on military issues, constitutional questions, and the nature of the international police force.[2]

---

1. General Framework Agreement for Peace in Bosnia and Herzegovina (GFAP), Annex 11 (International Police Task Force), Article I.1-2, available at http://www.ohr.int/dpa/default.asp?content_id=380 (accessed November 26, 2012).

2. Interviews with a State Department legal adviser and with Robert Gallucci, State Department official in charge of Dayton Accords civilian implementation, Washington, DC, January 21, 2000.

In the discussion of police, the United States presented the Contact Group with three models for an international police force for Bosnia: the traditional UN Civilian Police (CIVPOL) model of unarmed civilian police monitors with no executive authority, the Cambodia model of a UN CIVPOL force with limited executive authority and some arms, and a highly capable police force, including a rapid reaction unit. The United States preferred the third model, composed of Western European civilian police and gendarmes with some U.S. and Canadian participation. The entire force would be well trained, fully equipped, highly mobile, armed, and have executive authority. The rapid reaction unit would have helicopters and armored fighting vehicles. There would be no UN participation. European countries would recruit, equip, and fund the force. As the United States had primary responsibility for the Implementation Force (IFOR), policing would be left to the allies.[3]

The European members of the Contact Group opposed a strong international police force for Bosnia. They were afraid that such a force, with an aggressive mandate, would be drawn into dangerous confrontations and suffer casualties, a scenario that would be unacceptable to the European public. They questioned the appropriateness of foreign police taking responsibility for civilian policing in a third country—even a European one that was still being ravaged by violent ethnic conflict—and had strong doubts concerning the international community's ability to recruit, train, and deploy such a force in the short period between signing and implementing the agreement. And they were firmly, even angrily, opposed to the model that the United States preferred. The UK representative, Pauline Neville-Jones, said she could not accept, support, or even allow such a proposal. She maintained that British tradition and the legacy of Northern Ireland made it impossible for London to approve arming British police officers and authorizing them to make arrests on foreign soil. She argued that European police might have to enforce laws their governments found unacceptable. Local judges might throw out cases because they did not accept foreign police intervention. The European Union's representative, Carl Bildt, worried that a strong international police force would suggest an "occupation regime" rather than institution building.[4] The Europeans were determined to assign responsibility for the international police force to the United Nations and rejected anything beyond a force of unarmed UN police monitors.[5]

---

3. Interviews with legal adviser and Gallucci.

4. Interviews with a legal adviser and Gallucci.

5. Carl Bildt, *Peace Journey: The Struggle for Peace in Bosnia* (New York: Orion Press, 1999), 132–133.

At Dayton, the U.S. Department of Defense (DOD) shared the Europeans' preference for a weak IPTF mandate.[6] American military officials wanted to ensure that IFOR was the only legitimate armed force in Bosnia and feared that an armed international police force might be preyed upon for its weapons. They also feared an armed IPTF with an aggressive mandate would create problems and additional responsibilities for IFOR. If the IPTF got into trouble, IFOR would have to rescue the police and take over performing police functions. U.S. military officials argued that performing police functions would constitute mission creep, a politically potent term the U.S. military used when arguing against assignments it felt countered its interests. Beyond the hangover from Vietnam, military leaders remained deeply troubled by the loss of the Army Rangers in Somalia. They feared another imprecise mission like what had occurred there and did not really want U.S. troops in Bosnia. The result was to create what Ambassador Richard Holbrooke described as a "'Viet-malia syndrome," a Washington phobia against involving the U.S. military in peace operations.[7]

In the talks at Dayton, U.S. diplomats who favored a strong international police mandate thus faced the combined opposition of the U.S. military and the European members of the Contact Group. They also had to address a myriad of other issues, many of which were far more crucial to reaching a settlement of the conflict. The major issues of concern to Ambassador Holbrooke and the Balkan presidents were IFOR's mandate, the division of territory between the Bosnian Federation and the Republika Srpska (RS), and whether the High Representative would have authority over IFOR as well as civilian implementation. The three-week deadline Holbrooke set to conclude the negotiations placed a premium on the time allotted to considering any part of the agreement, prioritizing those issues that were critical to ending the conflict. Issues that related to peace implementation and nation building—such as the composition of police—received less attention. Among civilian questions, humanitarian assistance, return of refugees, and elections were viewed as more important than the role of the IPTF.[8]

In the closing days of the Dayton talks, Ambassador Holbrooke made a final effort to create a robust police mandate by getting agreement from Washington to pay the cost of organizing and arming a strong IPTF. Unfortunately, Holbrooke's appeal came as the Clinton administration was locked in a bitter budget fight with Congress that eventually led to a temporary

---

6. International Crisis Group, "Policing the Police in Bosnia: A Further Reform Agenda," *Balkans Report* no. 130, Brussels, May 10, 2002, 5.

7. Richard Holbrooke, *To End a War* (New York: Random House, 1998), 216–217.

8. Interview with Gallucci.

shutdown of the government. Without hope of obtaining adequate financial support, Holbrooke concluded that the United States could not "write the rules." The IPTF was given a weak mandate and assigned to the United Nations. As General Wesley Clark observed to Holbrooke, this "left a huge gap in the Bosnia food chain," with the United Nations and IPTF at the bottom.[9]

Under the agreement, the IPTF would be headed by a commissioner who would "receive guidance" from the high representative; the latter would be given overall responsibility for coordinating peace implementation. The IPTF was responsible for monitoring, observing, and inspecting law enforcement activities and facilities, "including associated judicial organizations, structures, and proceedings"; advising law enforcement personnel and forces; training law enforcement personnel; facilitating the parties' law enforcement activities within IPTF's mission of assistance; assessing threats to public order and advising on the capability of law enforcement agencies to deal with such threats; advising Bosnian government authorities on organizing effective civilian law enforcement agencies; and accompanying Bosnian law enforcement personnel in the performance of their duties, as the IPTF deemed appropriate.[10]

Missing from the list of IPTF functions was executive authority—the authority to enforce the law, conduct investigations, make arrests, and perform other crucial police duties. The IPTF was envisioned as an international civilian police force that would monitor, mentor, and train Bosnian police, who would be responsible for law enforcement and citizen protection. The IPTF would be unarmed and would rely on the local police and IFOR for protection. The IPTF's mandate was to advise and encourage local police; if the advice was ignored or rejected, the IPTF's recourse (Annex 11, Article V) was to notify either the high representative or the IFOR commander, who could bring failures to cooperate with the IPTF to the attention of local authorities, the United Nations, the Joint Civilian Commission, or relevant states. In cases of human rights violations, the IPTF could inform the Human Rights Commission established under Annex 6 of the agreement.

Given its weak mandate, it was clear the IPTF would have to interpret its mission flexibly and be prepared to push the limits of its authority. It would also need the cooperation of Bosnian law enforcement authorities to achieve Dayton's objectives of facilitating the restoration of law and public order, freedom of movement, and justice as the basis for a lasting peace.[11]

---

9. International Crisis Group, "Policing the Police," 5.

10. GFAP, Article II.1.

11. James Gow, *Triumph of the Lack of Will: International Diplomacy and the Yugoslav War* (New York: Columbia University Press, 1997), 294–295.

The prospect for the IPTF receiving such cooperation from the Bosnian police was highly problematic. The drafters at Dayton failed to appreciate that, postconflict, the police forces of the three rival parties were ethnically based. This meant local law enforcement authorities were unlikely to protect or serve minorities, particularly given the involvement of police in the conflict. Further, because the IPTF was unarmed and had no police powers, there would be no police force in Bosnia to protect minorities, nor any means beyond persuasion for the IPTF to compel compliance with the Dayton Accords. While IFOR could provide area security and reinforce patrolling to deter lawlessness, its forces would not be trained or equipped to control demonstrations or perform routine law enforcement functions. Appeals to the high representative would be of limited utility as that office had little authority and few resources. The IPTF could function effectively only with the consent of those it was assigned to monitor and advise.[12]

SIGNING THE DAYTON AGREEMENT

Immediately following the initialing of the Dayton Accords in late November, the UN Security Council authorized under Resolution 1026 the dispatch of a UN assessment mission to determine requirements for the IPTF. The team found that Bosnia's three ethnic-based police forces had expanded greatly during the conflict to a total of 44,750, including large numbers of former soldiers with no police experience. It determined the IPTF should number 1,721 officers, using a ratio of 1 IPTF member for every 30 local police, with an additional 229 officers to compensate for routine absences.[13] The assessment was followed by a month of frenzied diplomatic activity that culminated with IFOR's arrival in Bosnia in January 1996.

On December 8 and 9, 1995, a peace implementation conference was held in London to mobilize international support for the Dayton Accords. The conference endorsed the agreement, including the creation of the IPTF. It also established the Peace Implementation Council (PIC), composed of concerned states and relevant international organizations, to oversee the peace process in Bosnia.[14] Less than a week later, the three Balkan presidents,

12. Michael J. Dziedzic and Andrew Bair, "Bosnia and the International Police Task Force," in Robert Oakley, Michael Dziedzic, and Eliot Goldberg, eds., *Policing the New World Disorder* (Washington, DC: National Defense University Press, 1998), 270.

13. United Nations Report of the Secretary-General Pursuant to Security Council Resolution 1026 (1995), S/1995/1031, December 13, 1995, 6–7.

14. Bruce Pirnie, *Civilians and Soldiers: Achieving Better Coordination* (Santa Monica, CA: Rand Corporation, 1998), 72.

Alija Izetbegović, Franjo Tudjman, and Slobodan Milošević, met in Paris to sign the General Framework Agreement on December 14. The Bosnian Serbs and Croats had not been invited to Dayton. Milošević and Tudjman signed the accords on their behalf. On December 15 the UN Security Council adopted Resolution 1031, authorizing member states to establish IFOR under unified command, with ground, air, and maritime units from NATO and non-NATO countries. The Security Council authorized member states to take all necessary measures under the peace enforcement provisions in Chapter VII of the UN Charter to implement the Dayton agreement. On December 21 the Security Council adopted Resolution 1035, which created the United Nations Mission in Bosnia and Herzegovina (UNMIBH) and established the IPTF with an authorized strength of 1,721 international police monitors, 254 international staff, and 811 local personnel. On December 22, 1995, the UN Department for Peacekeeping Operations (DPKO) issued a note verbale to 45 UN permanent missions in New York, inviting their governments to contribute civilian police to the new Bosnian mission. Eventually, 43 countries responded, but the IPTF was extremely slow to deploy and did not reach its full complement until August 1996.[15]

IMPLEMENTING THE DAYTON ACCORDS

The IPTF faced its first test early in 1996, when the seven Bosnian Serb–controlled municipalities surrounding Sarajevo were transferred to the control of the federation. Under the Dayton Accords, the transfer of the seven Serb-held suburbs, located on the high ground surrounding the city, was to make Sarajevo less vulnerable to artillery attacks. More than 100,000 ethnic Serbs inhabited these areas; many were long-time residents. As the deadline for the transfer approached, hard-line Serb leaders in Pale ordered Serb residents to evacuate and destroy everything they could not carry, thoroughly ransacking, burning, and demolishing buildings so incoming federation authorities would find a wasteland. The Office of the High Representative (OHR) allowed Serb police to remain in the municipalities, assuming they would protect Serb residents. Instead, Serb police and groups of young Serb thugs engaged in ethnic self-cleansing, forcing as many as 30,000 Serb residents who might have stayed to withdraw. From late February to mid-March, all Serb residents were either evacuated or forced to leave for the RS, taking the wiring, windows, and pipes from their apartments and destroying

---

15. United Nations, Department of Public Information, *The Blue Helmets: A Review of United Nations Peacekeeping*, 3rd ed. (New York: United Nations, 1996), 562–563.

or booby-trapping what could not be removed. Some families exhumed the bodies of their relatives and carried them to the RS. Television pictures of burning buildings and fleeing refugees gave the world an image of general lawlessness that IFOR was unable to control.[16]

As the February 23 start date for the transfer approached, the IPTF was not yet operational. The first IPTF commissioner, Peter Fitzgerald, had not arrived in country, and only 230 of the 1,721 IPTF monitors had been deployed.[17] With a mass exodus of Serb residents already in progress, the transfer of the first municipality, Vogosca, "went wrong from the start." Federation police ordered the Serb mayor to leave and then ransacked his office under the pretense of looking for concealed bombs. This action violated an agreement with the federation that civilian administration in the suburbs was to remain untouched. As word of this incident spread, panic followed. IFOR gave permission for the Serb army to send trucks to complete the evacuation, ending any hope that a portion of the Serb population might be convinced to stay. Events on the first day in Vogosca made the subsequent transfers of the other municipalities more difficult. In Hadzici, Serb arsonists burned the town's municipal offices on the evening before the transfer. In Ilidza, gangs of hooligans ran through the streets terrorizing the remaining three or four thousand Serbs just before the transfer of authority took place.[18]

As the forced evacuation proceeded, IFOR, which was present in force, did nothing to stop it. Admiral Leighton Smith, the first U.S. commander of IFOR, smartly executed the military aspects of the Dayton agreement but considered civilian aspects of the implementation process, including police functions, outside of his responsibility. As the destruction of infrastructure and attacks on civilians proceeded, IFOR troops stood by and watched, refusing requests for protection from civilians who wished to remain and appeals from the OHR to intervene and arrest marauding arsonists. IFOR even kept its firefighting equipment locked inside IFOR compounds. An IFOR spokesman stated that while the burning of buildings was "unfortunate," the Serbs had the right to burn their own houses. As the violence increased, General Michael Walker, IFOR's second in command, rejected a personal appeal for military intervention from his civilian counterpart, Deputy High Representative Michael Steiner. IFOR could have prevented the destruction of property and the violent expulsion of thousands of residents, but refused to do so because police functions were not in its mandate. A NATO

16. Larry Wentz, *Lessons from Bosnia: The IFOR Experience* (Washington, DC: National Defense University Press, 1998), 149–150.

17. United Nations, *The Blue Helmets*, 563.

18. Bildt, *Peace Journey*, 196–197.

spokesman put it bluntly: "IFOR is not a police force and will not undertake police functions." The failure to prevent the violence was a defining moment, setting the tone for the initial phase of the peace operation.[19]

In addition to its problems with deployment and initial failure to maintain public order, the IPTF suffered from the poor quality of CIVPOL personnel. Although IPTF members were required to demonstrate a working knowledge of English and the ability to drive a four-wheel-drive vehicle, many failed the test on arrival and were repatriated.[20] IPTF also faced major logistics problems. Equipment that UNPROFOR left behind was transferred to IFOR. A companion UN military force could have provided logistical support, including a medical unit, but the IPTF was the first CIVPOL mission to operate without one. Instead, it had to rely on the inadequate UN procurement system and experienced extreme shortfalls in vehicles, communications, and other equipment. The IPTF was forced to turn to IFOR for such essentials as medical care, vehicle maintenance, access to food stores, and mail delivery. The IPTF did not share stations with local police; instead, it built separate police stations, a process that took time and further delayed effective operations.[21]

While the IPTF struggled operationally, it succeeded in its mission to downsize and restructure the Bosnian police and to develop and introduce principles of democratic policing. As was mentioned above, three ethnic-based police forces developed during the conflict. After the conflict, each ethnic group sought to maximize its security by transferring combatants into police units to avoid demobilization. When the IPTF arrived in Bosnia, the standard police uniform was military fatigues and the standard police weapon was the AK-47.[22]

One of the initial tasks of downsizing the Bosnian police was to remove nonpolice personnel. The goal was to create a police force with a police-officer-to-population ratio consistent with European standards,[23] an effort complicated by the Dayton agreement's confirmation of the wartime division of Bosnia into two separately controlled entities, the Bosnian Federation and the RS. Within the federation, internal security was the responsibil-

---

19. Holbrooke, *To End a War*, 327–337.

20. United Nations Secretariat, Report of the Secretary-General Pursuant to Resolution 1035 (1995), March 29, 1996, S/1996/210, 3.

21. Alice Hills, "International Peace Support Operations and CIVPOL: Should There Be a Permanent Global Gendarmerie?" *International Peacekeeping* 5, no. 3 (Autumn 1998), 35.

22. Dziedzic and Bair, "Bosnia and the International Police Task Force," 264.

23. Robert Wasserman, "Remarks," speech by the IPTF deputy commissioner, contributors meeting, United Nations headquarters, June 26, 1996, photocopy, 3–4.

ity of a federation police force and independent police forces in each of the ten cantons. In the RS, another police force was under tight central control by ethnic Serb authorities. In the initial stages of the peace operation, the various Bosnian police forces cooperated poorly with the IPTF—when they cooperated at all. Matters began to improve in April 1996, when the IPTF convened an international conference on police restructuring in the German town of Petersberg, a suburb of Bonn. Federation officials, UN representatives, and senior IPTF officers attended the meeting along with delegations from donor countries, including the United States. RS officials and police were invited but did not come.[24]

The Petersberg Declaration, signed on April 25, 1996, provided for a two-thirds reduction in the size of the federation police forces to 11,500. Restructuring was accomplished through a vetting process that screened applicants against IPTF-established standards—including graduation from a police academy, professional police experience, and a good record—to remove imposters, criminals, and human rights offenders. Applicants' names were checked against the database of the International Criminal Tribunal for the Former Yugoslavia (ICTY) in The Hague. They were also published in local newspapers with an invitation for persons with negative information to come forward. Candidates who met the criteria and survived the vetting would take a written examination and physical and psychological tests. Any police officer not certified by this process would be dismissed from the force. Any person who was armed but not a certified police officer would be handled by IFOR.[25]

The IPTF's goal was to reorient the Bosnian police from their previous role of protecting the state to protecting the rights of citizens, regardless of ethnicity, and adopting international standards of democratic policing. During 1997, IPTF completed the provisional certification of Bosniak (Bosnian Muslim) police officers in the federation and started to work on certifying the Croats. It also assisted in reopening the police academy in Sarajevo and enrolling the first multiethnic class. The academy's curriculum reflected a commitment from local police to respect human rights and protect democracy. This commitment was also important for the orientation of the IPTF itself, which was composed of police officers from a broad range of countries with a diverse understanding of how police should function in a democratic society.[26]

---

24. Wentz, *Lessons from Bosnia*, 153–156.

25. Agreement on Restructuring the Police Federation of Bosnia and Herzegovina (Petersberg Declaration), Bonn, Germany, April 25, 1996, 1–4, available at http://www.ohr.int/other-doc/fed-mtng/default.asp?content_id=3576 (accessed November 26, 2012).

26. International Crisis Group, "Policing the Police," 7.

At the March 6–7, 1997, meeting of the Brcko Implementation Conference in Vienna, the United Nations proposed enlarging the IPTF, including a special unit to monitor the RS police in Brcko. The primary objectives of the new unit would be to ensure freedom of movement, the return of refugees, and the restructuring and training of the local police. The goal was to reshape the local police force so it would represent the interests of all the people in the area, regardless of ethnicity. As the IPTF unit would consist of unarmed personnel without executive authority, the UN secretary-general requested that the international community support it and that the UN Stabilization Force (SFOR) closely cooperate with it in performing its duties.[27] On March 31, 1997, the Security Council authorized an additional 186 IPTF monitors and 11 civilian personnel for Brcko and called upon member states to contribute police personnel to staff the new mission.[28]

The expansion of the IPTF force in Brcko was among the steps to implement the February 14, 1997, interim decision of the Brcko arbitration tribunal. Unable to reach a final decision on the future of Brcko, the panel decided to retain jurisdiction for another year and establish the Office of the International Supervisor of Brcko. It also set requirements for RS authorities, including the return and resettlement of displaced persons and the creation of a multiethnic administration in Brcko, including the local police. Creation of a reinforced IPTF unit for Brcko was among the international community's steps to ensure that the instructions of the arbitration panel were carried out.[29]

In the aftermath of the Brcko incident and the September 1997 elections in Bosnia, attention in Washington and Brussels turned to SFOR's future. At the halfway point in the eighteen-month SFOR mandate, it was evident that the decision on whether to renew the mandate had to be made by December 1997 so that it could be implemented before the June 1998 deadline for SFOR's withdrawal. While the tasks enumerated in the military annex of the Dayton Accords had been accomplished quickly, the failure to make similar progress in civilian implementation required a continued military presence. From the outset of discussions on the future of SFOR, two things were clear: The Clinton administration and Congress favored transferring responsibility for peacekeeping in Bosnia to the

27. United Nations Secretariat, Report of the Secretary-General Pursuant to Security Council Resolution 1088 (1996), S/1997/224, March 14, 1997, 1–4.

28. UN Security Council Resolution 1103 (1997), March 31, 1997.

29. International Crisis Group, "Brcko: What Bosnia Could Be," Bosnia Project Report no. 31, Sarajevo, February 10, 1998, 6–8.

Europeans, and the Europeans would not remain in Bosnia without the United States.[30]

The prospects for resolving the dilemma and retaining an effective NATO presence were not promising. In December 1995, congressional support for a one-year deployment of 20,000 American troops to Bosnia was unenthusiastic. It disappeared almost entirely when President Clinton decided in December 1996 that 8,500 troops would remain for an additional 18 months. In June 1997 the House of Representatives passed the FY 1998 defense appropriations bill, which barred funding for the deployment of U.S. ground troops in Bosnia after June 1998. The Senate version of the bill did not include a ban on funding; instead, it adopted a nonbinding resolution calling for a U.S. troop withdrawal at the end of the SFOR mandate. The Senate resolution also called for the European allies to supply all the combat troops for the follow-on force in Bosnia. Senate action came after a raid by British SFOR that resulted in the capture of one accused war criminal and the death of another. The Senate urged that U.S. troops not take part in arrests of war criminals on the grounds that they could result in American casualties. In the end, the two houses adopted and President Clinton accepted a provision that barred funds for U.S. troops in Bosnia after June 1998 but allowed the president to waive the provision if he offered a strategic rationale for the extension and a detailed exit strategy.[31]

By fall 1997 it was clear that a substantial majority of both houses opposed an extension of the U.S. troop presence in Bosnia and wanted Europe to supply the follow-on force. In the conference report on the FY 1998 defense authorization bill, Congress repeated the negative provisions in the FY 1998 appropriations law and added a few more. This legislation (PL 105-85), which the president signed on November 18, 1997, stated that it was "the sense of Congress that U.S. ground forces should not participate in the Bosnian follow-on force, except to provide command and control, intelligence, and logistic support for European forces." Any presidential waiver that extended the U.S. troop presence would have to include assurances that U.S. forces would not be used as civil police in Bosnia. Other sections required the administration to report on the activities of U.S. troops to show what steps had been taken to transfer responsibility to a European-led peacekeeping force. It was going to be a hard sell if the administration was going to get Congress to acquiesce to U.S. troops

---

30. Alexander Nicoll, "NATO Studies Staying On in Bosnia," *Financial Times* (London), October 6, 1997, 2.

31. Lizette Alvarez, "Senate Is Cool to GI Mission in Bosnia But Doesn't Cut Off Funds," *New York Times*, July 11, 1997, 3.

remaining in Bosnia. At the same time, the administration would have to convince the Europeans to do more.[32]

There was no indication, however, that any European country was interested in leading or even participating in a post-SFOR force without the United States. European efforts to deal with the dissolution of Yugoslavia had ended in disaster. The end of the Bosnian conflict at Dayton reestablished U.S. leadership in NATO, which Europe warmly welcomed. The issue was not whether European countries could supply the required number of soldiers. Rather, European insistence on U.S. participation reflected concern about the credibility of an all-European force and the need for continued U.S. leadership within the alliance. U.S. intervention in Bosnia had revitalized NATO and was responsible for securing Russian participation in SFOR. It had also encouraged participation by NATO Partnership for Peace countries, such as Poland and the Czech Republic, that promised to create the basis for NATO enlargement. Awareness that these gains were at risk was the basis of the European "in together, out together" refrain in discussions on the future of SFOR.[33]

SUPPORT OF THE POLICE IN BOSNIA

There was little evidence of European interest in supporting the police program in Bosnia either by assisting the indigenous police or by contributing forces to an armed constabulary. U.S. efforts to support the Bosnian police had begun a year earlier. On September 29, 1996, a UN-sponsored donors' conference was held at Dublin Castle in Ireland to raise money for reforming and retraining the Bosnian police. UN under-secretary-general for peacekeeping affairs Kofi Annan opened the conference, cochaired by the high representative, Carl Bildt, and attended by the Irish prime minister and representatives of thirty-four countries that contributed police officers to the IPTF. Commissioner Peter Fitzgerald presented an elaborate program for equipping the Bosnian police, including provision of vehicles, communications equipment, uniforms, and forensics laboratories. Annan called on UN member states to review the extensive materials the IPTF had prepared on the needs of the Bosnian police and to make contributions so that the United Nations could purchase the $100 million worth of equipment and training required.[34]

---

32. Steven Bowman, Julie Kim, and Steven Woehrel, "Bosnia Stabilization Force and U.S. Policy," Congressional Research Service, Washington, DC, September 19, 1998, 12–14.

33. Ivo Daalder, "Bosnia after SFOR: Options for Continued U.S. Engagement," *Survival*, vol. 39, no. 4 (Winter 1997–98), 8–9.

34. John Maher, "Part of the Resources Needed for Bosnian Police Raised at Dublin Meeting," *The Irish Times* (Dublin), September 30, 1996, 4.

In response to the UN appeal, the United States spoke first by prearrangement with the conference organizers. Robert Gelbard, the leader of the U.S. delegation and assistant secretary of state for international narcotics and law enforcement affairs, said the United States was committed to the success of the IPTF and the police assistance program in Bosnia. The United States had 225 civilian police officers serving in the IPTF and would donate $19 million in equipment and training for local police. A series of European representatives followed Gelbard to the podium. Most said they would first have to study the UN documents before deciding if contributions might be possible. A few countries offered to make slots available for Bosnians in their own national police academies or donate small amounts of equipment. The Irish government offered to train eighteen Bosnian police officers at the Irish police college. Germany offered fifty Volkswagen vans for police transport. Most delegates said that beyond contributing police officers to the IPTF, it was unlikely they would make other contributions. Excluding the U.S. contribution, total pledges at the conference were not more than a few hundred thousand dollars. The French delegate began his remarks by asking in what language did alphabetical order allow the United States to speak first.[35]

In the year after the conference, Europeans contributed little to the UN police training effort in Bosnia, while the United States provided substantial technical assistance and training through the U.S. Department of Justice International Criminal Investigative Training Assistance Program (ICITAP). At the same time, Gelbard began a campaign to create an armed international police force for Bosnia. In March 1996 he had "watched in disgust" as the IPTF and IFOR stood by and refused to apprehend marauding Serb thugs and arsonists during the transfer of the Sarajevo suburbs. When Gelbard asked IPTF officers or IFOR soldiers to take action, they explained they could do nothing because it was not part of their mandate. In one case Gelbard appealed directly to a group of Italian soldiers manning a checkpoint to assist an injured Serb couple whose car had been stoned and flipped over by a mob. The soldiers looked up from their chess game and said they were sorry, but assisting civilians was not in their mandate. Appalled by this behavior, Gelbard protested directly to Iqbal Riza, the senior UN official in Sarajevo. Riza claimed the United Nations could do nothing because the IPTF was unarmed and its mandate was limited to monitoring the local police. Gelbard also raised the issue with IFOR commander Admiral Leighton Smith, who said IFOR could not intervene because its mandate excluded police functions.[36]

---

35. The author was a member of the U.S. delegation to the Dublin meeting.
36. Interview with Robert Gelbard, Washington, DC, August 20, 2002.

In Washington, Gelbard appealed directly to the secretary of state, the White House, and the Pentagon for a change in the IPTF and IFOR mandates. Gelbard explained that there was a serious gap in the "spectrum of response" of the security forces in Bosnia between IFOR and the IPTF, which meant no one could deal with civil disorder. After his appointment as U.S. special representative for the implementation of the Dayton Accords in April 1997, Gelbard met repeatedly with DOD officials at the Pentagon and with European allies on the need for NATO to create an international constabulary to handle the violence he had witnessed in Sarajevo. At the Pentagon, Gelbard encountered resistance from the chairman of the Joint Chiefs of Staff, General John Shalikashvili, who opposed U.S. military forces performing police functions and creating an armed police element within SFOR. General Shalikashvili's position was understandable: He had assumed office a few days before the failed attempt to arrest Somali warlord Mohamed Farah Hassan Aideed in Mogadishu that resulted in the death of eighteen U.S. Army Rangers. Gelbard also met with UN secretary-general Boutros Boutros-Ghali and under-secretary-general Kofi Annan in New York to discuss expanding the IPTF to include an armed constabulary. The United Nations proved unwilling to amend the IPTF mandate, and Gelbard returned to his preferred option of creating the constabulary unit within SFOR.[37]

On July 11, 1997, General Wesley Clark became NATO's Supreme Allied Commander Europe. Clark was intimately familiar with Bosnia, having served on Ambassador Holbrooke's negotiating team and as Holbrooke's senior military adviser at Dayton. Clark's arrival in Brussels followed the June 12, 1997 meeting of NATO's North Atlantic Council defense ministers, which endorsed a more aggressive strategy of military support for civilian implementation in Bosnia. At their first meeting, NATO secretary general Javier Solana informed Clark that SFOR "must actively help the civilians to succeed" if the entire international mission in Bosnia was to achieve its objectives. Solana told the new NATO commander that his mission was "not simply a matter of protecting your forces."[38]

NATO's more aggressive policy toward civilian implementation reflected a growing frustration and a change of attitude within the Clinton administration. General Clark's assumption of command coincided with SFOR's first arrest of a war criminal indicted by the ICTY. This followed a high-level and extremely contentious policy debate in Washington and a subsequent

---

37. Telephone interview with Andrew Bair, former special assistant to Ambassador Robert Gelbard, January 24, 2002.

38. Wesley Clark, *Waging Modern War* (New York: Public Affairs, 2001), 77–87.

U.S. effort to organize a NATO working group in The Hague to direct such operations. Clark's arrival also accompanied a new activism on the part of SFOR in the RS. In late summer 1997 SFOR took control of the RS police antiterrorist brigade, a Serb military police unit that had conducted ethnic cleansing and continued to perform clandestine duties for Serb hard-liners in Pale. Clark approved SFOR's active support for RS president Biljana Plavšić in her struggle against Radovan Karadžić. In mid-August, British SFOR troops intervened to thwart a coup attempt against Plavšić, seizing weapons caches, rounding up plotters, and surrounding the antiterrorist brigade's station in Banja Luka with armored vehicles. SFOR's support for Plavšić involved a series of operations to take control of police stations around Banja Luka from RS police who were loyal to Karadžić. In late August, General Eric Shinseki, the new U.S. commander in Bosnia, called Clark to report that a pro-Plavšić police captain was poised to attempt to take over the police station in Brcko.[39]

THE U.S. DEBATE ON EXTENDING SFOR

Despite opposition from Congress and dissent from senior administration officials, the White House began laying the groundwork to extend the U.S. military commitment in Bosnia in the fall of 1997. In late September the national security adviser, Samuel R. Berger, began offering a rationale for a continuing U.S. presence in Bosnia while stressing that the president had not made a decision. Berger publicly reiterated that the United States maintained a significant stake in the success of the Dayton peace implementation process and left open the possibility of longer-term U.S. involvement in Bosnia. This effort followed a meeting of the National Security Council on the future of SFOR in Bosnia. After the meeting, administration officials began an extensive round of consultations with members of Congress, explaining the rationale for extending the SFOR mandate and for U.S. troops remaining in Bosnia.[40]

On November 4, 1997, President Clinton held a White House meeting with more than a hundred members of Congress to discuss Bosnia. Invitations went to the leadership of both houses, committee chairmen, and key members of both political parties. The president, Secretary of State Madeleine Albright, and Ambassador Gelbard made the case for renewing the SFOR mandate and continuing the U.S. troop presence. Attendees asked questions but did not challenge the president's apparent intention to commit

---

39. Clark, *Waging Modern War.*

40. Bowman, Kim, and Woehrel, "Bosnia Stabilization Force," 10–11; interview with Gelbard.

the United States to a long-term engagement in Bosnia. After the meeting, Secretary Albright told the press that a "consensus was emerging" between the administration and Congress on the need to maintain a robust peacekeeping force in Bosnia, including a contingent of U.S. ground troops.[41]

Secretary of Defense William Cohen immediately challenged Albright's optimistic statement. On November 6 he denied that a consensus had emerged, saying the president would not make a decision until he had reviewed all the options, which ranged from complete withdrawal to extending the existing force. Beyond the expenses and the negative effect on troop morale, Cohen said the United States must weigh its global commitments and determine if the Europeans could play a larger role. Secretary Cohen's statement was consistent with his long-standing opposition to retaining U.S. troops in Bosnia. As a former Republican senator, he was well aware of many lawmakers' anger and frustration over Clinton's decision to extend the original December 1996 deadline by eighteen months to June 1998. At his confirmation hearing Cohen stated emphatically that U.S. troops would leave Bosnia as scheduled. Cohen warned his administration colleagues that congressional support was eroding and that the Pentagon could not continue to spend $2 billion annually to keep U.S. forces in Bosnia. He also believed the Europeans should be forced to do more. As a U.S. pullout appeared increasingly unlikely, Cohen attempted to use his position as the administration's chief critic on Bosnia to leverage a larger European contribution, particularly in assisting the Bosnian police and providing constabulary forces.[42]

In early November the U.S. proposal for an international constabulary force for Bosnia received qualified support from NATO secretary general Solana. Speaking in Berlin at a European forum on pan-European peacekeeping on November 8, he said that successful peace support operations required NATO to adapt to new demands in the security environment by creating new political and military structures. Among the lessons learned from Bosnia was that appropriately armed and trained forces were essential to the transition from hostilities to peace. Experience in Bosnia had revealed a gap between the ability of SFOR and the local police to provide a secure environment, and creating an international police force or gendarmerie to manage crises in Bosnia would help restore civil order. Some situations were too difficult for the IPTF and inappropriate for the military.[43]

---

41. "Bosnia: NATO Prepares New Force Options," *World News Digest*, December 4, 1997.

42. Bradley Graham, "Cohen Plays Skeptic Role on Bosnia: Defense Chief to Insist on Europe Doing More," *Washington Post*, November 30, 1997, A1.

43. Hills, "International Peace Support Operations," 26–28.

A DECISIVE DECEMBER

The role of civilian police in Bosnia emerged as the major point of contention between the United States and its European allies at the meeting of NATO defense ministers in Brussels on December 2, 1997. In discussions about the follow-on force to SFOR, Cohen recommended creating a deterrent force (DFOR) that would both reduce the number of NATO troops and transfer responsibility for maintaining public order to a multinational police force. Cohen made clear that the United States wanted to reduce the overall size of the NATO presence from 34,000 troops and draw down the 8,000 U.S. personnel serving in Bosnia. He suggested that U.S. participation in the follow-on force should be limited to logistics and intelligence support and supplying over-the-horizon protection from air power based in other countries.[44]

Cohen also called to substantially increase European assistance to the Bosnian police, pointing out that the United States had contributed $30 million to police reform in Bosnia, while European countries had contributed only $5 million. Cohen said the Bosnian police remained short of personnel and equipment because much of their $100 million budget had not been funded. He warned that President Clinton would have trouble persuading Congress to support continued U.S. troop presence in Bosnia unless he could demonstrate that the Europeans were prepared to carry a larger share of the peacekeeping burden and contribute more resources. Cohen said there was a "serious deficiency" in European commitment to building a well-trained local police force that was not under the control of obstructionists attempting to frustrate the Dayton peace process.[45]

Cohen's most controversial proposal, however, was to create an international police force drawn from the constabulary forces of the European allies. He noted that SFOR was not trained or equipped to do policing, which created a security gap exploited by local politicians, including suspected war criminals. There was a need for a specially trained international police force that could take over such tasks as crowd control, election security, and protecting returning refugees. Creating such a force would reduce the need for the United States and NATO to maintain large numbers of troops in Bosnia. Cohen did not specify which countries the United States wanted to contribute to such a force, but it was clear that the Italians, the French, and the Spanish were the most likely candidates. According to a senior Pentagon

---

44. Ennio Caretto, "America Wants Out, Looks to Allies for Relief," *Corriere della Sera* (Milan), December 1, 1997.

45. William Drozdiak, "NATO Commander Urges Follow-on Force in Bosnia," *Washington Post*, December 3, 1997, A41.

official, this could be done by "building a public security force that could take over the kinds of responsibilities that were in the hands of the international military presence."[46]

General Clark reinforced Cohen's message, telling the defense ministers that a substantial follow-on force would be needed to sustain the progress achieved in implementing the Dayton Accords. Clark warned that without a robust NATO presence, reconstruction efforts could collapse and war could resume in Bosnia. The military challenge remained formidable, as SFOR conducted more than 150 patrols a day to maintain a fragile truce between the former warring parties. In addition, NATO peacekeepers were overwhelmed by civilian tasks such as supervising elections and resettling refugees because the United Nations could not handle such responsibilities. Clark made a particular point of the need for an international police force that could stop the political corruption and rampant smuggling that undermined Bosnia's economic recovery and subsidized the "Mafia-type" activities of ethnic Serb hard-liners like Radovan Karadžić.[47]

For their part, the Europeans pressed Secretary Cohen to continue the U.S. military presence and resisted U.S. pressure to create an international police force in Bosnia. British defense minster George Robertson "chided" the Clinton administration for refusing to renew the commitment of forces, claiming a U.S. withdrawal could undermine the tenuous peace that had existed since IFOR arrived in January 1996.[48] The Europeans countered American requests for a constabulary by claiming they would be hard-pressed to find the highly trained police to handle such a sensitive mission. Only a small number of countries in NATO—France, Italy, Spain, Portugal, and the Netherlands—had such forces. To take police from only a few countries to perform dangerous tasks would represent an unfair burden and violate the NATO principle of sharing risks equally. The Europeans also claimed there were legal issues associated with using international police in a peace operation, including questions about whether the police would have law enforcement authority and under what conditions they could use deadly force. Some objected to sending an international force that might substitute for the local police. Others argued the police lacked the kind of firepower that deterred the former belligerents from attacking NATO peacekeepers. Yet Cohen's recommendation for an international constabulary was included

---

46. Jim Mannion, "Police Role in Bosnia a Point of Contention Among Allies," *Agence France-Presse*, December 2, 1997.

47. Drozdiak, "NATO Commander Urges Follow-on Force."

48. Steven Meyers, "Britain Presses U.S. for Pledge on Bosnia GI's," *New York Times*, December 5, 1997, A8.

in the instructions to the alliance's military planners to develop a set of options for a follow-on force to replace SFOR.[49]

On December 8, 1997, two influential daily newspapers gave Secretary Cohen explicit support. In an editorial, the *New York Times* noted that the Clinton administration was "sidling toward" a positive decision on maintaining troops past the June deadline. The editorial claimed that Secretary Cohen had "chosen his words more wisely" than Secretary Albright, placing two important conditions for a continued U.S. presence in Bosnia. According to the *Times*, Cohen wanted a shift of security responsibilities from soldiers to a stronger international police force and greater European participation to meet congressional concerns. Noting that the IPTF was composed of police monitors "hemmed in by a weak mandate and faulty UN recruiting procedures," the *Times* counseled that a new armed international police force needed to fill the gap between heavily armed NATO soldiers and unarmed UN police trainers. Such a force could come from the large, armed "paramilitary police forces" in many Western European countries. Sending European constabularies to Bosnia would relieve NATO's burden and "be a good way to increase Europe's share of the overall security burden." The editorial concluded that the United States should not stay in Bosnia unless a compelling need for U.S. troops had been established and "a clear strategy leading to their early replacement by an armed police force had been put in place."[50]

On the same day, *Newsday* said Secretary Cohen's plan for the NATO allies to form an international police force to take over from military peacekeepers in Bosnia made sense. "A police force," the newspaper stated, "in credible numbers and with appropriate powers and jurisdiction, can do what military peacekeepers cannot do without distorting their role: live among the population, cultivate informants, arrest suspects, quell civil disorder, and handle routine disputes." According to the editorial, NATO provided little more than a "wet blanket dampening down smoldering resentments that could flare up at any time." An international police force would be better suited to the long-term mission of maintaining civil order, with the provision that NATO troops could return if war erupted.[51]

The editorials foreshadowed the actions the United States and Europe would take to resolve their differences over the future of NATO's presence in Bosnia. Under arrangements that would emerge from high-level

49. "Obstacles Strew the Way of Bosnia's Future Force," Agence France-Presse, January 22, 1998.

50. Editorial, "Mr. Cohen's Caution on Bosnia," *New York Times*, December 8, 1997, A24.

51. "Call the Police: Cohen's Plan to Replace Bosnia Peacekeepers with a NATO Police Force Makes Sense," *Newsday*, December 8, 1997, A30.

political decisions and NATO military planning, the United States would agree to keep a smaller number of its troops in Bosnia and the Europeans would commit to providing a constabulary force that would be armed and experienced in dealing with civil disorder. The European contribution of such a force would be presented to Congress as proof that the NATO allies were prepared to shoulder more of the burden in Bosnia. As a consequence, U.S. military forces would be less likely to face hostile mobs and risk suffering casualties.

On December 9 and 10, the Peace Implementation Council convened in Bonn to review progress on civilian implementation of the Dayton Accords. The PIC stated that there had been considerable improvements in security and in addressing the prerequisites for reconciliation, such as protecting freedom of movement and strengthening the economy. It also noted that "much more could have been achieved if the Bosnian authorities contributed their full share to the construction of a civil and democratic society." As for the IPTF, the council endorsed the progress made in reforming and restructuring the local police. It also called to create new IPTF units that would specialize in "key public security issues," including managing civil disorder.[52]

While creating a constabulary force for Bosnia was not on the PIC agenda, it was the subject of a meeting "on the margins" between NATO secretary general Javier Solana; Gregory Schulte, the director of NATO's Bosnia Task Force; and a senior U.S. military officer. During the discussion, Schulte took out a piece of paper and drew two circles, marking one SFOR and the other UN IPTF. The participants then discussed the respective merits of locating the proposed constabulary unit in one or the other circle. The trio agreed that the United Nations was unwilling to arm the IPTF or expand its mandate. The senior U.S. military officer expressed concern about SFOR performing police functions. He was more concerned, however, about the proliferation of armed groups outside of SFOR. At the end of the discussion, Schulte placed the letters MSU, for "multinational specialized unit" within the circle marked SFOR. None of the three liked the name, but they could not think of another. Having privately reached agreement in principle, there remained the difficult task of achieving formal agreement on renewing the mandate and including a constabulary unit within the follow-on force to SFOR.[53]

At the December 16, 1997, meeting of NATO foreign ministers in Brussels, the United States and its allies moved closer to endorsing publicly the exten-

---

52. "Bonn Peace Implementation Conference 1997," December 10, 1997, 11.

53. Interview with Gregory Schulte, senior director, National Security Council, Washington, DC, August 20, 2002.

sion of the SFOR mandate beyond the June 1998 deadline. Emerging from the first day's session, French foreign minister Hubert Vedrine told the press that his colleagues had reached consensus on retaining a reduced NATO military presence in Bosnia, although a formal decision, including numbers, would have to await the military planners' report. NATO officials attending the conference were quoted as stating that the new "slim-line" unit, tentatively named DFOR, would be reduced to between 15,000 and 20,000 troops, roughly half the size of the existing force of 30,000 soldiers. U.S. troops would be included, but their number would be reduced to 8,500. There would also be a contingent of constabulary police to deal with crowd control and refugee return. The new force would not have an exit date, but its mandate would be reviewed every six months. The ministers said a final decision on the composition of the new force was required by March 1, 1998, to allow adequate time for redeployments.[54]

At the conference, Secretary of State Albright reiterated that the Europeans must contribute more toward police if the U.S. Congress was to support a continued U.S. military presence in Bosnia. Albright said it was unacceptable for the United States to provide 90 percent of the funding for training and equipping the Bosnian police when creating law and order was critical to "a sensible exit strategy" for all NATO countries. She reaffirmed the need to strengthen the international police in Bosnia to take responsibility for civilian reconstruction tasks that a smaller SFOR would be unable to perform, suggesting that NATO could support the IPTF by providing the "capabilities that are found in many countries in the form of Gendarmes and Carabinieri." Such forces could increase SFOR's flexibility, enhance force protection, and promote Dayton implementation. Secretary Albright had no problem praising the Europeans for their efforts but said they "must do much, much more."[55] To drive home her point about the need for constabulary forces, the secretary showed the NATO ministers a video of the August 28 riot in Brcko. If the soldiers had been unable to hold their position on the bridge, she said, the only fallback available was the helicopter gunship overhead—obviously, not a desirable option. Constabulary forces trained and equipped for crowd control would have provided an alternative.[56]

54. Norman Kempster, "NATO Seeks Plan to Extend Its Peace Mission in Bosnia," *Los Angeles Times,* December 17, 1997, A1; "NATO Stays in Bosnia Another Year," *Toronto Star,* December 17, 1997, A17.

55. Martin Walker, "No Exit for NATO's Bosnia Force," *The Guardian* (London), December 17, 1997, 12; U.S. Mission to NATO, "Statement by Secretary of State Madeleine Albright during the North Atlantic Council Ministerial Meeting," Brussels, December 16, 1997, available at http://www.nato.int/docu/speech/1997/s971216aa.htm (accessed November 26, 2012).

56. Interview with Schulte.

Two days later, on December 18, 1997, President Clinton announced the U.S. "commitment in principle" to extend its troop presence in Bosnia beyond the June 1998 deadline. Clinton noted the progress toward a lasting peace in Bosnia and the challenges that still had to be faced to finish the job. The international community had helped Bosnia create democratic institutions, improved the lives of the Bosnian people, and provided for their security by training ethnically integrated police forces in the Bosnian Federation and "taking the first step toward a professional, democratic police force" in the RS. This progress was "unmistakable, but not yet irreversible." The Bosnians still needed the "safety net and helping hand that only the international community, including the United States, could provide."[57]

To finish the work, the president said the international community must continue to provide a military presence to enable economic reconstruction and the return of refugees to proceed in an atmosphere of confidence. For this reason, the president had instructed the U.S. representative to NATO to inform our allies that "in principle, the U.S. will take part in a security presence in Bosnia when SFOR withdraws this summer." The agreement in principle would become a commitment only when the president approved the action plan NATO military authorities would present early the following year. While not wanting to prejudge the details of the plan, Clinton listed several criteria the plan would have to meet, including the ability of the follow-on force to protect itself. Although the force would be smaller than the present one, it needed to be sufficiently large to achieve its mission and defend itself. In addition, European allies would have to assume their share of responsibility. Clinton noted that the Europeans had done a great deal but said they could do more. Finally, he said the new force would have to enjoy the support of Congress and the American people. With that in mind, he announced that members of Congress from both parties had accepted his invitation to accompany him on a forthcoming visit to Bosnia.[58]

On December 22, 1997, the president, first lady Hillary Clinton, and their daughter Chelsea spent twelve hours in Bosnia delivering a political message to Bosnian leaders in Sarajevo and yuletide cheer to U.S. troops at Eagle Base in Tuzla. Accompanying the president were former senator Robert Dole, his Republican opponent for the White House, his wife Elizabeth Dole, and eleven members of Congress, including Senator Ted Stevens, chairman of the Senate Appropriations Committee, and Representative John Kasich, chairman of the House Budget Committee. Clinton met with the Serb, Croat, and Bosniak members of Bosnia's collective presidency and had a

57. "Decision in Bosnia," *New York Times,* December 19, 1997, A20.

58. "Decision in Bosnia."

private meeting with Biljana Plavšić. In a twenty-minute speech delivered to four hundred religious and political leaders crowded into Sarajevo's small National Theater, Clinton praised Bosnian leaders for the progress they had achieved but then went down a checklist of things they still had to do. This list included sharing power, returning refugees, ending corruption, freeing the media, and capturing war criminals. Clinton said leaders must also "take the police out of the hands of the warlords" and "reform, retrain, and re-equip a democratic police force that would foster security, not fear." At Club 21, a large shed with a sheet-metal roof at Eagle Base, Clinton told several hundred cheering GIs that the United States was determined to do its part in Bosnia but rightly expected Bosnians to do theirs.[59]

Clinton's Christmas visit was a defining moment in the Bosnian peace process. Until that time, hard-line Serbs and other opponents of the Dayton agreement believed they could wait until the United States and the international community left in June 1998. Clinton's decision that U.S. troops would remain indefinitely nullified that option, and his visit to Bosnia convinced the Europeans and the Bosnians that the United States was committed for the long term.[60] Once it was certain the United States would remain, the pace of the peace implementation process accelerated. Within the first two months of 1998, there was more progress toward national integration than in the previous two years. In rapid succession, a flag, a common currency, a unified telephone system, and common license plates were adopted; limited air, rail, and truck traffic began to operate.[61]

PLANNING FOR THE DETERRENT FORCE

NATO planning for the SFOR follow-on force accelerated in January 1998. At Supreme Headquarters Allied Powers Europe (SHAPE), four options for the deterrent force were under consideration: complete withdrawal, continuation of the current force levels, a smaller force with a broad military and civilian-assistance mandate, or an even smaller force limited to military tasks.[62] The first two options were throwaways; only the last two were serious. The third option included an international constabulary force—the new Multinational Specialized Unit (MSU), which would fill the security gap between

---

59. James Bennet, "Clinton on Tour, Presses Bosnians and Salutes GI's," *New York Times,* December 23, 1997, A1.

60. Interview with Richard Kauzlarich, former U.S. ambassador to Bosnia, Washington, DC, January 3, 2002.

61. Holbrooke, *To End a War,* 357.

62. Kempster, "NATO Seeks Plan."

SFOR and the IPTF and would be used primarily for crowd control. Its mission would be to protect returning refugees, ensuring the right of return that the Dayton Accords provided. It would also assist with installing minority mayors and municipal council members who had been elected in absentia in the fall of 1997 but had been unable to return to their hometowns to assume office. It was widely predicted in the media that international efforts to return refugees and seat minority politicians would be met with a wave of ethnic-related violence. The UN High Commissioner for Refugees, Sadako Ogata, urged NATO to include rapid reaction police units in its plans for the follow-on military force for Bosnia, as a strong international police force was important to completing Bosnia's refugee resettlement program.[63]

On February 20, 1998, the North Atlantic Council, composed of ambassadors from the sixteen NATO member states, agreed to continue the NATO military presence in Bosnia indefinitely beyond June 1998. The council's decision was subject only to approval by the UN Security Council, which was a formality. The NATO-led force would retain the name SFOR, primarily to avoid the $1 million cost of repainting signs and vehicles and issuing new identification cards. The new SFOR's mission would be to deter the renewal of hostilities and create an environment conducive to implementing the civilian aspects of the Dayton peace process. In this regard, the new force would have "enhanced capability to help promote public security" in close cooperation with the OHR, the IPTF, and the Bosnian authorities. The council instructed NATO military authorities to prepare a final operations plan for the new force that could be reviewed with non-NATO contributors.[64]

Included in the new, smaller version of SFOR would be tough new police units capable of dealing with ethnic-related civil disturbances that regular soldiers were not trained or equipped to handle. According to a senior Clinton administration official, the new multinational police unit would be drawn from European constabulary forces and would have "more balanced capabilities and training than just retreating or killing." It would be well armed and supported by regular SFOR troops, if necessary. The senior official noted that all three ethnic groups, supported by local police, were guilty of preventing the return of refugees of different ethnicities. The NATO police force would "try to coax local law enforcement to act," but

---

63. "Military Police Units Considered for SFOR Follow-On," Agence France-Presse, January 16, 1998.

64. North Atlantic Treaty Organization, "Statement by the North Atlantic Council on the Continuation of a NATO-Led Multinational Military Presence in Bosnia and Herzegovina," press release, February 20, 1998, available at http://www.nato.int/docu/pr/1998/p98-018e.htm (accessed November 26, 2012).

if it failed to respond the international police would take responsibility.[65] General Wesley Clark expressed a somewhat different view. According to Clark, the new force was a "step toward adapting the capability of SFOR to meet new requirements on the ground." It was "not a police force," but a force that would offer "tangible assistance" to the local police, filling the gap between them and the IPTF. It was unclear if the new force would arrest war criminals.[66]

CREATING THE MSU

Recruiting

Recruiting constabulary units for the new MSU was not easy, as despite U.S. appeals, European donor countries proved unwilling to participate. After a prolonged recruiting effort, only Italy stepped forward to volunteer three companies of Carabinieri. Additional platoons had to be recruited from non-NATO states to form the first battalion. The process of raising, training, and deploying the first MSU battalion took nearly eight months, so the first SFOR constabulary unit did not reach Sarajevo until August 1998. A second battalion was scheduled to arrive in Bosnia in November 1998, but efforts to recruit personnel from Spain, Poland, the Czech Republic, Hungary, and the Netherlands failed, and the second unit was never deployed.

For Italy, assisting with planning for the MSU and providing most of the personnel was part of a larger effort to increase its status in NATO. It was also part of a defensive strategy to exert greater influence in the Balkans, a region vital to Italian national interests. Sharing the Adriatic Sea coastline with Albania, Croatia, Bosnia, Montenegro, and Slovenia, Italy was a magnet for refugees and a target for Balkan organized crime. In 1994, when the European Union assumed responsibility for policing the southern Bosnian city of Mostar, Italy sent forty Carabinieri as part of the international police force organized by the Western European Union. In January 1996 some 3,200 Italian troops were part of IFOR when NATO troops arrived in Bosnia. In 1997 Italy took the lead in organizing Operation Alba, an eight-country, 7,000-member intervention force that restored order in Albania after the collapse of a series of pyramid investment schemes led to a situation of total anarchy. A coalition of the willing authorized by the UN Security

---

65. Norman Kempster, "NATO to Create New Police Force in Bosnia," *Los Angeles Times,* February 20, 1998, A10.
66. Elizabeth Neuffer, "NATO Plans Paramilitary Force in Bosnia," *Boston Globe,* February 23, 1998, A2.

Council, Operation Alba was the first peace enforcement mission composed entirely of Europeans.[67]

For the Italian press, the Carabinieri's performance in Operation Alba gave Italy the honor of leading the MSU. In January 1998, Italian newspapers reported that General Clark had been so impressed with the Carabinieri's operation in Albania that he personally asked the chief of the Carabinieri if Italy would take the lead in organizing the MSU for Bosnia. On January 20 the Carabinieri established an MSU working group in Rome to plan and initiate the MSU's formation. At the same time, the Italian government assigned a Carabinieri officer to the MSU working group at NATO headquarters in Brussels. A month later, on February 27, the Carabinieri established an MSU training base in Gorizia, Italy, and began preparations for deploying to Bosnia.[68]

The reaction to NATO's call for contributions to the MSU from the other two most likely NATO contributors—France and Spain—was less than forthcoming. The French were strongly opposed to the MSU from the start. For Paris the U.S. proposal to create a European-led constabulary force for Bosnia was a means for Washington to pass the buck to the Europeans. Because the United States did not have forces similar to the French Gendarmerie or the Carabinieri, the Americans could not be expected to participate, leaving the responsibility for filling the ranks of the new multinational police force solely to the few countries in Europe that had such forces. The French saw the role envisioned for the new specialized unit as highly risky and likely to set a negative precedent for future operations. To ensure proper burden sharing, the French argued that regular infantry, with some additional training, should handle crowd control and refugee return. The United Kingdom shared this attitude, reporting no problem dealing with mob violence in its sector: With experience in Northern Ireland, British troops were accustomed to dealing with civil disturbance and saw no need for a specialized police force for such contingencies.[69]

Madrid initially greeted the plan to include an MSU within SFOR with enthusiasm. On the eve of Ambassador Robert Gelbard's visit to Spain in January 1997, the Spanish press announced the Guardia Civil was preparing to send between 300 and 500 men to Bosnia as part of the new multinational police force. Reports noted there were already 144 members of the Guardia

---

67. Carlo Scognamiglio-Pasini, "Increasing Italy's Input," *NATO Review* (Summer 2001), 26–27.

68. "Missioni all'estero," on Carabinieri website, available at www.carabinieri.it/ (accessed October 17, 2012).

69. Luc Rosenzweig, "NATO Debates Mission of New Multinational Force," *Le Monde* (Paris), February 4, 1998.

Civil in Bosnia: 68 were serving as military police with Spanish forces, 56 were in the IPTF, and 20 were providing close protection for High Representative Carlos Westendorp, a Spaniard. As the new multinational police force would be armed and part of NATO, the press stated that the Guardia had attracted U.S. attention because of its discipline and its distinguished service in Bosnia.[70] The results of Gelbard's visit were positive and the Spanish seemed genuinely interested in participating. In the final analysis, however, the Spanish government decided not to join, despite the personal appeals from another Spaniard, NATO secretary general Javier Solana. The primary reason was that the Guardia was engaged in an intensive struggle against Basque separatists that badly stretched its limited resources. In May the Spanish defense minister announced that his country would "remain on the sidelines" and not participate in the MSU. Spain preferred to retain its military police in regular SFOR units; it would not reduce or reconfigure its military presence in Bosnia.[71]

Roles and Missions

On March 4, 1998, President Clinton certified to Congress that U.S. forces were required in Bosnia after June 1998 to facilitate the rapid implementation of the Dayton agreement. He called for a reduction of the number of U.S. troops from 8,500 to 6,900, but proposed that no end date or "arbitrary deadline" should be established to withdraw them. That said, deployment would not be open-ended; the United States would substitute an end date with an "end state." Clinton then outlined ten conditions that would permit a NATO-led withdrawal, including creating a restructured, retrained, and reintegrated police force; judicial reform; arrest of war criminals; press freedom; democratic elections; refugee returns; and a multiethnic administration in Brcko. The president asked Congress to provide $2.35 billion in 1998–99 to support the effort.[72]

In explaining the president's decision, Gelbard told the press that SFOR would retain its name and would not see a reduction in troop levels until after the September 1998 elections. The size of the U.S. combat force would remain at three battalions, but the number of other U.S. troops would

---

70. Miguel Gonzalez, "Civil Guard to Send Its Men to Bosnia under Order of NATO," *El Pais* (Madrid), December 28, 1997.

71. "Spain Rejects Military Police Plan for Bosnia," Agence France-Presse, May 4, 1998.

72. The White House, Office of the Press Secretary, "President Seeks $2.5 Billion for 1998 to Support Military Operations in Bosnia and Southwest Asia," March 4, 1998, available at http://www.usembassy-israel.org.il/publish/press/whouse/archive/1998/march/wh3306.htm (accessed November 26, 2012).

decline as the Europeans took over logistics and other support functions. What was new, Gelbard said, was that NATO was organizing specialized units composed of European military police that would handle the expected increase in civil unrest that increased refugee returns and the seating of minority municipal officials generated. These international police units would respond when the local police could not control the situation. They would also train local police and support the IPTF.[73]

In March 1998, NATO planners at SHAPE focused on the issues related to the role and mission of the new specialized unit in SFOR. As this was a totally new concept, planners had to determine what duties the new unit would perform, its rules of engagement, and the nature of its relationships with the IPTF and local police. To assist in this effort, General Clark invited Ambassador Robert Oakley and Colonel Michael Dziedzic to Brussels to brief NATO leaders and planners on their theory concerning the use of constabulary forces in peace operations. At the time, Oakley and Dziedzic were staff members of the National Defense University's Institute for National Strategic Studies in Washington, DC. They were accompanied by a military officer from the Joint Chiefs of Staff to emphasize the importance the Pentagon attached to their views.[74] In their book, *Policing the New World Disorder*, Oakley and Dziedzic had identified the "security gap" between military forces that were reluctant to engage in confrontations with civilians and international police monitors and local police that were unable or unwilling to do crowd control. To fill this gap the authors recommended constabulary forces trained and equipped to handle public disorder and better suited than the military to perform law enforcement functions. When the likelihood of military conflict had been reduced substantially, they argued, constabulary forces could substitute for regular military forces in peace operations and, ultimately, replace them altogether.[75]

On March 4, 1998, the day of President Clinton's congressional certification, Oakley and Dziedzic briefed General Clark's deputy and senior SHAPE planners on the possible roles and missions of a constabulary force in Bosnia. In their briefing, Oakley and Dziedzic stressed the importance of recruiting formed and fully integrated forces from only a limited number of countries with similar policing traditions and philosophies, as well as the necessity of providing the specialized unit with clear rules

---

73. "Slight Reduction in American Contingent of International Force in June," Agence France-Presse, March 4, 1998.

74. Interview with Ambassador Robert Oakley, Washington, DC, August 23, 2002.

75. Dziedzic, introduction, 12, and Robert B. Oakley and Michael J. Dziedzic, conclusions, 519, in *Policing the New World Disorder*.

of engagement and clearly defining its relationships with SFOR, OHR, and the IPTF. They envisioned that the new unit would be deployed in a central location and would use nonlethal means to deter and contain politically motivated unrest, to assist the IPTF and local police in handling spontaneous civil disorder, and to promote Dayton implementation in general. The unit would also assist the IPTF in training local police to perform crowd control functions. They cautioned that the new unit should not be used for arresting war criminals, local law enforcement, or as part of an American exit strategy.[76]

Three weeks later, Oakley and Dziedzic returned to Brussels on March 25, 1998, this time at Solana's invitation, to chair a workshop at SHAPE on the roles constabulary forces could play in a range of future NATO contingencies, from preventing state collapse and facilitating humanitarian relief to providing postconflict security. The workshop was unofficial, but the attendees included field grade officers from the Gendarmerie, the Carabinieri, the Guardia Civil, the Dutch Marechaussee, U.S. military police, and the Royal Canadian Mounted Police. The Swedish deputy foreign minister and a UN-MIBH representative also attended. Participants agreed that constabulary forces provided a valuable mix of capabilities, but that the mission and mandate must be clear and resources must be adequate. There was uniform opposition to constabulary forces exercising executive authority (e.g., arrest and detention). The preferred role, the meeting concluded, was for the constabulary to support the local police and hold them accountable to international standards. During the discussion, Solana was particularly concerned about the limited pool of qualified source countries, the need for an adequate mandate, command and control arrangements, and the development of common tactics and doctrine. At the end of the meeting, the Swedish representative offered to host a field exercise involving NATO military forces, the MSU, and UN IPTF personnel to address the issues Solana raised. Unfortunately, the proposed Swedish exercise was never held, and these issues would bedevil the MSU long after its arrival in Bosnia.[77]

Riot in Drvar

On April 24, 1998, an incident in the Bosnian municipality of Drvar reaffirmed the need for an international constabulary force in Bosnia. Once again opponents of the peace process used a rent-a-mob to engage international peacekeepers. Once again IPTF officers were forced to flee after the mob burned their police station and vehicles. Once again SFOR was forced

---

76. Interview with Colonel Michael Dziedzic, Washington, DC, August 28, 2002.

77. Interview with Dziedzic.

to engage civilian demonstrators. This time, however, the antagonists were ethnic Croats, not Serbs.

Before the war, the town of Drvar had a population of 17,000, of which 97 percent were ethnic Serbs. During the conflict, the combined Croat and Bosniak armies broke through Serb lines near Drvar, sending the population fleeing to Banja Luka. Surprisingly, the town suffered almost no damage. After the war, the Croatian Democratic Union (HDZ) party took advantage of the situation to resettle 6,000 Croat refugees and former soldiers and their families in Drvar. It also began a campaign of violence and intimidation to discourage Serb returns. On April 16 an elderly Serb couple that had just returned were murdered and their house was burned. The next day, the high representative, the UN's special representative of the secretary-general (SRSG), and the IPTF commissioner sent a joint letter to the authorities in Canton Ten (Livno) calling for the resignation of the cantonal interior minister and the deputy mayor of Drvar and the decertification of the town's police chief. The letter accused local authorities of failing over a period of several months to investigate and take action in dozens of incidents of assault, harassment, and arson against returning Serbs.[78]

On April 24 a highly disciplined mob of two to three hundred Croats attacked the municipal office building and assaulted the Serb mayor, who had been elected by absentee voting in September 1997. The mob then attacked and destroyed nearby non-governmental organization (NGO) offices and the IPTF station, assaulting and seriously injuring several IPTF officers and international NGO staff. Seven UN vehicles were destroyed and others were damaged. Finally, the rioters burned an apartment complex housing Serb returnees, leaving 160 people homeless and injuring SFOR soldiers who tried to protect the building and its residents. The Canadian SFOR troops, which were responsible for Drvar, operated under rules of engagement (ROEs) from Ottawa that prohibited them from performing police duties and engaging the rioters. The Canadian ROEs were different from those of SFOR, but the Canadians followed their national guidance. In the end, SFOR evacuated the IPTF, the mayor, and all the Serbs who wanted to leave for the safety of Banja Luka. During the chaos, the local police refused to intervene and were seen openly fraternizing with the rioters. It was clear from the mob's behavior that the day's events were orchestrated by Croat authorities.[79]

---

78. United Nations Secretariat, Report of the Secretary-General on the United Nations Mission in Bosnia and Herzegovina, S/1998/491, June 10, 1998, 5.

79. International Crisis Group, "Impunity in Drvar," Balkans Report no. 40, Sarajevo, August 20, 1998, 3–8; interview with Kauzlarich.

In the aftermath of the violence, a number of senior international officials visited Drvar. High Representative Carlos Westendorp, NATO commander General Wesley Clark, SFOR commander General Eric Shinseki, Organization for Security and Cooperation in Europe (OSCE) head of mission Robert Barry, and several congressmen arrived within weeks. They stated that the international community was not going to be intimidated, nor were Serbs going to be denied their right of return. General Clark was accompanied by tanks and helicopter gunships to make the point. But Serb returns stopped for two months, and the Serb population did not reach its preriot level for six months.[80]

The MSU Advance Team

On April 24, 1998, the day of the Drvar riot, the MSU advance team of the Carabinieri arrived in Sarajevo. The MSU executive officer, Colonel Vincenzo Coppola, began an extensive round of briefings at SFOR headquarters and at the headquarters of each of the multinational divisions. In these meetings Coppola sought to introduce the concept of a constabulary force and discuss its capabilities. He quickly discovered a general absence of familiarity with constabulary forces and a lack of understanding of their potential role and mission in a peace operation, particularly among U.S. and northern European military officers. Coppola also encountered a general reluctance to accept that the MSU would operate like "a police force with military characteristics." In Coppola's concept of operations, the MSU's primary mission would be to serve as a deterrent force. The unit would patrol widely, constantly interact with civilians, and spot and defuse trouble before it could start. This contrasted markedly with the general understanding of senior SFOR officers, particularly the multinational division (MND) commanders. In their view, the MSU should perform like a "riot squad" or "strategic reserve" that would remain in its barracks in Sarajevo and enter its areas of responsibility only when needed. When the initial round of briefings concluded, Coppola found that summer transfers and the influx of new officers required him to repeat his briefings for a new cast of characters.[81]

In addition to briefing SFOR, Colonel Coppola met with IPTF leadership to discuss possible areas of cooperation. Here again, Coppola found a general lack of familiarity with constabulary forces among the British, American, and German police officers who held the most senior positions

---

80. International Crisis Group, "Impunity."

81. E-mail interview with Vincenzo Coppola, former MSU executive officer, August 29, 2002.

in the IPTF. The IPTF was generally wary that the MSU would become a competitor and attempt to take over some of its functions. There was also a fear that the Bosnians would not be able to distinguish between the members of the MSU and their IPTF counterparts. Coppola sought to reassure the IPTF leadership that the MSU, in its distinctive blue uniforms with red berets and red armbands, would be easily identifiable from other SFOR units and the IPTF, which wore national police uniforms and blue UN berets. MSU vehicles would be painted blue with SFOR markings, in contrast to the IPTF vehicles, which were painted white with the letters UN in black on the side. Coppola also sought to reassure the IPTF that the MSU intended to cooperate fully and coordinate its operations with the United Nations through the SFOR commander. Yet he made it clear that, to be effective, the MSU would have to engage in information gathering, and once an intervention was ordered, the MSU would have responsibility for determining the force level, tactics, and timing of the operation. Coppola left his meetings with the IPTF officials feeling he had not entirely allayed their concerns.[82]

Final Approval

On May 28, 1998, the NATO foreign ministers met in Luxembourg and adopted the operations plan prepared by the alliance's military committee for extending SFOR beyond the June deadline. The plan, code-named Operation Joint Forge, called to reduce military force levels after the September elections. It also called to create an MSU in SFOR of six hundred men with the same mandate as other SFOR elements. The new unit would enhance "SFOR's ability to support local authorities in responding to civil disorder without engaging in police functions so as to assist the return of refugees and displaced persons and the installation of elected officials."[83] According to General Clark, the specialized police unit would be composed of police from the Carabinieri and the Argentine National Gendarmerie. The MSU, Clark said, would be based at a central location and would be dispatched as needed. It would operate under NATO ROEs, but it would not have responsibility for arresting war criminals. It also would not replace the local police or be responsible for local law enforcement. Clark noted that in the future, NATO would review the SFOR mandate

---

82. Interview with Coppola.

83. North Atlantic Treaty Organization, "Statement on Bosnia and Herzegovina Issued at the Ministerial Meeting of the North Atlantic Council held in Luxembourg on May 28, 1998," press release M-NAC1(98)60, May 28, 1998, available at http://www.nato.int/docu/comm/1998/9805-lux/ (accessed November 26, 2012).

every six months, but that there would be benchmarks to be met rather than an arbitrary end date for the mission.[84]

In recruiting for the MSU, General Clark turned to Buenos Aires after France, the Netherlands, Spain, and Portugal refused to participate. Like Italy, Argentina saw participation in NATO-led peace operations as a means of burnishing its international image. It also saw responding to Clark's request as a way to improve its ties with the United States. In December 1997 Argentina had contributed 140 gendarmes to the UN civilian police mission in Haiti. The Argentine mission was to provide for the security of UN personnel, including thirty-one American CIVPOL officers. Providing a similar number of gendarmes for the MSU in Bosnia was part of this larger effort to gain positive international recognition after a series of repressive regimes and the debacle of the Falkland Islands war.[85]

On June 11, 1998, the NATO defense ministers agreed to the activation order required to continue SFOR beyond the June deadline, subject to the resolution of the UN Security Council. SFOR's mission would be to continue to deter renewed hostilities and contribute to a secure environment. The NATO-led force would include an MSU, which would assist in the transition from military to civil implementation.[86] On June 15, 1998, UN Security Council Resolution 1174 formally authorized the extension of SFOR's mandate an additional twelve months and extended the mandate of UNMIBH and the IPTF for the same period.[87] On June 20, 1998, the NATO-led international military force in Bosnia became the new SFOR. Speaking at a NATO information seminar in Sarajevo a few weeks later, Gregory Schulte told the audience of local leaders that they "probably did not notice much of a change." After all the meetings, speeches, and planning, SFOR remained much as it had been the previous summer. What was new, Schulte said, was the addition of the MSU, which would be trained to deal with violent demonstrations such as the one that had occurred recently in Drvar. The unit would also assist SFOR in countering those who used thugs and criminals to prevent the return of refugees and the seating of elected

---

84. Philippe Rater, "Third NATO Peace Mission to Be Named 'Joint Forge,'" Agence France-Presse, April 22, 1998.

85. Interview with Gelbard.

86. North Atlantic Treaty Organization, "Final Communique, Ministerial Meeting of the North Atlantic Council, NATO Headquarters, Brussels, Belgium, June 11, 1998," press release M-NAC-D1(98)71, June 11, 1998; available at http://www.nato.int/docu/pr/1998/p98-071e.htm (accessed November 26, 2012).

87. UN Security Council Resolution 1174 (1998), June 15, 1998.

officials. By introducing such a force, Schulte said, "we want to promote public security, which is a key to a lasting peace."[88]

88. Gregory Schulte, director, Bosnia Task Force, NATO International Staff, "SFOR Continued," speech at NATO information seminar, Sarajevo, July 2, 1998.

4

Blue Box: The Multinational Specialized Unit in Bosnia

On August 2, 1998, Colonel Leonardo Leso, the Italian commander of the Multinational Specialized Unit (MSU), arrived in Ploče, Croatia, with "350 well-equipped soldiers and 100 vehicles" en route to his head-quarters at Camp Butmir, Sarajevo.[1] Despite the efforts of Colonel Vincenzo Coppola and the MSU advance team to brief UN Stabilization Force (SFOR) officers about the role of constabulary forces, opinions in Sarajevo on the new unit's role and mission varied widely. Senior U.S. military officers in SFOR viewed the MSU as another military unit, subject to the same command structure and rules of engagement as all other SFOR units. The MSU would be part of the SFOR strategic reserve, deployed in extremis if the International Police Task Force (IPTF) and the local police were unable to handle mob violence. In the view of one U.S. general, the MSU was "one more club in the SFOR bag." Another described the MSU as "just another bunch of guys in tree suits," a reference to the camouflage uniforms worn by SFOR troops.[2]

Colonel Leso's view could not have been more different. He understood the MSU as a "police force with military status" and believed it would prioritize patrolling and community policing to prevent friction among ethnic groups. The MSU would also have credible military capabilities, the capacity to control territory, the ability to collect human intelligence, and, if necessary, the ability to respond rapidly to riots and other types of civil disorder. It would close the operational gap between SFOR and the local police and work in perfect harmony with the IPTF in public security and public order management. Preparation of the new unit in Italy included training in firearms, combat techniques, riot control, martial arts, intelligence gathering,

---

1. Alexis Mersch, "MSU Arrives in BiH," SFOR Informer Online, August 12, 1998, available at http://www.nato.int/sfor/sfor-at-work/msu/arrival/msu.htm (accessed November 27, 2012).
2. Interviews with American SFOR officers, Sarajevo, August 3–8, 1998.

principles of international law, use of communications equipment, and spoken English. While the MSU was trained to handle worst-case scenarios, its primary goal would be conflict prevention through its professionalism and the use of basic police skills to defuse potentially violent situations.[3]

For its part, the United Nations had already taken steps within the limited IPTF mandate to meet the need for police who were capable of managing civil disorder. In 1997 at its December 9 and 10 meeting in Bonn, the Peace Implementation Council called to modify the IPTF structure to provide maximum support for "the most pressing needs of civilian implementation" and recommended creating a special ten-member IPTF public order and major incident management unit, made up of gendarmes serving in an individual capacity as UN civilian police monitors. The unit was tasked with organizing and training crowd control units among the Bosnian police. Creating similar specialized IPTF units was also recommended to deal with refugee returns, organized crime, and terrorism.[4]

The council's recommendations were subsequently endorsed in UN Security Council Resolution 1144, which extended the IPTF mandate until June 21, 1998, unless there were "significant changes in the security arrangements provided by SFOR." The council "encouraged" the secretary-general to implement its recommendations, particularly the creation of the specialized IPTF units to address "key public security issues." It also encouraged member states to increase their contributions of training and equipment for the local police.[5]

During the summer of 1998, the IPTF worked with the U.S. Department of Justice's International Criminal Investigative Training Assistance Program (ICITAP) to organize, train, and equip a 350-man, multiethnic civil disorder management unit in the Bosnian Federation. Nine of the ten cantons in Bosnia and the federation police provided officers. Canton Ten (Livno) was excluded because ethnic Croat authorities refused to remove an offensive nationalist shoulder patch from police uniforms. Units from canton police forces were brought together in Sarajevo and trained to operate in integrated formations. The goal was to encourage cantons and the federation to work together and call on each other for assistance. Subsequently canton-level crisis management operations centers were established in each canton to coor-

---

3. Mersch, "MSU Arrives in BiH."

4. Bonn Peace Implementation Conference, Bosnia and Herzegovina 1998: Self-Sustaining Structures, Section IV, Public Order and Police Issues, paras. 1 and 3, Bonn, December 10, 1997, available at http://www.ohr.int/pic/default.asp?content_id=5182 (accessed November 27, 2012).

5. UN Security Council Resolution 1144 (1997), December 19, 1997.

dinate emergency response, including police, fire, and rescue services, and the IPTF carried out a similar program to create riot control units in the RS.[6] Meanwhile, the UN leadership in Sarajevo saw the NATO decision to deploy the MSU as the international community's vote of no confidence in the unarmed IPTF and its ability to properly train and motivate local law enforcement authorities. UN officials believed it was a mistake for the international community to assume a larger role in peace implementation rather than place increasing responsibility on the Bosnians. They also felt strongly that it was counterproductive to turn over responsibility for managing civil disorder to the military while the international community was attempting to build democratic institutions and introduce community-oriented policing based on democratic principles.[7]

For its part, the IPTF saw the MSU deployment as a potential threat to relationships painstakingly developed with local authorities. Senior UN police officials were wary that the MSU might try to assume responsibility for training, reforming, and advising local police, particularly in civil disorder management. Bosnia's ethnic-based police forces had demonstrated a strong disinclination to protect returning refugees and a general unwillingness to confront demonstrations against refugee resettlement. IPTF officers were afraid reliance on the MSU would give local police an excuse to avoid responsibility for protecting minorities. IPTF leaders also feared MSU involvement in violent clashes with Bosnians might spell danger for IPTF officers. MSU personnel would wear their national police uniforms rather than military attire, which might make them indistinguishable from members of the IPTF. Senior IPTF officers feared that Bosnians would take revenge on unarmed UN Civilian Police (CIVPOL) officers for the actions of their armed MSU counterparts.[8] As a result, the IPTF leadership ordered the IPTF public order and major incident management unit to avoid contact with the MSU. The MSU would have no role in training the local police. Liaison between the MSU and the IPTF would be limited to single officers assigned to their respective headquarters. Neither SFOR nor the the IPTF briefed the Bosnian police and their newly created civil disorder management units on the role and mission of the MSU. The Bosnians were angry, feeling that the IPTF and SFOR should have sought their cooperation and held joint exercises.[9]

6. Interview with ICITAP project manager James Tillman, Sarajevo, July 1, 2002.

7. Telephone interview with Mark Kroeker, former UN IPTF deputy commissioner, February 5, 2002.

8. Interview with Kroeker.

9. Interviews with UN and Bosnian officials, Sarajevo, August 3–8, 1998.

MSU MANDATE AND ORGANIZATION

The lead elements of the MSU arrived in Sarajevo in July 1998. As stated in Annex JJ of Supreme Headquarters Allied Powers Europe (SHAPE) Operation Plan 10407 and later in SFOR's operations plan, the mission of the MSU was to promote public security by utilizing the unit's ability to serve as a strategic reserve force and to operate throughout the theater; assist with refugee return by establishing local area security and ensuring freedom of movement across the Inter-Entity Boundary Line (IEBL) and within the Bosnian Federation; support installation of elected minority government officials; perform crisis management to maintain public order, including the use of force in riot and crowd control; collect intelligence and process information for operational purposes; and enforce directives of the Office of the High Representative related to public security. Under these guidelines, the MSU would operate primarily as a police rather than a military force. To gather police-related information before conducting operations, the MSU would make contacts with the local population to establish confidence and develop sources. It would conduct patrols to provide area security, conduct surveillance, and engage in crisis management, using persuasion and other nonviolent means to prevent or defuse conflicts. It would rely on nonlethal force for riot and crowd control to restore public order, though if necessary, it could use lethal force, including snipers, to suppress armed instigators.[10]

The description of the prospective duties of the MSU was important, but there was an equally long list of operations the MSU would not undertake and tasks it would not perform. The MSU would intervene to maintain public order but would not engage in law enforcement. Under its restricted mandate, the MSU would not act as an international police force by conducting routine police operations such as traffic control or escorting convoys; replace the IPTF, which would remain responsible for monitoring, reforming, and retraining the local police; replace the local police, which would retain primary responsibility for law enforcement and maintaining public order; conduct criminal investigations unless directed by the SFOR commander; make arrests or detain suspects longer than the time required to turn offenders over to the IPTF or the local police; engage in war crimes investigations; deal with official corruption; conduct hostage rescues, although it maintained a special weapons and tactics capability to intervene in such situations; engage in counterterrorism operations; or train local police—not even in crowd control, the MSU's specialty.[11]

---

10. Vincenzo Coppola, "Briefing on the Multinational Specialized Unit," paper presented at the U.S. Army Peacekeeping Institute, Carlisle Barracks, PA, June 16, 1999, photocopy, 1.
11. Coppola, "Briefing," 2–3.

As the only NATO member willing to contribute forces, Italy was given the lead in organizing and commanding the MSU. The Italians contributed 386 Carabinieri, or 75 percent of the MSU's personnel. Argentina was the second largest donor, contributing 76 members of its Gendarmería Nacional. The remainder of the force was composed of a platoon of 24 Romanian Politia Militari and a platoon of 23 Slovenian military police, plus 3 American and 2 Dutch liaison officers. The MSU's organization included a regimental headquarters with an operational battalion, a support company, and a maneuver unit. The MSU commander reported directly to the SFOR commander. The unit was structured so that up to three additional battalions could be added. The first operational battalion was made up of four companies. Alpha Company was composed of four platoons, three Italian and one Romanian. Companies Bravo and Charlie each comprised three Italian platoons. Delta Company had three Argentine platoons and the Slovenians.[12]

The MSU maneuver unit was made up entirely of Carabinieri and included a special weapons and tactics (SWAT) team, an intelligence unit, snipers, and a K-9 unit. The dog team had three "Italian speaking" German shepherds, trained in riot control techniques, and their Carabinieri handlers.[13] The MSU support company performed standard logistics, personnel, and administrative duties. All units in the operational battalion were equipped with flak jackets, leg and arm protection, shields, batons, tear gas grenade launchers, pistols, submachine guns, assault rifles, and machine guns; they could convert quickly to light infantry if required. The MSU was logistically autonomous. Housed originally in tents at Camp Butmir, in early 1999 it occupied a new compound next door called Butmir II. Italy paid almost all the costs of constructing the camp and gave logistical support for the MSU in return for a per-person, per-day fee paid by the other participating countries for their units.[14]

The Italians chose officers with broad experience in a wide range of police disciplines and in previous peace operations. Many of the Italians had already served a tour of duty as members of the IPTF. The Argentines were veterans of the mobile battalions of the Gendarmería Nacional, antiriot forces with specialized training in maintaining public order. To enhance the prospects for cooperation with the Italians, the Argentines chose officers

12. Paolo Valpolini, "The Role of Police-Military Units in Peacekeeping," *Jane's Europe News,* July/August 1999.

13. Alexander Montagna, "MSU Dog Team," SFOR Informer Online, January 6, 2000, available at http://www.nato.int/sfor/indexinf/78/msudogs/t000712j.htm (accessed November 27, 2012).

14. Valpolini, "Role of Police-Military Units."

with Italian or Spanish ancestry. Argentine MSU members joked that the official language of the unit was Italo-Español, although their officers also spoke English, the official language of the Bosnian mission. Before departing for training with the Carabinieri in Italy, the Argentines underwent a month's training at the Training Center for Missions Abroad in Argentina on the specifics of serving in Bosnia.[15]

The MSU arrived in Bosnia as an integrated unit, having received classroom instruction and participated in field exercises before deployment. The Italians and Argentines received six weeks of training in Gorizia, Italy, at the headquarters of the Thirteenth Friuli-Venezia Giulia Battalion of the Carabinieri, using the standard Carabinieri curricula, procedures, vehicles, and equipment. After the training, senior officials from NATO, the United Nations, and the IPTF—including Supreme Allied Commander Europe (SACEUR) General Wesley Clark and IPTF deputy commissioner Mark Kroeker—attended a demonstration of riot control tactics, during which Clark asked Kroeker, who was deputy chief of police in Los Angeles during the 1992 Rodney King riots, for his evaluation of the MSU. Kroeker said the MSU appeared to be a highly professional and well-trained force. Its tactics and formations for crowd control were consistent with international standards and all major civilian police forces used them. Kroeker questioned the effectiveness of their use of voice commands rather than hand signals during noisy street confrontations, but otherwise believed they would contribute positively to peacebuilding and looked forward to working with the Italians.[16] After the Italians and Argentines arrived in August, NATO added units from non-NATO countries. They received in-country training and were certified as meeting NATO standards on September 11, 1998, after participating in a thirty-hour field exercise held in Doboj, Bosnia. The exercise culminated in a military parade and ceremony attended by the commander of Multinational Division (MND)–North, U.S. Major General Larry Ellis.[17]

COMMAND AND CONTROL

The Italians arrived in Sarajevo full of positive expectations that they could contribute in numerous ways to the peace implementation process. They

---

15. Luis Barber, "SFOR Argentinean Contingent," SFOR Informer Online, November 8, 2000, available at http://www.nato.int/sfor/indexinf/100/s100p03a/t0011083a.htm (accessed November 27, 2012).

16. Interview with Kroeker.

17. Angel Brufau, "MSU Certification Ceremony," SFOR Informer Online, September 23, 1998, available at http://www.nato.int/sfor/sfor-at-work/msu/msucert/msucert.htm (accessed November 27, 2012).

believed that the MSU would have full freedom of movement and unlimited access to all areas in Bosnia, and that it was essential that the MSU become thoroughly familiar with the territory, major roads, and urban centers through frequent patrolling, reconnaissance operations, and mixing with local officials, police, and citizens. The MSU thus would have operational autonomy in the choice of routes, timing, and forces to develop detailed knowledge of the country, particularly areas where there was refugee resettlement. The Italians believed the MSU's most important contribution would be its ability to warn early of potential threats to public order and to gather and analyze information on criminal activities, particularly organized crime. This information would be provided to the SFOR commander on a daily basis, then disseminated widely throughout the command. The concept of operations was based on normal police practices and on the manner in which the Carabinieri conducted its operation in Italy.[18]

Unfortunately, little had been done to prepare SFOR for the arrival of the MSU. Created as the successor to IFOR, SFOR—under Operation Joint Guard, or Operation Joint Forge—was established on December 20, 1996. Its primary missions were to prevent resumed hostilities and new threats to peace, to promote the peace process, and to support civilian organizations selectively—"within its capabilities." SFOR was composed of troops from NATO members and fifteen other countries.[19] By the time the MSU arrived, the three multinational divisions—MND-North (United States), MND-Southwest (United Kingdom) and MND-Southeast (France)—had developed substantial autonomy. Known popularly as the Three Kingdoms, they were large organizations with multinational headquarters, complex commands, complicated procedures, and thousands of troops wearing an array of national uniforms. The MSU was quartered in a compound adjoining SFOR headquarters at Camp Butmir in Sarajevo. Just getting the attention of SFOR, however, was initially a challenge for the MSU battalion.

From the outset, the MSU had to cope with unfamiliarity, misunderstandings, and outright prejudices within SFOR. Beyond determining what tasks the MSU would and would not perform, no doctrine had been developed concerning the MSU's relationship to the SFOR command structure or the conduct of SFOR operations. Acting on preconceived notions or their own national doctrine concerning military police, the

---

18. Information provided by the Office of the Commander of the Multinational Specialized Unit, Camp Butmir, Bosnia, June 28, 2002.

19. "History of the NATO-led Stabilization Force in Bosnia and Herzegovina," SFOR website, available at http://www.nato.int/sfor/docu/d981116a.htm (accessed November 27, 2012).

SFOR commander and the MND commanders initially regarded the MSU as another infantry unit, subject to the same tactics, techniques, and procedures as all other military units under their command. As MND commanders were responsible for all activities conducted in their sectors, they were initially unwilling to allow the MSU to enter, to move freely between sectors, or to conduct operations within their sectors without express prior permission. As such permission was not readily forthcoming, the restriction made it difficult for the MSU to conduct mobile patrols, provide security, or gather information. The MSU requests to conduct operations across MND boundaries were often misdirected or lost in the SFOR chain of command. The MSU was generally seen as a strategic reserve, a force that should remain in its barracks until it was called out in response to an emergency.[20]

Under the above restrictions, MSU operations initially were confined to patrolling and information gathering. From August 7, 1998, to January 25, 1999, the MSU conducted 243 reconnaissance missions, 87 information-gathering operations, and 33 public order interventions, of which only a small number involved crowd control. Procedures were developed under which the MSU planned security patrols and information-gathering missions, coordinated with the MND and approved by SFOR. In such operations, the MSU reported to the commander of SFOR, which allowed it to move between MND sectors and operate throughout the country. In practice the MSU had contact with local civilians and established relations with local police. Under its mandate to collect information, the MSU gathered it on local political and social conditions and on the activities of organized crime by following the normal police practice of engaging in informal conversations in roadside markets, bars, and restaurants. The MSU made it a practice to visit local officials and police stations during vehicle patrols, viewing this as following standard police procedures and essential to its function of serving as SFOR's eyes and ears. Information concerning local conditions was collected according to a weekly plan, processed by fifteen experienced Carabinieri analysts assigned to MSU headquarters, and disseminated within the MSU and through the SFOR commander to MND commanders. Apparently unaware that the MSU had this capability, SFOR initially made few requests to the MSU for information, which further restricted its utility.[21]

---

20. Coppola, "Briefing," 4–5.
21. Coppola, "Briefing."

PUBLIC ORDER AND REFUGEE RETURNS

While SFOR restrictions on routine operations frustrated the MSU, the procedures and command relationships SFOR established for dealing with civil disturbances were nearly disastrous. Three MSU platoons engaged in daily operations, keeping one platoon in reserve as a rapid reaction force for unexpected contingencies. In case of a potential threat to public order, the MND would submit a request for MSU assistance to the SFOR commander, who, in turn, would task the MSU to provide a mission analysis and operational plan, which the SFOR commander would pass back to the MND. SFOR would task the MSU for the operation, transferring tactical command of the MSU to the MND. In emergencies where the MSU was used as a rapid reaction force, the same procedures were followed, except the MSU would deploy without doing a mission analysis or operations plan. Instead, it would rely on its advance units to conduct on-site surveillance and to report to the most senior MND officer available. In both scenarios, the leader of the MSU detachment would be under the command of the senior MND officer present. The MSU commander would not control his own forces, nor would he be able to direct the operation based on his experience and standard operating procedures.[22]

On October 1, 1998, the MSU faced its first test when demonstrators blocked the road between Sarajevo and Ploce near Capljina in southern Bosnia. This was the first time the MSU was used for crowd control and to assist with the return of displaced persons and refugees. The incident occurred during an Office of the High Representative (OHR) attempt to return internally displaced persons to their original homes. The demonstrators were ethnic Croats who had been displaced from central Bosnia and had resettled in Tasovčići. They were protesting the return of fifty Bosniak families to houses in Tasovčići they now occupied. Croatian television's news coverage of the incident showed "Italian policemen" with helmets, shields, batons, and firearms charging a group of mostly women and children. The broadcast also showed "the Italians" using their shields to protect themselves from stones and bottles thrown by the crowd. Three MSU officers received superficial wounds. A grenade thrown from a vehicle killed one returnee and wounded three others.[23] A similar attack on returnees occurred in the nearby town of Stolac. An SFOR spokesman stated that the MSU had been

---

22. Coppola, "Briefing."

23. "Official Condemns SFOR Action to Unblock Road at Capljina," HINA News Agency, October 2, 1998, translated in Foreign Broadcast Information Service, document FBIS-EEU-98-275.

used as a "last resort" because the local police failed in their duty to protect minorities.[24]

When the MSU platoon reached the roadblock, it found an SFOR contingent facing a growing crowd of hostile demonstrators. The MSU platoon commander, an Italian captain, requested permission to conduct his own reconnaissance and to talk with the protesters to determine the reasons for the demonstration. The senior SFOR officer present, a Spanish major, overruled the captain and ordered him to attack the roadblock and clear the area of protesters. The MSU carried out the order, using force to break through the barrier and disperse the crowd. The MSU officer then requested permission to remain in Capljina overnight to ensure that the protesters would not reassemble. At sundown, however, the Spanish major ordered the MSU to return to its barracks. During the night, widespread violence erupted in the town. Without the MSU, SFOR was forced to deploy armored vehicles to quell the disturbance.[25]

The arbitrary misuse of the MSU, the resulting violence, and Italian protests caused SFOR to reevaluate its procedures for using the MSU to control civil disturbances, resulting in a new doctrine governing MSU use for crowd control. In dealing with civil disorder, the senior MSU officer present would not only command his own unit, but all other forces within the immediate area of responsibility (AOR) during the operation. The AOR, or blue box— for the color of the Italian Carabinieri uniforms—was established in both space and time. Once the operation began, any forces coming into the box were under MSU command until the operation was completed. All other SFOR troops in the surrounding AOR, or green box, would remain under the command of the senior MND officer present and support the MSU. Under this arrangement, the MSU officer would be able to decide whether to use nonviolent tactics to attempt to defuse the situation or to use force, if necessary. This allowed the MSU to operate like a police force, utilizing persuasion followed by ascending levels of nonlethal force to control the situation.[26]

The revised doctrine was tested in early November 1998 in Mrkonjic Grad in the Republika Sprska (RS). Nearly two hundred former workers at Udarnik, the state transport company, protested in front of their former factory, which the British SFOR contingent had appropriated as the MND-Southwest headquarters. The protesters demanded either the return of their

---

24. "NATO/SFOR Joint Press Conference," Coalition Press Information Center, Tito Barracks, October 7, 1998.

25. Coppola, "Briefing."

26. Coppola, "Briefing."

factory and reinstatement of their jobs or compensation for the use of the building. Previous efforts to resolve the problem had been met by British statements that they were there under orders from the SFOR central command, so the problem had to be resolved in Sarajevo. The British requested MSU assistance to remove the crowd, which was blocking the road in front of one of the buildings.[27]

Operating under the new guidelines, the MSU officer in charge, a Carabinieri captain, positioned his forces out of sight. He then approached the barricade the Bosnians had erected across the road, accompanied by his interpreter. The officer discovered from talking with the demonstration's leaders that when the workers had lost their jobs, they were promised compensation that had not been forthcoming. Repeated appeals to SFOR and RS authorities had produced nothing. The people had erected the roadblock because they had expended their savings and had no food or oil to heat their homes. With winter approaching, they were desperate. In response, the Italian captain offered the protesters a deal: If they would remove the roadblock and disperse peacefully, he would invite the leaders to a nearby coffeehouse to discuss their grievances. If they could prove their case, he would intervene with the authorities to see they received the compensation to which they were entitled. The roadblock disappeared and the crowd returned to their homes. After the conversation in a nearby café, the MSU officer intervened on behalf of the community.[28] On November 10 the RS Ministry of Transport and Communication informed the workers that until the future of the factory was resolved, they would receive 200,000 dinars in place of their salaries for October and 30 metric tons of oil to meet the needs of the community.[29] Using standard police tactics, the MSU had defused a potentially explosive situation through negotiation, without resorting to a show of force or using violence.

In early 1999 events in Brcko came full circle. On Friday, March 5, High Representative Carlos Westendorp announced the final award of the arbitral tribunal for the dispute over the IEBL in the Brcko area. The arbitration panel ruled that Brcko would become a part of neither the Bosnian Federation nor the RS; instead, it would become a self-governing neutral district under international supervision. Administration was placed in the hands of an elected,

---

27. Belgrade Tanjug Domestic Service, "B-H: Workers Protest against SFOR Using Factory Premises," November 2, 1998, translated in Foreign Broadcast Information Service, doc. FTS19981102002064.

28. Coppola, "Briefing."

29. Srpski Radio, "RS Minister to Help Get SFOR to Vacate Firm's Premises," November 10, 1998, translated in Foreign Broadcast Information Service, doc. FTS19981110001587.

multiethnic district government, which would operate under the supervision of the Brcko Supervisor. In the language of the final award document, Brcko would be governed by a "new institution, a new multiethnic democratic government to be known as the Brcko District of Bosnia and Herzegovina." The new municipal authority would be composed of an elected district assembly, an executive board selected by the assembly, an independent judiciary, and a "unified police force under a single command structure with one uniform and badge and complete independence from the police establishments of the two entities." The entire territory within the boundaries of the prewar Brcko municipality (opstina) would be "held in condominium by both entities simultaneously: The territory of the RS will encompass the entire opstina, and so also will the territory of the Federation. Neither entity, however, will exercise any authority within the boundaries of the district, which will administer the area as one unitary government."[30]

On the day the arbitral award was announced, two unrelated events combined with news of the Brcko decree to produce an angry Serb response. Westendorp announced his decision to sack the Bosnian Serb president, Nikola Poplasen, for obstructing the peace process. That evening, an American Special Forces sergeant in a town near Brcko shot dead a Serb ultranationalist. In what was apparently a premeditated attack, a group of Serbs accosted four U.S. Special Forces soldiers having dinner at a café. When one of the Serbs struck the sergeant with a club, the soldier shot his assailant.

The reaction from political hard-liners in the RS was virulent. Živko Radišić, the Serb representative in Bosnia's joint presidency, suspended his participation. The RS prime minister, Milorad Dodik, announced his intention to resign, and the republic's parliament passed a law withdrawing all Serb representatives from Bosnian state institutions and barring Serb officials from speaking to representatives of the international community. Demonstrations were staged in the RS and in Brcko; UN vehicles were attacked and destroyed. Tensions were further heightened by the breakdown of the Kosovo peace talks in late February and the beginning of the NATO bombing campaign against Yugoslavia on March 24, 1999. During the air campaign, NATO jets on their way to targets in Belgrade and Pristina flew over Brcko several times a day, raising anti-American sentiment among Serbs to a fever pitch.[31]

---

30. "Final Award of the Arbitral Tribunal for Dispute over the Inter-Entity Boundary in the Brcko Area," March 5, 1999, 3–6, available at www.state.gov/www/regions/eur/bosnia/990305_arbiter _brcko.html (accessed October 24, 2012).

31. "Bosnian Serbs United in Anger," BBC News Online, March 8, 1999, available at http://news.bbc.co.uk/2/hi/europe/292441.stm (accessed November 27, 2012); Ivo Daalder and Michael O'Hanlon, *Winning Ugly: NATO's War to Save Kosovo* (Washington, DC: Brookings

Unlike the Brcko riot in 1997, this time SFOR had the proper mix of forces to deal with any eventuality. The MSU battalion headquarters, together with two companies and part of the maneuver unit, was deployed to Brcko before the announcement and remained until after tensions had eased. The center of town was declared a blue box and the MSU prevented demonstrations while SFOR secured the town perimeter and UN police reinforced the IPTF contingent. With professional riot control units in place, regular SFOR troops were not called upon to confront civilian demonstrators.[32] Within a week, the protests over the decision died away. In the words of one reporter, "Less than a hundred people showed up. Waving banners and posters of their president, marching behind a battered car with loudspeakers mounted on the roof. It was a poor turnout for the disciples of hate."[33]

Although the MSU's primary mission was crowd control, its primary contribution was its apparent ability to deter civil disorder. The announcement of the arbitration award in Brcko was only one of numerous incidents in which deploying the MSU was enough to dissuade would-be troublemakers. Over time, MSU deployments became a routine part of SFOR operations for public events and ceremonies. During the Israeli army's incursion into the West Bank and Gaza in the spring of 2002, the Israeli national soccer team played against the Bosnian team in Zenitsa, which is in a Muslim area. Supported by SFOR troops, the MSU deployed en force, including stationing officers in plain clothes inside the stadium. There were no incidents. The MSU was also deployed for the annual July 11, 2001, return of the Women of Srebrenica to the town in the RS to commemorate the wartime massacre. The MSU collected information on public attitudes and provided highly visible support for the RS police. The event was held without incident. It is impossible to say with certainty that deploying the MSU deterred violence, but senior SFOR officers believed the presence of professional, armed police in full riot gear had a salutary effect.[34]

The potential for widespread violence caused by the massive return of displaced persons and refugees did not materialize in Bosnia. This was due

Institution Press, 2000), 230–31; interview with former Brcko supervisor Robert Farrand, Washington, DC, July 31, 2002.

32. Valpolini, "Role of Police-Military Units."

33. Nick Thorpe, "Returning to Brcko," BBC News Online, March 15, 1999, available at http://news.bbc.co.uk/2/hi/programmes/from_our_own_correspondent/294839.stm (accessed November 27, 2012).

34. Interview with Lieutenant Colonel Michael Meese, executive officer, assistant chief of staff (Operations), SFOR, Camp Butmir, Sarajevo, June 28, 2002.

to both the pace and the volume of returns, which was slower and smaller than international experts had predicted. A prolonged process meant that returnees faced decreasing antagonism over time as communities resolved to overcome wartime differences. By summer 2002, SFOR relied primarily on regular military units to provide security for returning refugees, limiting the MSU contribution to routine patrolling and information collection.[35]

COMBATING ORGANIZED CRIME

Increased SFOR confidence in the MSU coincided with the appearance of the next problem to confront the international community in Bosnia: the emergence of organized crime and official corruption as major impediments to Dayton implementation. During the conflict, international sanctions and the exigencies of war forced the political leadership of all three ethnic groups to rely on the criminal underworld to perform essential services. Faced with an international arms embargo, the Bosniak leadership in Sarajevo depended on military weapons and equipment smuggled by criminal groups to provision its military forces. For the Serbs, smuggling and black marketing of consumer goods and primary products generated the revenue to fund the war effort and enabled hard-liners such as Radovan Karadžić to retain their hold on power. All sides relied on armed gangs and paramilitary groups that engaged in illicit trafficking. Groups with names like Arkan's Tigers and White Eagles profited from the war, fomented terror, and conducted ethnic cleansing. Even after the leaders of some of the groups involved were subsequently indicted as war criminals, many people continued to regard them as war heroes.[36]

After the conflict, the criminal groups allied with extreme nationalists and corrupt politicians continued their illegal activities under various kinds of commercial or quasi-official front organizations. All three ethnic communities remained under the control of autocratic elites who relied on extralegal intelligence, police, and security services and organized criminal syndicates to retain power and obstruct Dayton implementation. In addition, Serb hard-liners continued to receive political and financial support from the Milošević regime in Belgrade, while Croat extremists received assistance from the Croatian Democratic Union party in Croatia. Members of these unholy alliances exercised control through intimidation and violence and

---

35. Interview with Meese.

36. Michael J. Dziedzic and Andrew Bair, "Bosnia and the International Police Task Force," in Robert Oakley, Michael Dziedzic, and Eliot Goldberg, eds., *Policing the New World Disorder* (Washington, DC: National Defense University Press, 1998), 260.

their ability to make appointments and set salaries for judges, prosecutors, and police officers. They cooperated across ethnic boundaries for personal profit, even when such cooperation was against the best interest of their communities. By 1999 organized criminal elements began to play a central role in the Bosnian power structure. Between 40 and 60 percent of Bosnia's economy was based on black-market commerce. A wealthy criminal class allied with extremist politicians diverted public revenues, ensuring the country's continued dependence on outside assistance. It became apparent that organized crime and official corruption posed a greater threat to security and stability than the increasingly unlikely possibility of renewed military conflict. Unless the situation was rectified, the international community's efforts to empower Bosnians would do little more than further consolidate power in the wrong hands.[37]

For the United States, a particularly embarrassing manifestation of the emergence of organized crime was the Arizona Market. Established by SFOR in 1996 with $40,000 in U.S. funds, the market was named after the NATO designation for the adjacent highway and was located near Brcko in the NATO-enforced Zone of Separation between the RS and the Bosnian Federation. The market was envisioned as an area where "free enterprise would flourish." Within three years, the sprawling complex of stalls, shacks, and temporary structures employed more than 2,500 people and attracted 25,000 customers on an average weekend. As the market was located in a kind of no-man's-land, criminal gangs easily took over its operations, and it soon became a center for tax cheats, prostitutes, and sellers of contraband cigarettes, counterfeit CDs, narcotics, and stolen vehicles. The Bosnian government lost an estimated $30 million a year from untaxed sales of goods at the market. Much of the illegal activity occurred with the complicity or active participation of local police. The Brcko supervisor, Robert Farrand, viewed the market as a potential source of revenue for the municipality, if properly regulated. The senior UN official in Bosnia, Jacques Klein, disagreed; he saw it as a center for organized crime and said the site should be reclaimed by SFOR and bulldozed.[38]

Given the IPTF's limited mandate and the timidity of local judges and police, only SFOR had the intelligence assets and coercive capacity to

37. Mac Warner, "SFOR Lessons Learned in Creating a Secure Environment with Respect for the Rule of Law," paper prepared for the Joint Chiefs of Staff Peace Operations seminar on the role of the military in establishing the rule of law in peace operations, U.S. Army Peacekeeping Institute, Carlisle Barracks, PA, June 13–15, 2000, photocopy, 5.

38. R. Jeffrey Smith, "Bosnian Mart Becomes Den of Criminal Enterprise: Thieves, Tax Cheats Thrive in U.S.-Sponsored Venture," *Washington Post*, December 26, 1999, A33.

confront organized crime in Bosnia. In this regard, the MSU, with its hybrid military and police capabilities, appeared particularly suited for operations that SFOR conducted but required law enforcement skills. The prominence of the Italian Carabinieri in the MSU also seemed particularly fortunate. The Italians were highly experienced in dealing with organized crime as a result of their experience in fighting the Italian mafia. They were also extremely professional in analyzing criminal data and using highly sophisticated information technology, such as crime mapping and link analysis. Unfortunately, under Italian law, the Carabinieri could not perform criminal investigations or engage in law enforcement unless they were under the authority of the Italian Ministry of the Interior. In Bosnia, the Carabinieri assigned to the MSU were under the authority of the Ministry of Defense, and in any case, law enforcement was outside the MSU's mandate.[39]

Within the MSU's limitations, however, its ability to conduct patrols, collect and analyze information on criminal activity, and conduct covert surveillance contributed substantially to SFOR efforts to counter organized crime. With the exception of U.S. Special Forces, the MSU was the only element in SFOR in which members could wear civilian clothes and conduct operations out of uniform. This gave the MSU the ability to engage in plainclothes surveillance and obtain information from informants without attracting attention. In addition, the MSU's ability to provide armed escorts for prisoners and assist with witness protection proved extremely useful to SFOR in its efforts to counter organized crime.[40]

In 1999, facing the evident weakness of the local judicial system, NATO decided to involve SFOR directly in the fight against organized crime and other illegal activities aimed at obstructing implementation of the Dayton peace process. On January 18, 1999, Herzegovina-Neretva Canton police arrested Jozo Perić, the local organized crime boss and owner of the infamous Renner Transport Company, which was a front for a number of illegal operations. A number of Perić's criminal associates were also arrested.[41] The local police acted with MSU support, which deployed to the town and carried out surveillance and information gathering over an extended period. The arrests temporarily disrupted the group's illegal operations, though Perić received advance warning and removed incriminating documents and material before the police arrived. After spending six months in jail, he was released for lack of evidence.

---

39. Warner, "SFOR Lessons Learned," 22.

40. Interview with Meese.

41. "Police Arrest Croat Accused of Organized Crime in Stolac," HINA News Agency, January 18, 1999, translated in Foreign Broadcast Information Service, doc. FTS1999121700319.

On October 14, 1999, SFOR raided the Mostar headquarters of the National Security Service (SNS), a covert Bosnian-Croat intelligence agency with links to its Croatian counterpart and the nationalistic Croatian Democratic Union (HDZ) party. Dubbed Operation Westar, the SFOR action netted computers, databases, encryption software, and equipment for producing forged credit cards and bankcards and for distributing pornographic materials throughout Europe. Troops discovered a cache of illegal weapons and ammunition. The raid also found substantial evidence that the SNS was engaged in four separate intelligence operations aimed at disrupting the work of the International Criminal Tribunal for the Former Yugoslavia (ICTY) and the Dayton peace process. Although SFOR troops seized substantial amounts of illegal property, they found the SNS offices empty. There were no arrests and no injuries.[42]

From an analysis of the materials seized in the raid, it was evident that the SNS had engaged in financial crimes to fund its activities. The four intelligence operations—code-named Puma, Grom (Thunder), Munja (Lightning), and Panter (Panther)—aimed to monitor the activities of the OHR and other international organizations, compromise and recruit their local staff, and gain access to OHR, SFOR, and UN facilities. Operation Puma involved photographic surveillance, wiretapping of ICTY personnel, and monitoring of their investigations, which included collecting information on local citizens who contacted ICTY representatives and recruiting ICTY local interpreters. Operation Munja involved surveilling OHR, international military and civilian humanitarian organizations, and the Agency of Investigation and Documentation, the Bosniak security service. The operation focused on collecting embarrassing or damaging personal information on international and local employees. Included in the materials seized were reports on the sexual preferences of shadowed persons and photos of international representatives in compromising positions. Operation Panter was directed toward collecting information on individuals and international organizations outside the ethnic Croat regions of Bosnia. It was designed to counter alleged efforts by the international community to destabilize the Bosnian Croat leadership and to place responsibility for the failure of Croat-Bosniak cooperation on the Croats. Operation Grom aimed to counter the alleged activities of foreign intelligence agencies, whose agents SNS believed made up the vast majority of the foreign personnel assigned to international organizations in Bosnia. Here again, the goal was to collect information on and to recruit ethnic Croats who worked for international organizations

---

42. "B-H: More on Illegal Intelligence Activities Discovery," HINA News Agency, December 17, 1999, translated in Foreign Broadcast Information Service, doc. FTS19991217001319.

as informants and operatives.[43] Under the limitations of its mandate, the MSU's role was restricted to surveillance, information collection, and supporting the SFOR units that conducted the raid.

In the spring of 2001 pressure from OHR and SFOR on nationalist politicians and organized crime in ethnic Croat areas of Bosnia produced political insurrection and an explosion of violence against the international community. In March, Ante Jelavić, the Croat member of Bosnia's tripartite presidency, and local officials of the HDZ party announced they were withdrawing from the Bosnian Federation and establishing Croat self-government in parts of Herzegovina. A new Croat national assembly began to set up self-rule in five Croat-dominated cantons. It appealed to ethnic Croat military forces to withdraw from the federation army and to ethnic Croat police to defect to the new regime. On March 3, High Representative Wolfgang Petritsch dismissed Jelavić from the presidency and banned him and his followers from engaging in future political activity. SFOR's deputy commander, Major General Robert Connatt of the United Kingdom, made clear that SFOR would prevent any attempt by Croat military units to withdraw from the federation's army. IPTF Commissioner Vincent Coeurderoy warned canton police chiefs that police officers would be dismissed if they engaged in political activity. Despite these actions, substantial numbers of Croat military and police personnel left their posts and identified themselves with the new regime. The new Croat "government" raised prices on public utilities, levied taxes, and intimidated local businesses into providing financial support.[44]

Faced with a growing insurrection, SFOR struck against the financial underpinnings of the illegal Croat ministate. On April 6, 2001, SFOR troops, including elements of the MSU, attempted to seize records and audit the accounts of the Herzegovacka Bank in Mostar and other cities. The bank was controlled by a group of ethnic Croats known locally as the Young Generals, men who made fortunes smuggling arms and food and were rewarded with military rank during the conflict. Many of these individuals held senior positions in the Bosnian branch of the hard-line nationalist HDZ party. They were also the leaders or close allies of local organized crime. These Croat extremists used the bank to launder profits from an illegal trade in oil, cigarettes, liquor, and stolen

43. "B-H Croat SNS Secret 'Operations' Details," *Slobodna Bosna* (Sarajevo), December 23, 1999, 18–19, translated in Foreign Broadcast Information Service, doc. FTS19991225000291.

44. Amra Kebo, "Croat Troops Mutiny: Tension Mounts in Bosnia as Croat Officers Leave the Federation Army," Institute for War and Peace Reporting, Balkans Crisis Report no. 229, London, March 23, 2001.

vehicles, as well as to divert contributions from international organizations that were supposed to be distributed to veterans' organizations and local charities. The bank was the financial citadel of organized crime and Croat political extremists in Mostar who were engaged in establishing the independent Croat political entity. Through it, HDZ party officials enforced discipline through payments to police and local politicians and controlled public information through cash transfers to local newspapers and radio stations.[45]

To take down the Croats' illegal financial empire and undermine the foundations of the Croat insurrection, OHR launched Operation Athena, SFOR's forcible seizure of the headquarters and branch offices of the Herzegovacka Bank, so that accountants from the U.S. firm of Kroll-O'Gara could audit its accounts. Under the plan for inspecting the records of the bank's main headquarters in Mostar, a small number of MSU officers would escort teams of American auditors into the building. They would order the employees to leave and then provide security while the auditors collected incriminating information. Boxes of bank records would be removed in SFOR vehicles. If the blue-box contingent required backup, MSU officers inside the bank would radio for assistance from the green box: regular SFOR troops positioned outside of town.[46]

Unfortunately, the plan to seize the bank headquarters was compromised from the start. The audit teams and their MSU escorts entered the bank's modern, high-rise office building in downtown Mostar in late morning and ordered the employees to depart. Once the MSU officers and the auditors entered the bank offices, groups of tough-looking men with shaved heads appeared outside the bank and began pelting the building with eggs and rocks. Organized groups of Croat schoolchildren were placed at the front of a growing crowd of protesters, who threw objects and shouted abuse at the MSU officers. Groups of armed thugs then rushed the main door of the bank, closing off any possibility of escape and pushing their way inside. Croat thugs grabbed, beat, and threatened to kill the auditors. They also attacked and beat the MSU guards. Under death threats from the mob, the auditors were forced to return all the records they had collected.[47]

During the mob's assault, MSU calls for assistance from SFOR troops stationed outside the town went unanswered. Although equipped with armored vehicles, the SFOR reaction force was deterred by the prospect

45. R. Jeffrey Smith, "Criminal Gangs Challenging West in Bosnia: Separatist Croat Threat Alters Troops' Mission," *Washington Post,* June 24, 2001, A1.

46. Smith, "Criminal Gangs."

47. Aida Cerkez-Robinson, "Bosnian Croats Stoned NATO," Associated Press, April 7, 2001.

of threading its way through roadblocks of trucks and burning trash cans and the possibility that the incident might become more violent if they intervened. This scenario was repeated at several branch offices where there was similar mob violence with serious consequences. At one branch a U.S. auditor suffered serious eye damage from broken glass, while an EU monitor from Ireland was beaten unconscious and suffered permanent brain damage. The most dangerous standoff occurred in the town of Grude, where the auditors and their escorts were held for twelve hours at gunpoint. Mob leaders refused to release their hostages until all the seized bank records that had been taken away in a truck were returned. During the entire operation, twenty-nine internationals and Bosnians were injured, several seriously. Eleven of the injured were members of the MSU. Ten days later, SFOR returned to the bank headquarters in Mostar. Armored personnel carriers were parked bumper to bumper to "ring the building in steel," and heavily armed troops entered the bank's offices. They found the files empty and the computerized records they had seen previously had disappeared.[48]

In addition to dealing with organized crime, the MSU's purview was expanded to include supporting SFOR efforts to conduct investigations and arrest persons indicted for war crimes by the ICTY. MSU platoons were trained in both seizing war criminals and dealing with the possibility of adverse public reaction to such operations. In these exercises the main force of the MSU provided area security and crowd control, while the MSU SWAT team actually made the arrests.[49]

In the spring of 2002, SFOR assisted investigators from ICTY with collecting information in Bosnia. One hundred ICTY investigators were sent to search eight sites in MND-North, including four local police stations. This was the first time ICTY had attempted to enter Bosnian police stations, and there was concern about the reaction. On the day of the operation SFOR placed two MSU platoons on standby as a rapid intervention force. MSU officers in civilian attire were assigned to "drink coffee" at cafés near the targeted police stations, where they could report developments by cell phone. Their reports provided the SFOR commander with situation awareness that he could not have obtained in any other manner. The operation was conducted without incident.[50]

---

48. Smith, "Criminal Gangs."

49. Lisa Simpson, "MSU Trains Slovenians and Romanians," SFOR Informer Online, April 25, 2002, available at http://www.nato.int/sfor/indexinf/137/p07a/t02p07a.htm (accessed October 24, 2012).

50. Interview with Meese.

COUNTERTERRORISM

The events of September 11, 2001, resulted in a change in the original MSU mandate and the addition of counterterrorism to the list of its assigned responsibilities. The MSU was instructed to carry out antiterrorism operations as a special mission under the direction of the SFOR commander.[51] Involving SFOR and the MSU in the war on terrorism resulted from NATO's September 11 decision to invoke Article 5 of the North Atlantic Treaty. This action triggered the collective defense arrangements—this time, to protect the United States—that European countries had relied on during the Cold War. Seven NATO airborne warning and control system (AWACS) aircraft were deployed to watch the skies over the eastern United States in Operation Eagle Assist, which freed U.S. aircraft for service in Afghanistan. The unprecedented use of NATO assets to protect the United States ended when the planes returned to Europe on May 16, 2002.[52]

The MSU's involvement also resulted from threats that Islamic extremists in Bosnia posed to U.S. diplomatic facilities and to U.S. and Western European military units in SFOR. Hundreds of Arab fighters joined the war in Bosnia to fight alongside Bosniak forces. These mujahideen displayed great courage and their fellow Muslims held them in high esteem. After the war, most returned home, but some remained, married local women, and acquired Bosnian citizenship. Arab nationals who came after the war to work for international humanitarian organizations joined them. Together, these two groups gave financial aid and other types of support to Islamic extremist organizations, and they operated undisturbed until U.S. and European intelligence agencies began to investigate al-Qaeda's activities in Europe following September 11.[53]

The war on terrorism changed the focus of the MSU's surveillance, information collection, and analysis functions to concentrate on Islamic organizations that might directly threaten SFOR security. It also involved the MSU in takedown operations against terrorist cells in Bosnia. On September 25, 2001, SFOR stormed the Saudi High Commission for Assistance to Bosnia in Sarajevo. Code-named Operation Hollywood Hotel, the operation netted computers, documents on how to fly crop-dusting aircraft, large amounts of cash, and fake U.S. embassy identification badges. Four

---

51. Interview with Colonel Antonio Colacicco, MSU commander, Camp Butmir, Sarajevo, June 30, 2002.

52. "NATO Prepares to End Its Patrols of U.S. Skies," Reuters, May 2, 2002.

53. "NATO: Terrorists Are Still in Bosnia," Associated Press, April 2, 2002.

men were arrested, two of them Egyptians.[54] The MSU provided area security and support for the raid, which was executed by U.S. Special Forces.

Over the next month, Bosnian police, working with the MSU and SFOR, conducted a number of operations under the supervision of the Joint Coordination Committee for the Fight Against Terrorism in Bosnia, a group that brought SFOR together with U.S., international, and Bosnian intelligence and law enforcement agencies. Their raids resulted in the arrest of some twenty persons suspected of belonging to a terrorist cell that planned attacks on U.S. facilities in Bosnia. Among those taken into custody was Densayah Belkacem, who worked for a humanitarian assistance agency in the town of Zenica. Investigators obtained telephone records showing that Belkacem was in frequent contact with Abu Zubaydah, one of Osama bin Laden's senior lieutenants. On October 16 the American and British embassies in Sarajevo closed when a plot was discovered against both installations and Eagle Base, the main U.S. military facility, located in Tuzla. The discovery resulted in the arrest of six suspected terrorists for plotting to bomb the embassies. On December 15, Bosnian federal police staged raids against two Arab humanitarian agencies, Taibah International and the Global Relief Foundation, that were suspected of fundraising and providing logistical support for al-Qaeda.[55]

On January 18, 2002, U.S. forces in Sarajevo took custody of the six suspected terrorists—five Algerians and one Yemeni—whom Bosnian police had arrested in October. As the United States was unwilling to release intelligence reports for use in a trial, the Bosnian supreme court ruled that there was insufficient evidence against the suspects. The Bosnian government then agreed to allow American SFOR troops to seize the men as they were released from detention. Nearly four hundred family members, friends, and supporters attempted to disrupt the operation by surrounding the SFOR vehicles. U.S.-trained Bosnian riot-control police were called in and controlled the situation. The MSU was positioned to provide backup for the local police to ensure the operation's success. According to a U.S. embassy statement, the men posed a credible security threat to U.S. personnel and facilities. U.S. Army general John Sylvester, the American SFOR commander in Bosnia, said they were part of a group with direct links to al-Qaeda. The men, five of whom were Bosnian citizens, were transported to the U.S. military's terrorist internment facility in Guantánamo Bay, Cuba.[56]

---

54. "Bosnia Terror Suspects Quizzed," BBC World News, October 2, 2001, available at http://news.bbc.co.uk/hi/english/world/europe/newsid_1547000/1574678.stm (accessed October 24, 2012).

55. Andrew Purvis, "Targeting 'Eagle Base,'" *Time Europe,* October 16, 2001.

56. Peter Finn, "U.S. Troops Seize 6 Terror Suspects Freed by Bosnia," *Washington Post,* January 18, 2002, A16.

TRAINING BOSNIAN POLICE

On May 7, 2001, a mob of ethnic Serb nationalists attacked a group of international officials and Bosnian Muslims during a ceremony to mark the start of reconstruction of the sixteenth-century Ferhadija Mosque in the RS capital of Banja Luka. Serb forces had destroyed the mosque in 1992. In 1999 the Human Rights Chamber, an international human rights commission, ordered its reconstruction. Nearly three hundred Muslims attended the ceremony to lay a new cornerstone, intending to demonstrate that it was safe to return to the city, which had a large prewar Muslim population. As the ceremony began, a crowd of two thousand protesters attacked the visitors, severely beating ten people, overturning vehicles, and setting buses on fire. Muslim clergy and a group of international dignitaries—including the senior UN official in Bosnia, Jacques Klein, and the ambassadors from the United States, the United Kingdom, Sweden, and Pakistan—were forced to take refuge in the Islamic Community Center, where they were trapped during the rampage. A riot squad of IPTF-trained RS police was present, but its members were seen shaking hands and joking with the demonstrators. After several hours, RS authorities responded to threats from Klein to call in SFOR and ordered the police to create a cordon to evacuate the dignitaries and visiting Muslims.[57]

The incident left the international community in Bosnia badly shaken. Klein remarked that it was "a sad day when brave Serb men throw stones at old Muslim women." High Representative Wolfgang Petritsch said he was "shocked that the RS still appeared to be a place with no rule of law, no civilized behavior, and no religious freedom." U.S. ambassador Tom Miller condemned the riots and called on Bosnian Serb officials to punish the perpetrators. In the riot's aftermath, the United Nations and several Western governments expressed renewed interest in providing civil disorder management training and equipment to the Bosnian police.[58] As a result, the IPTF overcame its reluctance to work with the MSU on police training.

Representatives from the IPTF Public Order and Major Incident Management Unit sought MSU assistance to update and refurbish the training of the Bosnian crowd-control units that the IPTF and the ICITAP had created by 1998. The program, which started in January 2002, brought

---

57. "UN Condemns Serb 'Sickness,'" BBC World Service, May 8, 2001, available at http://news.bbc.co.uk/hi/english/world/europe/ newsid_1318000/1318283.stm (accessed October 24, 2012).

58. "Diplomats Freed After Bosnia Riot," CNN World, May 7, 2001, available at http://articles.cnn.com/2001-05-07/world/bosnia.violence.02_1_republika-srpska-bosnian-serbs-serb-republic?_s=PM:WORLD (accessed November 27, 2012).

together one platoon of police from each ethnic area for two weeks of intensive training at Camp Butmir. Units were housed together in the MSU compound and participated in a series of joint planning and operational exercises. Trainers from the IPTF, MSU, and ICITAP provided instruction. The first three units to receive training were from Brcko, Banja Luka, and Sarajevo. The course covered such topics as strategic planning, civil disorder management, crowd control, vehicle searches, identification checks, and arrest procedures. To encourage participation, the IPTF and MSU provided transportation and paid for meals and lodging. The goal was to train a group of three platoons each month for nine months, with the program ending in September, just before the general elections scheduled for October. As the elections might be the first in which the old guard of nationalist politicians was seriously challenged, there was the possibility that the newly retrained units would need to deal with campaign-related violence.[59]

The MSU also trained Bosnian special police units for an April 8, 2002, raid on a brothel suspected of employing women who had been brought to Bosnia against their will and forced to engage in prostitution. The brothel, located at the top of a hill at the end of a long road, could be approached successfully only by helicopter. To prevent compromise, the Bosnian police were told only that they were being trained to conduct helicopter assaults. Their graduation exercise, however, was an actual night assault on the brothel that liberated several captive women.[60]

MSU EXPANSION

With the addition of counterterrorism and training to MSU's mandate and the continuing drawdown of SFOR military forces, the overall personnel strength of the MSU increased from 550 to 750 in the fall of 2002. On December 2 the Argentine contingent concluded its assignment in Bosnia and returned to Buenos Aires. The Argentines would have preferred to continue their participation, but deteriorating economic conditions at home made it impossible for them to continue the mission, and 150 Hungarian police were scheduled to take their place in August. The Carabinieri trained the Hungarians in Hungary during the spring and early summer of 2002. At the same time, NATO headquarters in Brussels began efforts to recruit the second MSU battalion that had been part of the original plan. Italian participation in the new battalion was questionable, as the Carabinieri's par-

---

59. Interview with Tillman.
60. Interview with Meese.

ticipation in constabulary forces in Bosnia, Kosovo, and Albania was already stretching the organization's budget and material resources.[61]

Despite the expanded mandate and new resources, the MSU leadership remained frustrated by the restraints that its location in SFOR placed on its operations. The Carabinieri could play a larger role in the fight against organized crime and assist local police with civil disorder management, the MSU's primary mission. Following the Herzegovacka Bank debacle, the MSU was used sparingly and, during the first six months of 2002, did not undertake crowd-control operations. This was due in part to the generally peaceful environment in Bosnia, but it was also the result of SFOR wariness about deploying the MSU. Despite the development and further refinement of MSU doctrine, there remained considerable misunderstanding within SFOR over the MSU's role and mission. The entire MSU battalion was quartered in Sarajevo and made at least one platoon available each week to every MND. The Americans in MND-North were the largest consumers of MSU services. French and Italian forces in MND-South routinely declined the offer. Even in the American sector, problems with language and terminology precluded the MSU from playing a more prominent role. Few members of the Carabinieri spoke English, which made it impossible for them to undertake high-risk arrests and other missions in which real-time communication was vital. But overall, the MSU mandate had grown from crowd control and refugee return to include organized crime, counterterrorism, and training local police. The unit had established itself as an integral part of SFOR, and American commanders were grateful for its presence and its service.[62]

---

61. Interview with Colacicco.

62. Interview with Meese.

5

Odd Jobs: Constabulary Forces in Kosovo

The United Nations had little time to prepare to provide civil administration and the rule of law in Kosovo. During the conflict, it appeared these responsibilities would be assigned to the Organization for Security and Cooperation in Europe (OSCE). Before the NATO bombing campaign began, the OSCE's Kosovo Verification Mission (KVM), a force of two thousand unarmed monitors that included five hundred police officers, had a broad mandate that included verifying an agreed-upon reduction of Yugoslav security forces and the training of a new ethnic Albanian communal police.[1] After the bombing ended, however, Moscow and Belgrade would not accept the OSCE option, and responsibility for the administration of Kosovo fell to the United Nations. Security Council Resolution 1244 created the UN Interim Administration Mission in Kosovo (UNMIK).[2]

The United Nations was responsible for the entire spectrum of civil administrative functions, from health and education to finance and telecommunications to police, courts, and prisons. At the same time, it was tasked to create democratic self-government institutions that would ensure a peaceful life and prosperous future for Kosovo's inhabitants. There was, however, a critical contradiction in the UN mandate. While UNMIK was supposed to develop institutions of self-government, Security Council Resolution 1244 did not define a specific end state. Instead, it left to future deliberations whether Kosovo should be prepared for eventual independence, reintegration into Serbia, or some other final status.

UNMIK was unprecedented not only for its scope but also because no previous peacekeeping mission had been designed with multilateral organizations as partners under UN leadership. The mission was composed of

---

1. Steven Meyers, "2,000 Monitors Go to Kosovo, But Their Power Is Unclear," *New York Times*, October 15, 1998, A6.
2. UN Security Council Resolution 1244 (1999), June 10, 1999.

four pillars, with an international or regional organization as the lead agency for each component. The special representative of the UN secretary-general (SRSG) led the mission, assisted by a principal deputy special representative. The first pillar was the UN High Commissioner for Refugees, responsible for humanitarian assistance; second was the United Nations, overseeing civil administration and law enforcement; third was the OSCE, facilitating democratization and institution building; and fourth was the European Union, responsible for reconstruction and economic development. The senior official for each pillar had the rank of deputy SRSG and reported through the senior deputy SRSG to the chief of mission. The first SRSG was Dr. Bernard Kouchner, the former French health minister.[3]

THE KOSOVO FORCE

On June 9, NATO lieutenant general Mike Jackson (UK) and Yugoslav general Svetozar Marjanović signed the military technical agreement under which all Serb security forces would withdraw from Kosovo and peacekeeping forces enter it. The Kosovo Force (KFOR), a NATO-led military force of 50,000 troops from 30 countries, was responsible for creating a safe and secure environment and ensuring that conditions would permit the safe return of refugees and the implementation of the UN mandate. KFOR entered the province on June 12, 1999, two days after the adoption of UN Security Council Resolution 1244. In accordance with the military technical agreement, KFOR's deployment was synchronized with the withdrawal of Yugoslav military and police, which was completed without incident. Responsibility for security in Kosovo was divided among five multinational brigades (MNBs), with a major NATO partner in charge in each sector. The United Kingdom was the lead country in MNB-Center (Pristina), France in MNB-North (Mitrovica), Germany in MNB-South (Prizren), the United States in MNB-East (Urosevac), and Italy in MNB-West (Pec). Twelve non-NATO countries, including Russia, contributed forces. The MNB-East included military units from Russia, Ukraine, Lithuania, Poland, and Greece, in addition to U.S. forces. KFOR's initial challenge was to ensure the safe return of more than 800,000 ethnic Albanian refugees. Once this reverse migration was completed, KFOR was forced to deal with a fury of vengeful attacks by ethnic Albanians against Serbs and other minorities and an ensuing period of general lawlessness.[4]

---

3. United Nations Secretariat, Report of the Secretary-General on the United Nations Interim Administration in Kosovo, S/1999/779, July 12, 1999, 9.

4. For more on the Kosovo Force's Multinational Brigades, see "KFOR Structure," KFOR website, available at http://www.nato.int/kfor/ (accessed November 27, 2012).

Benefiting from the lessons learned in Bosnia, NATO had prepared for handling widespread civil disorder by including constabulary units in KFOR. Four of the five NATO nations commanding the MNBs deployed with military police units as an integral part of their military contingents. In addition, KFOR included a stand-alone multinational specialized unit modeled on the MSU in Bosnia. For its part, the United Nations included ten special police units (SPUs) in the civilian UNMIK police force. For NATO, including constabulary forces also reflected that KFOR's mandate was broader than SFOR's in Bosnia. Under UN Security Council Resolution 1244, KFOR was responsible not only for establishing a safe and secure environment, but also for ensuring freedom of movement, conducting border patrols and demining operations, and supporting and cooperating closely with UNMIK.

In MNB-North, the French KFOR included 140 gendarmes that were an integral part of the French brigade. In MNB-Central, the British contingent included 140 Royal Military Police and 13 military investigators from the Special Investigation Branch. In MNB-East, the U.S. military brought along a company of U.S. Army military police that performed constabulary functions. In MNB-West, the Italians could call upon the Carabinieri and Spanish Guardia Civil. These units were under the command of the NATO general in charge of each sector and had the same rules of engagement as other KFOR units. This meant they could perform public order functions such as conducting patrols, detaining people they witnessed committing crimes, weapons searches, disarmament, and riot control. The presence of these units gave each MNB its own capacity to handle situations with appropriately trained and equipped military police units instead of relying on regular infantry and armored forces.[5]

In addition to military police units, KFOR's force package included an MSU, which reported directly to the KFOR commander and conducted operations in all five MNB areas of responsibility. This stand-alone constabulary force was composed of 277 Italian Carabinieri, 51 French gendarmes, and 23 Estonian military police. As in Bosnia, the Italian Carabinieri force was assigned the lead and supplied the unit's commanding officer. The MSU's primary function was to provide a security presence by conducting patrols in all MNB areas; it was also assigned the tasks of maintaining public order, crowd control, information gathering, antiterrorism activities, and obtaining intelligence on organized crime. The MSU maintained one company full-time in Pristina, with four operative detachments composed of at least one

5. Peter Jakobsen, "The Role of Military Forces in Managing Public Security Challenges: As Little as Possible or Filling the Gap?," paper presented at the International Studies Association's 43rd Annual Convention, New Orleans, March 27, 2002, 10–12.

platoon allocated to each MNB and located in the towns of Mitrovica, Dja-kovica, Prizren, and Silovo. Specific assignments and the strength of these MSU detachments fluctuated, based on the specific needs of each MNB commander.[6]

With its Italian and French components, the MSU brought substantial ability and experience in criminal investigation, civil disorder management, and the maintenance of public order. As a part of KFOR, however, the MSU was subject to the same restrictions as NATO military forces. The MSU did not have executive authority to engage in law enforcement. It could collect intelligence on organized crime—and many observers believed the MSU was concerned with targets more of interest to Rome than to Pristina—but it could not conduct criminal investigations or legally collect evidence that could be submitted directly to court. This mismatch between capability and mandate resulted in misunderstandings between the MSU and other elements in KFOR, and there were clashes over authority, roles, and mis-sions between the MSU and the UNMIK police, which included formed police units. The presence of highly capable international military and civil-ian constabulary forces with different mandates, authorities, and chains of command caused confusion. As part of KFOR, the MSU was reluctant to acknowledge UNMIK regulations or to comply with the criminal procedure code the UNMIK police used in Kosovo. This resulted in situations in which the MSU would turn over suspects and contraband to the UNMIK police but not detain the individuals or collect evidence in a manner that could be admitted in court to obtain convictions. For their part, the UNMIK police, particularly the formed police units, had little incentive to cooperate with the MSU, considering their redundant capability and the difficulty of com-municating via KFOR's chain of command.[7]

In MNB-East, the American sector, the MSU mission was to collect criminal intelligence on organized crime and detain perpetrators. Many his-toric smuggling routes lay across the Macedonia-Kosovo border, and the MSU was assigned the task of conducting reconnaissance on potential drug and weapons routes and storage areas; it also monitored cross-border traf-ficking in women for prostitution. Yet the U.S. KFOR contingent's lack of familiarity with constabulary forces limited the MSU's effectiveness. With-out a clear understanding of MSU capabilities, U.S. commanders often had false expectations concerning the MSU's contribution to joint operations.

---

6. "Multinational Specialized Unit," KFOR website, available at http://www.nato.int/kfor/ structur/units/msu.html (accessed November 27, 2012).

7. Annika Hansen, *From Congo to Kosovo: Civilian Police in Peace Operations* (London: Inter-national Institute for Strategic Studies, 2002), 73.

This led to underutilizing the true strengths of the MSU as a peacekeeping force. Additional problems between the MSU and U.S. forces arose because of language barriers. In June 2000 an MSU team of between fifteen and twenty personnel was deployed to MNB-East to assist in riot control and counterinsurgency efforts. Unfortunately, only two members of the unit spoke English. Although they were adequately equipped with weapons and secure communications, the Italians found they could not communicate effectively with U.S. forces and thus could not conduct joint operations.

The MSU's accomplishments and frustrations were captured in the following description of its achievements provided by a senior Carabinieri officer:

> We charged one thousand persons with violations, of which five hundred were arrested [by UNMIK police]. We seized thirty-five thousand items, including mortars, bullets, grenades, and other explosives. We seized over a hundred tons of contraband cigarettes. We freed fifty young women who had been forced into prostitution. We identified thirty-five criminal groups and compiled criminal records on ten thousand individuals. We achieved this through the use of the Ulysses computer system, which allowed us to make real-time connections between incidents and criminal groups. Moreover, we did this in Kosovo, where there was no local police force and we had to start from zero.[8]

As in Bosnia, the Italian-led MSU chafed under its restrictive mandate. Its leadership recognized the contribution the MSU could make to local law enforcement. In Kosovo, however, this responsibility rested with the civilian UNMIK police and a new institution, the Kosovo Police Service.

THE KOSOVO POLICE SERVICE

Unlike Bosnia, there were no local police in Kosovo. During the conflict, the Yugoslav Interior Ministry's special police units were responsible for some of the worst incidents of ethnic cleansing. Under the terms of the military technical agreement between NATO and the Federal Republic of Yugoslavia, Yugoslav security forces, including the civilian police, were withdrawn from Kosovo. Initially a force of 3,155 UNMIK police filled the vacuum, with full executive authority, including the right to make arrests, detain suspects, and use deadly force. Paragraph 11(i) of UN Security Council Resolution 1244 provided that the principal responsibilities of the international civil presence would include "maintaining civil law and order, including establishing

---

8. "Missioni all'estero," on Carabinieri website, available at www.carabinieri.it/ (accessed October 17, 2012).

local police forces and meanwhile through the deployment of international police personnel to Kosovo." This was the first time the United Nations had provided an armed, executive police mission where there was no host government and no local police. UNMIK was responsible for providing police services while supervising the establishment of the new, multiethnic Kosovo Police Service (KPS). This meant the United Nations faced the challenge of creating UN and Kosovo police forces at the same time.[9]

While the United Nations was responsible for overall supervision of the KPS, the OSCE provided training. This involved establishing the Kosovo Police Service School (KPSS) and training a cadre of police officers with proportional representation of all ethnic groups, including Serbs. The KPSS was located in the town of Vucitrn, twenty-five kilometers north of Pristina, on the fully remodeled campus of a former special police unit training center. It opened on September 7, 1999, with an initial class of 200 multiethnic students selected from more than 19,500 applicants. When fully operational in March 2000, the KPSS was staffed by 200 international police instructors from 22 OSCE member states with a complement of 600 cadets in training at any time. The U.S. Department of Justice's International Criminal Investigative Training Assistance Program (ICITAP) supplied a director, a quarter of the school's training staff, and the basic curriculum. The newly renovated facility had the residential capacity to house up to 705 students, with separate quarters for men and women. The school also had two gyms, a weight room, a mess hall, a laundry, a warehouse, an armory, medical and administrative offices, and twenty-eight classrooms. The KPSS was the only multiethnic institution functioning in Kosovo.[10]

The OSCE's mandate was to provide "democratically oriented police training" for 5,300 KPS officers by December 21, 2002. At the KPSS students underwent twelve weeks of basic police instruction. OSCE international police instructors delivered lessons in English, which local language assistants translated into both Serbian and Albanian. The core curriculum emphasized community service and respect for human rights. Courses included patrol duties, use of force, basic criminal investigation, forensics, traffic control, defensive tactics, first aid, applicable laws, interviewing techniques, and report writing. Following graduation, UNMIK assigned officers to fifteen weeks of structured field training under the supervision of UNMIK police and KPS field training officers, also trained by the international KPSS staff. Trainees

---

9. International Crisis Group, "Kosovo Report Card," Balkans Report no. 100, Pristina/ Brussels, August 28, 2000, 42–43.

10. OSCE Mission in Kosovo, "Kosovo Police Service School Fact Sheet," Pristina, August 2, 2001.

spent nine weeks of this time in the field and six weeks at the KPSS or a regional training center in the classroom. After completing a total of twenty-seven weeks of classroom and field instruction, the new officers were eligible for certification and independent assignment. In addition to basic training, the KPSS offered a first-line supervisors' course, training for senior police managers, and advanced courses in a number of specialized police skills, such as criminal and accident investigation. It also offered a trainer certification program for KPS instructors, who were taking increasing responsibility for teaching at the school.[11]

The KPS was created as a multiethnic, community-oriented police organization that would eventually replace the UNMIK police. To ensure that all ethnic groups were represented, recruiting quotas were established for women (20 percent) and minorities (15 percent), including Serbs. The United Nations agreed that half of the original cadre of 4,000 officers would be former members of the Kosovo Liberation Army (KLA). To ensure a leavening of experience, the United Nations also agreed that 25 percent would be drawn from the ranks of those who previously had served as police officers in Kosovo during the period of provincial autonomy that ended in 1989. Unfortunately, this left little room for unaffiliated, ethnic Albanian men who were otherwise qualified. Recruits were required to be between twenty-one and fifty-five years old with a secondary education, good health, and strong moral character. Applicants had to pass a UN-administered interview, a written examination, a psychological test, a medical exam, and a physical agility test. They were also required to undergo a background investigation, including a vetting process to remove anyone who had committed human rights abuses or engaged in criminal activities. The screening process had an 80 percent failure rate, primarily from educational deficiencies and inability to pass the written examination.[12]

After graduating from the KPSS and completing field training, KPS officers were assigned to UNMIK police stations with ethnic Serb police, serving only in areas where Serbs were a majority. The KPS operated under the UNMIK police's Planning and Development Department and the watchful eye of its international counterparts. KPS officers were stationed with UN-MIK police and functioned as auxiliaries of that force because the United Nations was unwilling to create a separate institution pending a decision on Kosovo's final status. In its first months on the job, the KPS made a positive impression. Despite problems of low pay (380 deutsche marks per month), ill-fitting Norwegian uniforms, and inadequate vehicles and equipment,

---

11. OSCE Mission in Kosovo, "Kosovo Police Service School," Pristina, May 1, 2002.

12. Eileen Kovchok, "Kosovo Police Service Trainers," *Law and Order* (March 2001), 57–61.

KPS members took their responsibilities seriously. Officers initially worked unarmed, as it took the United Nations four months to supply them with sidearms. On several occasions, they came face-to-face with armed criminals; fortunately, there were no casualties. KPS officers had to deal with public distrust of the police, a leftover from the days of communist rule. There was also the problem of inadequate judicial and penal systems, which took much longer to begin functioning.[13]

UNMIK POLICE

Within UNMIK, the interim civil administration pillar included a police component under the command of the UNMIK police commissioner assisted by two deputy commissioners responsible for operations and administration. The UNMIK police had three separate but coordinated components: the UN Civil Police Unit, a UN Border Police Unit, and a UN Special Police Unit. The Civil Police Unit was responsible for routine police functions such as patrol, criminal investigation, and traffic control. It also covered more specialized police functions, such as narcotics trafficking and organized crime. The civil police were divided among five regional commands and maintained forty-five police stations. The unit's goal was to assume primacy for law enforcement and maintenance of public security from KFOR in each of the five regions. It also had responsibility for establishing and monitoring the KPS, including providing field training officers. Practically every member of the UN Border Police Unit came from the Bundesgrenzschutz, the Federal Republic of Germany's border guards and customs service. They provided a police presence on Kosovo's international borders with Albania and Macedonia, but not on the internal boundary with Serbia. While KFOR had primary responsibility for border control, the UNMIK border police advised KFOR on managing border traffic and controlling the transit of goods and people. When KPS border police were trained and deployed, the UNMIK police monitored their performance.[14]

SPECIAL POLICE UNITS

The special police units (SPUs) were responsible for crowd control and other special police functions related to maintaining public order. This was the first time a UN Civilian Police (CIVPOL) mission had included constabulary

---

13. Kovchok, "Kosovo Police Service Trainers."

14. United Nations, Civilian Police Division, *Concept of Operations for the UNMIK Police* (New York: United Nations, 2001), 1–8.

forces that were armed and had executive authority. Ten formed units were drawn from the constabulary forces of member states. The SPUs were fully integrated, national units with internal discipline and their own weapons, equipment, transport, and communications. They assisted the regular UN-MIK police, including the Border Police Unit, and KFOR with maintaining internal stability.[15]

The Civilian Police Division of the Department of Peacekeeping Operations at UN headquarters in New York conducted planning for the SPU. As the United Nations had no previous experience in fielding constabulary forces, the task was assigned to the only staff member with relevant experience, a French gendarme. Not surprisingly, in concept and organization, the SPUs were modeled on the French National Gendarmerie.[16] The UN Civilian Police Division developed a plan for ten identical, independent, and self-sustaining SPUs, each with 115 officers. Personnel could come from existing constabulary forces or regular police units. Each SPU had a command element, three operational platoons with thirty-two officers each, and a thirteen-member logistical support element made up of a medical team, mechanics, and technicians who could maintain the unit's vehicles, weapons, and communications equipment. The United Nations ensured that each SPU had the same complement of vehicles, weapons, and equipment. It also made certain that personnel joining these units received common training and deployed with their equipment to Kosovo.[17]

In recruiting for the new SPUs, the United Nations allowed member states to ignore the usual requirement that CIVPOL personnel must individually meet certain standards for serving in an international civilian police mission. These selection criteria were established at the beginning of the Bosnian mission and included at least five years of professional experience, proficiency in the mission language, familiarity with driving a police vehicle, and ability to use firearms. In the Kosovo mission, the SPUs were accepted as formed units without examining the qualifications of every participant, the approach used in recruiting UN military forces. The rationale for this decision was that the units would be used primarily for crowd control and would deploy in force, at the platoon level or higher. In theory, this meant that only commanding officers needed to speak the mission language and professional drivers would take care of troop transport. In practice, it meant that the units could not be expected to

---

15. UN Secretariat, S/1999/779, 12.

16. Interview with Joelle Vatcher, UN CIVPOL Division desk officer, New York, December 1, 2001.

17. Interview with William De Meyer, UNMIK police special adviser, New York, December 1, 2001.

break down below the level of a ten-man group, and most preferred to operate at the platoon or company level. Other CIVPOL officers who were required to speak English could be given individual assignments or dispatched in two-person teams to perform specific duties. The SPU had to move in strength and could undertake only certain specific functions.[18]

As with other CIVPOL missions, contributing nations were responsible for preparing and training police officers serving in SPUs. The CIVPOL Division, however, specified the training that the SPU should receive. It also sent out special police assessment teams to pretest the SPU personnel and ensure they had received the proper training and achieved an acceptable level of competence. The UN-prescribed regime included training in several areas: individual and collective crowd-control techniques and procedures up to the company level, with special attention to negotiation, maneuver, and weapons; individual and collective area security and patrol procedures in urban areas, including the use of night vision and global positioning systems; rules of engagement observed by UNMIK; the organization and mandate of UNMIK and its area of operations; map reading and communications; the geographic, historical, and cultural background of Kosovo, including the origins of the conflict; and mine awareness.[19]

COMMAND AND CONTROL

The SPUs were under the overall command and control of the UNMIK police commissioner and his deputy for operations, but they reported to the UNMIK police regional commanders for day-to-day operations. The SPUs were also responsible to the office of the SPU special adviser to the UNMIK police commissioner, which advised on SPU operations and supervised the administrative aspects of SPU participation in the UN mission. The special adviser's office oversaw the management and coordination of SPU operations, including preparation of orders and mission assignments. It conducted inspections of SPUs on arrival and at five-month intervals to ensure operational readiness and effective maintenance, handled administrative matters, such as leave and equipment acquisition, and was responsible for coordinating unit rotations. In addition, the SPU adviser or his staff were present when SPU elements deployed en force to ensure that such operations were properly coordinated with the UNMIK police and KFOR. Once all ten of the SPUs were in place, the special adviser's office began developing

---

18. Interview with Adalbert Gross, UNMIK police deputy commissioner of operations, Washington, DC, February 21, 2002.

19. UN, CIVPOL Division, *Concept of Operations*, 11.

joint training programs to ensure that the various national contingents could work together effectively.[20]

As a component of the UNMIK police, the SPUs were subject to the same rules of engagement and UN rules for the use of force and firearms as the rest of CIVPOL in Kosovo. Under the UN CIVPOL Division's concept of operations, each SPU could function independently and perform the same functions, which included the management of civil disorder during violent demonstrations through the use of nonlethal weapons and the minimum amount of force (including firearms) needed to control the situation; a rapid reaction capability to deal with emergencies and unforeseen threats to public order; operational support and backup for the UNMIK police, KPS, and KFOR; area security and information collection through preventive vehicle patrols, including light armored vehicles; protection and security for UN officials and UN border police in the performance of their duties; assistance to humanitarian organizations, UN agencies, and the International Criminal Tribunal for the Former Yugoslavia (ICTY); and radio communication and liaison in English for units in the field and international authorities.[21]

FINANCIAL ARRANGEMENTS

Under the memoranda of understanding with contributing countries, the United Nations agreed to pay the standard UN financial reimbursement for every officer in each of the SPUs. Under the UN schedule for personnel expenses, SPU members received payments each month in addition to their regular salary, paid in the contributing country's national currency: troop cost, at the rate of $988 per month per unit member; a daily allowance at the rate of $1.28, plus a recreational leave allowance of $10.50 per day for up to seven days of leave during each six-month period; a personal equipment allowance at the rate of $65.00 per month per unit member; a weapon and ammunition allowance at the rate of $5.00 per month per member; and a specialist's allowance at a rate of $291.00 per month per unit member for up to 10 percent of the contingent.[22] Under this payment schedule, the monthly personnel costs to the United Nations for a standard SPU of 115 members was $131,987.00; annually, that meant $1,583,844.00, plus an additional

---

20. Interview with Colonel Gery Plane, SPU special adviser to the UNMIK police commissioner, Pristina, June 24, 2002.

21. UN, CIVPOL Division, Concept of Operations, 11.

22. United Nations Secretariat, "Memorandum of Understanding with Jordan for UNMIK," October 9, 2000, A-1.

$16,905.00 in vacation allowances. At this rate, the total annual personnel cost to the United Nations for all ten of the SPUs in Kosovo was in excess of $16,007,490.00.

In addition to personnel costs, the United Nations agreed to reimburse contributing countries for the equipment they provided according to standard UN rates. This reimbursement was done under a wet lease arrangement that gave contributing countries financial compensation for the use of the equipment their units brought to Kosovo. For a representative SPU vehicle package of three unarmed armored personnel carriers, twelve Jeeps, and eleven trucks and other support vehicles, the monthly compensation was $40,500. The UN paid monthly compensation for weapons, ammunition, generators, containers, and other types of equipment, from loudspeakers to tear gas launchers, each SPU brought from its own national inventories. Each memorandum of understanding spelled out the type and condition of equipment, performance standards, maintenance requirements, provisions for replacement in case of damage or loss, and ultimate disposition. The agreements also specified the financial compensation and performance standards for SPU self-sustainment, covering catering, communications, medical and dental care, and office equipment. Each SPU received compensation for bringing its own cooks and doctors as well as nuclear, biological, and chemical weapons protection. Interestingly, the agreements specified the telephone as the primary means of communication and required that SPU kitchens have "hot dish-washing capabilities."[23]

DEPLOYMENT

With almost no time for advance preparation, the various elements of UN-MIK were very slow to deploy; this was particularly true of the UNMIK police. Kosovo was the first UN experience with fielding a police organization that required the capacity to perform all police functions, from traffic control to fighting organized crime. An initial component of 169 members of the UN International Police Task Force (IPTF) was immediately transferred from Bosnia, but this group of officers was unarmed and did little more than try to establish a headquarters operation.[24] Logistics were also a problem, as the United Nations was unprepared to equip a substantial force of police officers with everything required for comprehensive police services. The UNMIK police arrived with none of the facilities and materials police

---

23. UN Secretariat, "Memorandum of Understanding with Jordan for UNMIK."

24. United Nations Secretariat, Report of the Secretary-General on the United Nations Interim Administration Mission in Kosovo, S/1999/987, September 16, 1999, 4.

departments used—no police stations, desks, radios, telephones, office furniture, stationery, heat, water, mail—and very few vehicles.[25]

From the point of view of the UN CIVPOL Division, however, the deployment of the SPU to Kosovo was one time when the UN system worked more quickly than might reasonably have been expected. That the first SPU arrived in Kosovo in April 2000, ten months after the start of the UN mission, was viewed as an achievement by the CIVPOL Division. It was the first instance in which the United Nations had deployed formed constabulary units in a police mission, and time was required to conceptualize and plan the creation of the force. Since the United Nations did not take existing units, potential donors had to wait until planning for the force structure and the concept of operations was completed before determining whether they could participate in the mission. The countries that decided to go forward then negotiated with the United Nations and ultimately signed agreements covering the terms of participation, including a specific list of duties their forces would perform. At the same time, the CIVPOL Division had to obtain funding through the complicated UN budget process to lease or purchase the equipment needed to outfit ten units. Donor countries also had to recruit, organize, and train the new forces.[26]

Another reason for the delay in deploying the SPU was the need to locate and refurbish suitable facilities to house the units before they arrived. While these formed units came equipped with vehicles and communications gear, they were not outfitted like military units and were unprepared to live in the field. They could not set up camp and operate independently of the local infrastructure. They required the elements associated with a police headquarters—offices, barracks, and garages—plus electricity, heat, and water. Each unit required a kitchen and dining facility able to feed 120 people twice a day, with food service available for duty personnel around the clock. All units brought along medical personnel, requiring an infirmary.[27]

In searching for suitable facilities, UNMIK officials were competing with their UN counterparts and representatives from other international agencies in a postconflict environment where undamaged buildings were at a premium. Representatives of donor countries also had to approve the sites and their preparation. In one case, the Spanish government refused to allow its SPU to be quartered in a new, unoccupied, and only slightly damaged prison facility because they considered it inappropriate for their police to be housed in a jail. For most of the SPUs, the United Nations refurbished war-damaged buildings and constructed camps using containers

---

25. International Crisis Group, "Kosovo Report Card," 44.
26. Interview with Vatcher, 2001.
27. Interview with De Meyer.

and prefabricated buildings erected on concrete slabs. In some cases, the availability of housing actually determined where the SPU was stationed. The tenth SPU, the Romanian unit, arrived on February 22, 2002, and was quartered in Ferizaj because suitable buildings were available. The Romanians were a late selection by the UN CIVPOL Division, but responded quickly after several other countries turned down UN requests to provide the final unit.[28]

As police units the SPUs could not deploy without military support and could not operate in areas where KFOR had yet to establish a level of reasonable security. The SPUs were more capable of operating independently than the UNMIK police, but required military backup to conduct operations. The rapid escalation of ethnic violence and criminal activity that greeted UNMIK's arrival created additional disincentives for donor countries to rush their newly created constabulary units to Kosovo.

CRIME AND ETHNIC CONFLICT

Short of personnel and resources, the United Nations could not manage the wave of violence that swept Kosovo following the mass return of ethnic Albanian refugees from camps in Albania and Macedonia. Returning Kosovars took revenge on the Serbs, the Roma, and other minorities, which were accused of looting and pillaging following the Serb security forces' ethnic cleansing of Albanian villages. In the absence of international and local police, KFOR intervened to stem the violence and attempted to restore public order. In mid-July 1999, within six weeks of the start of the UNMIK mission, KFOR commanders were already beginning to chafe under the responsibility of performing police functions. In Washington, Defense Department and U.S. military officials went before Congress to criticize the slowness of UN efforts to deploy international police and to relieve the military of the responsibility for arresting and detaining local citizens.[29]

There was also confusion within the United Nations about what law the UNMIK police should enforce. Initially, the United Nations declared the laws of the Federal Republic of Yugoslavia and the Republic of Serbia[30] would continue to apply insofar as they did not conflict with international human rights standards and the UN mandate.[31] Local judges and prosecu-

---

28. Interview with UN CIVPOL Division official, New York, February 22, 2002.

29. Bradley Graham, "Pentagon Faults UN in Kosovo," *Washington Post*, July 21, 1999, A17.

30. The Republika Srpska refers to the ethnic Serbian half of Bosnia as determined by the Dayton Accords. The Republic of Serbia was a constituent republic of the former Yugoslavia.

31. UN Secretariat, S/1999/779, 5.

tors, who associated Yugoslav law with Serb oppression, challenged this decision. Kosovo Albanians advocated using the legal code from before 1989, when the province enjoyed substantial autonomy. Under pressure to reestablish the Kosovo criminal justice system, the United Nations agreed in December 1999 to the last suggestion. Thereafter, the applicable law in Kosovo became an almost unfathomable combination of old law, international and European human rights conventions, UNMIK regulations, and police directives. According to an UNMIK publication, the applicable law in Kosovo was literally "the regulations promulgated by the Special Representative of the Secretary-General and subsidiary instruments issued there under, and the law in force in Kosovo on March 22, 1989, according to UNMIK Regulation 1999/24 ("On the Law Applicable in Kosovo"), as amended by UNMIK Regulation 2000/59."[32]

In September, UN secretary-general Kofi Annan informed the Security Council that "the level of violence in Kosovo, especially against vulnerable minorities, remained a major concern."[33] With only 1,100 officers, the UNMIK police struggled to control the reemergence of Albanian organized crime; massive smuggling of cars, cigarettes, narcotics, fuel, and general contraband; and exploding street violence. UNMIK police commissioner Sven Frederiksen acknowledged the growing magnitude of crime and attacks on minorities but said he did not have the police personnel to stop it.[34] In December 1999, with serious security incidents on the rise, the murder of a newly arrived UNMIK international staff member, and the first assassination of an ethnic Albanian political leader, the Security Council acted on the secretary-general's recommendation and increased the authorized strength of the UNMIK police to 4,718 personnel. Unfortunately, only 1,817 CIVPOL had arrived in country, including 78 IPTF members who were transferred from Bosnia.[35]

The senior UN official in Kosovo, Bernard Kouchner, called the failure of UN member states to honor their commitments to supply personnel a "scandal" that was contributing to general lawlessness.[36] The new NATO commander, German general Klaus Reinhardt, reversed his predecessor's policy and ordered his troops back onto the streets to assist the UNMIK police to

---

32. United Nations Secretariat, "Report of the Secretary-General on the United Nations Interim Administration Mission in Kosovo," S/1999/1250, December 23, 1999, 5.

33. UN Secretariat, S/1999/987, 1.

34. R. Jeffrey Smith, "With Few Police to Stop It, Crime Flourishes in Kosovo," *Washington Post*, October 23, 1999, A19.

35. UN Secretariat, S/1999/1250, 5–6.

36. Peter Finn, "Gunman Kills Serb in Café in Kosovo," *Washington Post*, December 19, 1999, A51.

restore order.[37] In his December 1999 report to the Security Council, Annan noted the deteriorating security situation in Kosovo. He also pointed out that six months after the start of the UN mission, none of the SPUs that had been expected to spearhead the effort to control civil unrest had reached Kosovo. Annan blamed the problem on "logistical and other constraints" that delayed their arrival.[38]

MITROVICA

In early 2000 the full fury of ethnic hatred in Kosovo was felt in Mitrovica. Located in the northern part of the province, Mitrovica was situated astride the Ibar River just south of Kosovo's only major industrial center, the Trepca mining and smelter complex. The Ibar's meandering course marked an informal boundary between ethnic Serb areas extending northward forty kilometers to the border with the Republic of Serbia and areas occupied by ethnic Albanians to the south. North of Mitrovica, Serbia paid its civil servants, newsstands sold only Belgrade papers, prices were quoted in dinars, and schools used the Serbian curriculum. Initial NATO reluctance to establish control over Mitrovica's northern section resulted in a de facto division of the region. A short bridge in the center of town became the principal crossing point between the Serb and Albanian sectors. When French KFOR troops stationed tanks behind tumbles of razor wire and established a checkpoint on the bridge, Mitrovica became a divided city,[39] a condition that KFOR helped perpetuate when it failed to protect ethnic Albanians living north of the bridge or stop a similar process of ethnic cleansing of Serbs in the southern part of the city.

As tensions escalated and clashes became more frequent, a group of several hundred young Serbs organized to control the north end of the bridge and prevent an influx of ethnic Albanians into the northern part of the city.[40] These so-called bridge watchers gradually became more organized as they rallied behind a leader, Oliver Ivanović, and equipped themselves with Motorola radios, sirens, and truncheons. Formally identified as the Citizens' Association of Bridge St. Demetrios, the group claimed to be a community self-defense and philanthropic organization. According to an

---

37. Carlotta Gall, "German General's Kosovo Peacekeepers Are Fighting Crime," *New York Times*, December 21, 1999, A10.

38. UN Secretariat, S/1999/1250, 5.

39. Guy Lawson, "The View From the Bridge," *New York Times Magazine*, August 20, 2000, 48.

40. International Crisis Group, "Kosovo Report Card," 9, 19.

International Crisis Group report, the bridge watchers were paid operatives of the Serbian Ministry of the Interior in Belgrade whose mission was to incite violence against ethnic Albanians and the international community. Bridge watching became a regular job with wages and shifts. Some members were employed as hospital security staff and paid by the Serbian Ministry of Health, supplementing their incomes through donations from local citizens. Others enriched themselves by engaging in intimidation and protection rackets, illicit trafficking, and other forms of organized crime. In time, the bridge watchers became a parallel security force that checked identification, responded to complaints, and detained petty criminals. This security function was bolstered by the presence of plainclothes officers from the Serbian Ministry of Interior who were former police officers in Mitrovica.[41]

Belgrade's maintenance of parallel administrative and security structures in Mitrovica and the rest of northern Kosovo directly violated UN Security Council Resolution 1244. It was also a direct challenge that UNMIK and NATO seemed powerless or unwilling to counter. With the continuing violence, northern Mitrovica and neighboring Zvencan were exceptional as the only Kosovo municipalities where it was too dangerous to station KPS officers. Only in Mitrovica was Albanian confidence in KFOR in doubt, given the seemingly pro-Serb attitude of French troops. It was also the only place where local residents repeatedly demonstrated their willingness to use violence against the international community. UNMIK police conducted daily weapons searches in Albanian areas but could not conduct similar operations in the north. The Serbs seemed intent on defying UNMIK in order to establish self-rule. The Albanians seemed equally determined to prevent Kosovo's de facto partition.

In February 2000 a series of violent clashes occurred in Mitrovica between crowds of ethnic Albanians and Serbs. On February 2 a UN High Commissioner for Refugees bus carrying 49 Serbs was bombed, leaving two dead and three injured. In Mitrovica, the two days of rioting that followed severely tested relations between KFOR and the UNMIK police. Primacy for maintaining public order in Mitrovica rested with the 250-man infantry battalion of French KFOR troops. The UNMIK police had an understrength detachment of 65 officers that attempted to patrol on both sides of the Ibar. During the riots, French KFOR troops failed to respond numerous times to UNMIK police requests for support. In one incident, a U.S. CIVPOL officer and a detachment of French paratroops were attempting to reach a

41. International Crisis Group, "UNMIK's Kosovo Albatross: Tackling Division in Mitrovica," Balkans Report no. 131, Pristina/Belgrade/Brussels, June 3, 2002, 1–10.

small group of Albanians trapped by a Serb mob. When the UNMIK police officer was knocked to the ground, he expected the French to rescue him. Instead the French soldiers retreated to the protection of their armored personnel carriers. Eventually a company of Danish KFOR troops responded and rescued the Albanians. Such incidents created bad blood between the French KFOR contingent and the UNMIK police and between KFOR and local Albanians, who felt the French were acting on their historical affinity for the Serbs.[42] On February 13 a grenade attack on a Serb café in northern Mitrovica was followed by sniper attacks on French KFOR positions that wounded two soldiers. In an exchange of gunfire, one sniper was killed and another wounded; both were Kosovo Albanians.[43]

In March, Secretary-General Annan informed the Security Council that the deteriorating security situation in Mitrovica highlighted the "policing gap" that existed in Kosovo because of the failure of member states to contribute police personnel. He also noted that the continued absence of the ten SPUs meant that KFOR bore responsibility for maintaining public order.[44] In April 2000, the first SPU, a unit from Pakistan, arrived in Kosovo and was assigned to Mitrovica, but UNMIK police did not have primacy there and KFOR retained responsibility for law enforcement and maintaining public order.[45] In repeated incidents requiring riot control and civil disorder management, the French KFOR contingent relied on its own resources and the Pakistani SPU was not used, even as French troops suffered casualties in violent clashes with local Serbs.

The French unwillingness to allow contact between the Pakistanis and Serbs was particularly obvious on June 21, 2000, when a group of Serb bridge watchers clashed with UNMIK police, leaving twenty Serbs wounded and thirteen UN police and other international vehicles burned or damaged. The incident began when a group of Serbs threw rocks and broke windows in three eleven-story apartment buildings located in a UN zone of confidence near the north end of the bridge. Three-quarters of the buildings' inhabitants were ethnic Albanians, but one-quarter were ethnic Serbs. UNMIK police responded to complaints about the rock throwing from building residents and seized one of the vandals. A crowd of bridge watchers quickly

---

42. R. Jeffrey Smith, "French Troops in Kosovo Accused of Retreat," *Washington Post,* February 2, 2000, A14.

43. United Nations Secretariat, Report of the Secretary-General on the United Nations Interim Mission in Kosovo, S/2000/177, March 3, 2000.

44. United Nations Secretariat, Report of the Secretary-General on the United Nations Interim Administration Mission in Kosovo, S/2000/538, June 6, 2000, 10.

45. UN Secretariat, S/2000/538, 6.

surrounded the police to prevent his arrest.[46] Some of the UNMIK police wanted to release the suspect, but the American officer in charge placed the Serb under arrest and radioed for the Pakistani SPU to provide backup. After a considerable delay, the Pakistani SPU arrived at the southern end of the bridge. Standing in formation, the Pakistanis were pelted with rocks, but French KFOR troops and armored vehicles on the bridge prevented them from crossing.[47]

The French unwillingness to allow the Pakistani SPU to participate in the incident and others that followed was never officially explained. The French apparently did not trust the Pakistanis, who had a reputation for using violence against demonstrators in their own country and were untested in riot-control situations in Kosovo. The French also seemed concerned about the appearance of Pakistani Muslims clashing with Orthodox Christian Serbs. French motives may have derived from France's long-term commercial interests in Serbia and a belief that the region's future stability required an ethnic Serb presence in Kosovo. The French seemed to feel morally responsible for preventing the numerically superior Albanians from expelling the Serb minority.[48] As a practical matter, the presence of a force of French gendarmes within the French KFOR contingent gave French commanders an option for dealing with crowd-control situations that did not require going outside their own force or command structure. Gendarmes were colocated with French military forces, immediately available, fully trained and equipped, and totally compatible in language, communications gear, and doctrine. In contrast, the Pakistani SPU members spoke English and had incompatible radios, so the two forces could not communicate during an operation. There was also the possibility of problems arising because of differences in doctrine and tactics. For some or all of these reasons, the French chose to rely on their own forces in dealing with civil disorder management in Mitrovica.[49]

The only exception to the general practice of not using the SPU for security functions in Mitrovica was Operation Vulcan, the UNMIK takeover of the Trepca mining and industrial facility. Located just north of Mitrovica, Trepca was a complex of forty mines and processing plants that produced a range of metals and employed two thousand Serbs. Trepca was

46. Musa Mustafa, "Serbs Burned Police Vehicles and Attacked Albanians in Their Apartments," *Koha Ditore* (Pristina), June 21, 2000, 4.

47. Interview with General William Nash, U.S. Army, retired, former UNMIK commissioner for Mitrovica, Washington, DC, February 5, 2002.

48. Interview with Nash.

49. Interview with official in the Office of the SPU Special Adviser to the UNMIK Police Commissioner, Pristina, June 24, 2002.

the last major industrial unit operating in Kosovo and the primary source of employment for Serbs in Mitrovica. More than a year after the UN arrival in Kosovo, Trepca remained under the control of Serb engineers who took orders from Belgrade and exported the plant's entire production to Serbia. On August 14, 2000, a force of five hundred British, French, and Danish KFOR troops supported by helicopters and armored vehicles seized control of the facility. According to a KFOR spokesman, the action was taken to force closure of the Zvecan lead smelter, which was pumping more than two hundred times the safe level of lead fumes into the atmosphere. The UN's Kouchner, a physician and former French health minister, called Trepca an environmental disaster and said its continued operation was hazardous to public health. He noted the plant's management repeatedly refused requests to close the smelter and rejected the right of the United Nations under various Security Council resolutions to manage former Yugoslav state factories for the general good of Kosovo. Kouchner said the United Nations was prepared to invest $16 million to renovate the plant's buildings and outdated equipment. He also guaranteed that workers would continue to receive their salaries while the facility was undergoing renovation. The plant's managers called the UNMIK takeover "a classic case of robbery."[50]

Arriving before dawn, the first British KFOR elements clashed with workers protecting the front gate of the complex. As more employees arrived for work, the violence escalated, with the crowd throwing rocks and pieces of wood at the soldiers. At the Zvecan smelter, a group of thirty to forty Serb engineers locked themselves in the building and refused to shut down the furnace. By afternoon, resistance was overcome and UN experts closed down the facility. Meanwhile, in Mitrovica, a Serb mob clashed with British soldiers, who retaliated by firing rubber bullets. In a related incident, UNMIK police closed down a nearby Serb radio station that had been used to broadcast anti-UN and anti-KFOR propaganda.[51] Following the takeover in Trepca, the Pakistani SPU was brought from Mitrovica to provide area security and guard the Zvecan smelter. The SPU established two guard posts and conducted area patrols, but the large size of the facility defeated efforts to secure it effectively. Given the high levels of environmental pollution in the area, the United Nations was acutely aware of the dangers to its personnel. During the brief period of their deployment to

---

50. "Kosovo Serbs React Angrily to NATO Shutting Smelter," Reuters, August 15, 2000.

51. "Serbs and NATO Clash in Mitrovica," BBC World Service, August 14, 2000, available at http://news.bbc.co.uk/2/hi/europe/879474.stm (accessed November 27, 2012).

Trepca, SPU personnel were subject to weekly blood tests and their uniforms were cleaned every day to prevent contamination.[52]

TWO YEARS OF VIOLENCE

Throughout the winter of 2000 and spring of 2001, continued high levels of politically motivated violence, illicit trafficking, organized crime, and street crime in Kosovo reflected the generally unsettled conditions in the region. A series of attacks on ethnic Serbs in January 2001 was followed by a major incident on February 16, when a bus loaded with Serbs in the weekly KFOR-escorted convoy from Niš in Serbia to Gracanica near Pristina was bombed, resulting in 10 deaths and injuries to 40 others. Demonstrations were staged in more than 15 Serb enclaves, often involving up to 6,500 people. Tensions increased generally in the Mitrovica, Gnjilane, and Pristina regions, imposing severe limitations on freedom of movement for ethnic Serbs. Criminal behavior shifted toward increased violence against the international community, including aggression toward UNMIK law enforcement and KFOR personnel. One Russian KFOR soldier was killed.[53]

Mitrovica remained the focal point for ethnic violence and civil disobedience. On March 14, 2001, a Serb crowd surrounded an UNMIK police station, trapping police officers inside. Demanding the release of three Serbs who had been detained for assaulting UNMIK police officers, the crowd caused extensive damage to the station and burned or damaged seven police vehicles. In the melee, twenty-one UNMIK police were injured. KFOR troops dispersed the crowd, firing tear gas and stun grenades at the rioters and blocking the bridge across the Ibar.[54] Afterward UNMIK police temporarily suspended patrols in northern Mitrovica, resuming them only in late May with KFOR assistance. The incident appeared to be part of an orchestrated effort to drive UNMIK out of northern Mitrovica.[55] On April 19 a similar clash occurred when KFOR attempted to remove roadblocks established by Serbs protesting UN efforts to collect taxes on goods arriving from Serbia, a means of controlling the black

---

52. Interview with Joelle Vatcher, UN CIVPOL Division desk officer, New York, March 4, 2002.

53. United Nations Secretariat, Report of the Secretary-General on the United Nations Interim Administration Mission in Kosovo, S/2001/218, March 13, 2001, 2–3.

54. "Kosovo Serbs Attack UN Police," BBC World Service, March 14, 2001, available at http://news.bbc.co.uk/2/hi/europe/1219712.stm (accessed November 27, 2012).

55. UN Secretariat, S/2001/565, 3.

market. Ten Serbs were injured when KFOR fired tear gas to disperse the demonstration.[56]

On May 21, 2001, UNMIK established a new first pillar in the UN administrative structure, which realigned UNMIK's police and Department of Judicial Affairs into one structure headed by a newly arrived deputy SRSG, Ambassador Gary Matthews. This replaced the previous humanitarian assistance pillar, the residual functions of which were assumed by the UN's civil administration in the second pillar. Creating the new pillar brought the police, security, and justice structures under common management. It also brought greater coherence and centralized control of efforts against crime and improved UNMIK's ability to deal with street violence and organized crime. Matthews, a former U.S. State Department foreign service officer, had served previously as deputy high representative in Bosnia and was an auxiliary police officer in his hometown in Virginia. In organizing the new structure, Matthews sought to better focus UN law enforcement efforts while promoting judicial system reform through increasing the number and quality of judges and improving penal facilities. He also sought to take advantage of new UN legislation imposing heavier penalties for illegal weapons possession, weapons trafficking, and illegal border crossing. The new pillar created a single point of contact for cooperative efforts with KFOR, which continued to play a major role in ensuring public order.[57]

By June 2001 nine of the ten SPUs had arrived in Kosovo. India and Jordan sent two each; the others came from Spain, Pakistan, Poland, Ukraine, and Argentina. Their 1,089 personnel brought the total number of UNMIK police to 4,378, more than 90 percent of the authorized force strength. The new SPUs provided the UNMIK police with substantially increased capacity to engage in civil disorder management and to perform tactical police functions.[58] Despite repeated incidents of civil disorder and ethnic violence, however, none of the SPUs was used for crowd control, which was their primary function; rather, they were put to use in a hodgepodge of security-related tasks.

THE "ODD JOBS" UNIT

The reasons the SPUs performed a variety of odd jobs were many and varied themselves. First, the senior leadership of the UNMIK police was drawn

---

56. "Serbs Stone KFOR Troops," BBC World Service, April 19, 2001, available at http://news. bbc.co.uk/hi/english/world/europe/newsid_1286000/1286203.stm (accessed October 26, 2012).

57. Interview with Gary Matthews, former deputy SRSG in Kovoso, Washington, DC, April 16, 2002.

58. UN Secretariat, S/2001/565, 12.

from police forces in northern Europe and North America. These officers came from policing traditions that did not include constabularies. Officers who were unfamiliar with constabulary forces were reluctant to deploy them in sensitive situations.[59] At the same time, between 15 and 20 percent of the duties assigned to the UNMIK police were not related to law enforcement but were requests for police services.[60] As the arriving SPUs did not have assigned duties, UNMIK police officials saw them as an available labor pool that could perform a variety of necessary tasks and free regular UNMIK CIVPOL for duties related to law enforcement. SPUs had their own vehicles, communications, and weapons, which made them natural candidates for escort duty, close protection work, and other police services that required mobility. As they were trained to deploy in strength, they had a natural comparative advantage over regular UNMIK police in handling assignments that required large numbers of personnel. SPUs were called upon to serve as static guards for buildings, provide security for events, and handle other situations that required a large-scale security presence. As one senior UNMIK police official said, "In the beginning, UN commanders did not know what to do with the SPU. Now they cannot do without them."[61]

Second, the United Nations had expected that most of the SPUs would come from countries in Western Europe. In fact, European countries, which were also members of NATO, preferred to have their gendarmes serve as members of KFOR and not in the UNMIK police. After efforts to recruit European units were unsuccessful, the United Nations turned to countries in the Middle East, South Asia, Latin America, and the former Soviet republics. This meant dealing with donor countries with a broad range of military and police traditions and cultures.[62] It also meant accepting some forces that were more military in character and others that were an unknown quantity in how they might react in a violent confrontation. UNMIK officials were leery of employing the SPUs in situations where they might use tactics that would cause civilian casualties. Following their arrival, several of the SPUs received additional training in civil disorder management with an emphasis on nonviolent means of maintaining public order. In sectors where KFOR maintained primacy for law enforcement and public order, military commanders preferred to rely on constabulary units that were part of their own

59. Interview with De Meyer.

60. UN Secretariat, S/2000/538, 6.

61. Interview with De Meyer.

62. Halvor Hartz, "The Role of Civilian Police," paper presented at a conference on building a durable peace in Kosovo, sponsored by the Role of American Military Power Program of the Association of the United States Army, Arlington, Virginia, October 16, 2001, photocopy.

commands rather than cross jurisdictional boundaries and use forces that had different chains of command and rules of engagement. At the same time, senior UN officials were reluctant to press KFOR to utilize the SPUs, particularly in Mitrovica, fearing KFOR might seize the opportunity to shed responsibility for frustrating and dangerous assignments.[63]

Third, Kosovo was missing what one UNMIK police official described as the "European cultural context" for using gendarmes in civil disorder management. In Western Europe, there was a tacit understanding between police and demonstrators about how demonstrations should be conducted and the limits of acceptable behavior for both parties. In democratic countries, riot control forces were trained to regard protesters as fellow citizens and not as enemies. At the same time, protesters knew the arrival of constabulary forces meant the demonstration had reached the limits of official tolerance and that further escalation would provoke a violent response from the authorities. With its history of communist rule, Kosovo lacked such traditions and understandings. Demonstrations were most often staged not by citizens with a complaint or legitimate problem, but by a rent-a-mob of paid and disciplined partisans with a specific political objective. Groups such as the Mitrovica bridge watchers used civil disorder and violence to continue the original conflict. In such circumstances, provoking violence was the aim of civil action rather than an unfortunate by-product of a situation that got out of control.[64]

Finally, the passage of time, the growing number of UN and indigenous police, and KFOR's assertive presence brought a decline in the number of violent crimes and the restoration of more normal conditions. In 2001 the number of murders declined by 50 percent from the previous year. Incidents of arson fell by 58 percent and looting by 73 percent. Only the number of sexual assaults increased, probably the result of an increased willingness to report such crimes. The decline in violence was likely assisted by the departure of large numbers of Serbs and the retreat of those remaining into KFOR-guarded enclaves. With the exception of Mitrovica, which remained a flashpoint and center of interethnic violence, tensions in the remainder of the country began to ease. At the start of the Kosovo mission, a climate of impunity had prevailed; there were too few UNMIK police to provide security, no judicial system, and no prisons. By December 2001, trained KPS officers patrolled the streets, a judiciary was hearing cases, and the penal system was functioning. The UNMIK police had primacy for law enforcement for all areas except Mitrovica. Cities in Kosovo had lower crime rates than

---

63. Interview with police adviser, U.S. Office, Pristina, June 26, 2002.

64. Interview with De Meyer.

most communities in the United States.[65] In a more relaxed environment, there were almost no demonstrations and little call for formed police units to control civil disorder. Instead, UNMIK officials used the SPUs for a wide variety of duties.

First was static guard duty. SPUs guarded UNMIK facilities, courthouses, and other sensitive facilities, such as the Trepca industrial complex. A platoon of the Indian SPU and a Ukrainian K-9 unit provided airport security. The Indian SPU also provided security for the minor offenses court and the detention center in Pristina. Eighteen officers from five SPUs and two Ukrainian K-9 teams were assigned to guard the exterior of the Dubrava prison. Five-member SPU teams provided backup at roadblocks for UNMIK civil administrative officers, checking licenses, registration, and ethnic ridership levels of buses in Pristina.

Second, SPUs manned checkpoints, conducted patrols, and took other security measures to protect minority communities, cultural sites, and people in the witness protection program. In Obilić, the Indian SPU conducted routine foot and vehicle patrols to protect Serb residences. In Dubrava, the Spanish SPU provided a group of ten officers to guard the residence of a family of a witness in a trial.

Third, SPUs provided security at major public events, such as political ceremonies, soccer matches, and graduations. In February 2002 five platoons from three SPUs were deployed in connection with the annual ceremony commemorating the massacre of Adam Jashari, a KLA leader, and his family by Serb forces in February 1999. One Jordanian platoon and two Polish platoons were assigned as a rapid intervention force at three pedestrian checkpoints, while three Pakistani platoons were on standby at the local police station. Some 30,000 people attended the ceremony, which proceeded without incident. On March 9 three platoons from the Argentine SPU were dispatched to deal with a gang fight and riot following a basketball game in Prizren. Hooligans threw rocks and bottles at the SPU officers, who responded with tear gas to control the situation. Following the incident, SPU platoons were routinely deployed at sporting events where violence might occur.

Fourth, SPUs assisted the UNMIK border police at checkpoints on the border with Albania and Macedonia. The SPUs conducted vehicle searches, including the use of K-9 teams to identify drugs and weapons, and provided security and armed support. Under an agreement reached in the spring of 2002, the SPUs conducted joint patrols with the border police along the

---

65. International Crisis Group, "A Kosovo Roadmap (II): Internal Benchmarks," Balkans Report no. 125, Pristina/Brussels, March 1, 2002, 13–18.

frontier and, as a rapid reaction force, intercepted illegal crossings discovered by foot patrols and helicopters.

Fifth, SPUs supported the UNMIK special operations unit during high-risk arrests. The SPUs provided backup teams for the UNMIK police and, in cases where forced entry was required, actually made arrests. They were also deployed en force when it appeared the arrest might spark public demonstrations. On February 21, 2002, seven SPU platoons were deployed to the UNMIK police station in northern Mitrovica in connection with the arrest of two ethnic Serbs. The deployment was later reduced to one platoon that remained in place for several days. No incidents were reported.

Sixth, SPUs provided close protection for high-risk persons, including visiting dignitaries, international judges and prosecutors, UN personages, and local government officials. SPU officers were routinely assigned to escort provisional government officials and assembly members, particularly ethnic Serbs, from their homes to meetings in Pristina. This was a major commitment for the SPU, requiring up to one hundred officers and dozens of armored vehicles two or three times a week. A platoon of the Indian SPU conducted routine patrols within Pristina to protect UN buildings and the residences of senior international officials. SPUs also supported the close protection unit of the UNMIK police for particularly sensitive missions.

Seventh, SPUs provided election security. In November 2001, elections were held for a 120-member Kosovo assembly that would in turn select a president and provisional government. During the election campaigns, SPUs provided escorts for candidates and security at election rallies. During the voting, the SPU secured voting stations, transported ballot boxes, and ensured that voters of all ethnicities could reach the polls.

Eighth, SPUs provided security for payrolls and the transfer of large amounts of currency. Between December 15, 2001, and early February 2002, SPUs were continually involved in escorting shipments of up to $100 million worth of currency in the change from the deutsche mark to the euro. Units also secured roads, the Bank of Kosovo, and the airport during the arrival and departure of special chartered aircraft. The Pakistani SPU routinely escorted the transfer of prisoners from Dubrava prison to the courthouse in Mitrovica. Two SPUs provided an escort and rapid reaction force during the politically sensitive return of 120 ethnic Albanian prisoners that had been held in Serbia since June 1999.

Finally, it was envisioned that the SPUs would work closely with KFOR in conducting joint security operations. In MNB-East, the Romanian SPU and U.S. KFOR troops conducted joint training exercises and joint operations in manning checkpoints. Also in MNB-East, the Ukrainian SPU worked with KFOR to provide security for shipments of explosives used in commercial mining operations. In fact, however, these joint operations were the exception rather than the rule.[66]

A CAMPAIGN FOR LAW AND ORDER

In January 2002, UNMIK began a concerted effort to crack down on organized criminal activity in Kosovo. The primary targets of this campaign were a small number of ethnic Albanians who were formerly members of the KLA and current members of its successor organization, the Kosovo Protection Corps (KPC). Some were also leaders of the Democratic Party of Kosovo, led by former KLA commander Hashim Thaçi. UNMIK believed these persons were guilty of wartime atrocities and postwar involvement in organized crime. They were also suspected of harassing, intimidating, and assassinating members of Ibrahim Rugova's more moderate political party, the Democratic League of Kosovo. Many in the public regarded these individuals as war heroes who enjoyed a privileged status. UNMIK's intention was to remove these negative elements from society and demonstrate that in a democratic society, no one was above the law. While this operation was fully consistent with UNMIK's rule-of-law mandate, it was not without risks for the UN interim administration. The KPC was composed of 5,000 combat veterans who wore military uniforms, had authorized access to weapons, and were formally tasked by UNMIK with a number of functions, including search and rescue operations and responding to natural disasters. It was uncertain how the general public would react to arrests of KPC members or if criminal elements could whip up public demonstrations in support of their comrades. It was also not certain how the UNMIK police, the KPS, and the SPU would handle the widespread civil disorder that might result from a province-wide law enforcement effort against a number of well-known and presumably popular individuals.[67]

The answers to these questions were not long in coming. On January 28, UNMIK police arrested three ethnic Albanians suspected of wartime atrocities and postwar criminal activities. The three were former KLA members and current KPC members. They were also identified with former KLA commander Thaçi's political party and with the National Intelligence Service, a shadowy organization Thaçi formed after the conflict. One of those arrested was also a

---

66. United Nations Secretariat, Report of the Secretary-General on the United Nations Interim Administration Mission in Kosovo, S/2000/878, September 18, 2000, 6. Specific incident reports were provided by the Office of the SPU Special Adviser, Pristina, July 10, 2002.
67. Interviews with UNMIK police officials, Pristina, June 26, 2002.

member of the KPS. The arrests resulted in a series of public demonstrations in Pristina by KPC members and KLA veterans' organizations, the first demonstrations in the provincial capital since KFOR's arrival. On February 8 the third such demonstration in a week turned violent when 3,000 demonstrators attacked UNMIK police, broke windows, and then attacked bystanders sitting at a nearby café for failing to join the demonstration.[68] In response, one platoon of the Jordanian SPU and two platoons of the Indian SPU were deployed to control the protesters and prevent them from reaching UNMIK headquarters. This was the first time the SPU had faced rioters in the capital. There was a tense standoff, but, when confronted by trained riot control police in full riot gear, the crowds dispersed without incident.[69]

While the appearance of trained and properly equipped riot control police was enough to dissuade the demonstrators, this first use of the SPU for crowd control brought out several of its shortcomings. The first difficulty involved communication, as individual members of the SPUs were not required to demonstrate proficiency in English, the mission language. The first members of the Jordanian SPU to arrive on the scene could not speak English and could not communicate with other UNMIK police who were attempting to control the situation. UNMIK police had to find Arabic-speaking CIVPOL who also spoke English to act as liaison officers and interpreters for the SPU. The second problem involved command and control of the elements below the company level. The first SPU element on the scene arrived by armored vehicle without a senior officer present. As there was no one to command them to deploy, the officers stayed in their vehicle, ignoring the mayhem that was taking place around them, until a sufficiently senior officer arrived to order them to disembark.[70]

A second attempt in early 2002 to deploy the SPU to deal with civil disturbances also encountered difficulties. Three years after the start of the UN mission, Mitrovica remained a divided city with no meaningful UN law enforcement or administrative presence north of the Ibar. On April 8 the most violent attack against UNMIK personnel occurred since the inception of the UN presence. At 2:00 P.M. UNMIK police established a traffic inspection checkpoint at the north end of the main bridge that links the two parts of the city. The checkpoint was in front of the La Dolce Vita Café, a well-known bridge-watcher hangout. The

68. David Mullins, "UN Crime Crackdown Provoked a Backlash by Kosovo Albanian Radicals," Balkan Crisis Report no. 317, February 13, 2002.

69. Interview with Plane.

70. Interview with Gross.

action was part of a new program to ensure that vehicles were regis-
tered and that motorists had proper documentation. At 4:30 P.M., the
UNMIK police stopped a car and arrested the driver, an ethnic Serb
member of the bridge watchers. Word of the arrest spread quickly and a
group of about forty bridge watchers gathered, supported by a crowd of
about three hundred other Serbs. The arresting officers called for backup.
A platoon of the Polish SPU responded but found that a company of
gendarmes from the French KFOR contingent that was observing the
confrontation had closed the main bridge. The Poles were delayed for a
time but were finally allowed to cross.[71]

The mob threw stones at the SPU, which responded with tear gas. Slavoljub
"Pagi" Jović, a leader of the bridge watchers, was arrested for throwing rocks
and inciting the crowd against the police. When Jović tried to resist arrest
and threatened the UN police officers with a switchblade knife, the confrontation escalated sharply. This was the first time the SPU had engaged
in crowd control in Mitrovica. It was also the first time the Polish SPU was
called out to deal with a riot. Instead of accompanying the prisoner through
the French lines and across the bridge to safety, the UNMIK police and the
Polish SPU held their positions and then attempted to break up the crowd.
The Serb rioters responded by throwing two fragmentation grenades into
the Polish ranks. The Poles retreated behind their vehicles but came under
fire from Serb snipers. The SPU returned fire against the snipers and used
rubber bullets and tear gas to disperse the crowd.[72]

The grenade blasts injured nineteen SPU members, who were hospitalized
with shrapnel wounds. One critically injured officer was treated by KFOR
medical officers and evacuated to Poland. Seven UNMIK civilian police—
five Americans and two Germans—also received injuries. According to a local Serb leader, twelve Serbs were injured. At least two Serbs received bullet
wounds; one was in critical condition. With the Polish SPU out of action,
the UNMIK police commissioner turned responsibility for controlling the
situation over to French KFOR soldiers. Units from the Spanish and Romanian SPUs also were deployed but were not involved in the violence.[73]

Immediately after the incident, UNMIK and KFOR officials claimed
that the injuries had occurred because of a poorly organized police action

---

71. UNMIK Police Situation Center, "Security Situation Summary for April 10, 2002," Pristina, April 10, 2002, photocopy, item 6.5; interviews with staff members of UN Department
of Peacekeeping Operations/Civilian Police Division, New York, April 8, 2002.

72. UNMIK Police Situation Center, "Security Situation."

73. "UN Kosovo Police Attacked," BBC World Service, April 8, 2002, available at http://
news.bbc.co.uk/2/hi/europe/1917278.stm (accessed November 27, 2012).

and a breakdown of communication between the UN police and KFOR. A more thorough internal investigation discovered that the incident occurred because of the confusion and miscommunication between organizations and nationalities that often occurs in peace operations. The traffic inspection checkpoint was a cover for a snatch operation to arrest Jović, the leader of the bridge watchers, who was wanted for previous crimes. Team Six, a special operations unit of the UNMIK CIVPOL composed mainly of Americans, had orchestrated the operation, establishing the checkpoint in front of the café knowing Jović was likely to be there. To ensure that he would come out, the first motorist they arrested was Jović's brother.

Team Six ran its operation without informing UNMIK police headquarters or the regional UNMIK police commander. It also failed to inform the Polish SPU and the French KFOR contingent in advance of the operation. Once Jovic was arrested and transported across the bridge to the UNMIK police station in southern Mitrovica, the Team Six commander on the scene had neither the experience nor the authority to handle the mob action that ensued. At the time, the regional commander was attending a meeting in Pristina and his deputy was away on leave. The Polish SPU responded to the call for backup without knowing the true purpose of the arrest operation or that its target was already in custody. Rather than escorting the UNMIK police across the bridge to safety, however, the Polish SPU attempted to ease the pressure on the UNMIK police checkpoint by forcing the rock-throwing mob backward, away from the bridge and deeper into the ethnic Serb stronghold. As the Poles engaged the mob, they were attacked with grenades and automatic weapons fire. Throughout the incident, French KFOR gendarmes in full riot gear stood within a few feet of the bridge watchers, who were throwing rocks and grenades at the SPU, but they did not intervene.[74]

The injury of twenty-six UN police in a single incident sent shock waves across Europe. The day after, Polish prime minister Leszek Miller traveled to Pristina accompanied by Poland's interior minister and the head of the Polish police. Miller visited the wounded Polish police officers in the hospital and met with the newly arrived head of UNMIK, Michael Steiner, to discuss the situation in Kosovo. During a visit to the hospital with the prime minister, Steiner strongly condemned the violence that, he said, not only injured the police who were performing their duties under difficult circumstances, but also "hurt the legitimate interests of Serbs in Kosovo." The SRSG said the United Nations would not be "bullied" into leaving Mitrovica. The next day, thousands of Serbs returned to the Mitro-

---

74. Interview with senior UNMIK police officer, Washington, DC, February 21, 2002.

vica streets to protest the imprisonment of their leader, but they dispersed without violence. As a precaution, UNMIK police were withdrawn from patrolling the northern parts of the city and were confined to their fortified compound.[75]

In any case, that UNMIK police could not stop vehicles without fear of armed attack suggested that the United Nations needed to do something to reclaim northern Mitrovica and to make it a suitable environment for civilian police.[76] On July 2, 2002, UNMIK and French KFOR commander General Yves De Kerambon signed an agreement to ensure improved cooperation and coordination in Mitrovica. This coincided with a major change in attitude in the French KFOR. The new MND-North commander arrived with apparent instructions from Paris to cooperate with UNMIK in extending the UN writ beyond the Ibar. UNMIK officials were grateful for the change, which made real cooperation between the two parts of the international mission possible. The security situation was further enhanced as a result of renewed dialogue between UNMIK and Belgrade. On May 31, UNMIK, the Federal Republic of Yugoslavia, and the Republic of Serbia signed a protocol on police cooperation that provided for increased exchanges of information on terrorism and organized crime. On July 9 the Serbian justice minister, Vladan Batić, and the chief of the UNMIK justice system, Jean Christian Cady, signed another agreement to return forty Serb judges and attorneys to work in Kosovo courts. This was reached in the context of an understanding that Serbia would take steps to eliminate parallel security and judicial structures in Mitrovica and northern Kosovo. Pristina and Belgrade also agreed to encourage Serbs in northern Kosovo to apply for admission to the KPSS to increase the number of Serbs in the police.[77]

Finally, the UNMIK campaign to crack down on organized crime met with increasing public acceptance. On June 18, 2002, UNMIK police arrested six members of the KPC for alleged involvement in the killing of four ethnic Albanians from a rival faction immediately after the war. One

---

75. Nick Woods, "Polish PM Visits Kosovo Wounded," BBC World Service, April 9, 2002, available at http://news.bbc.co.uk/hi/english/world/europe/newsid_1917000/1917278.stm (accessed October 26, 2012); "Analysis: Gangs Target Kosovo Police," BBC World Service, April 9, 2002, available at http://news.bbc.co.uk/2/hi/europe/1919546.stm (accessed November 27, 2012); UNMIK Press Office, "Kosovo: UN Mission Chief Condemns Recent Attacks on UN Police," *UNMIK News,* April 9, 2002, available at http://www.un.org/apps/news/story.asp?NewsID=3339&Cr=kosovo&Cr1=unmik (accessed November 27, 2012).

76. International Crisis Group, "UNMIK's Kosovo Albatross," 5.

77. United Nations Secretariat, Report of the Secretary-General on the United Nations Interim Administration Mission in Kosovo, S/2002779, July 17, 2002, 5.

of those taken into custody was Daut Haradinaj, a former commander of the KPC Third Zone and war hero. Haradinaj was arrested in Peja by a team from the Romanian SPU when he walked into a trap set by UN authorities. Following the arrests, demonstrations occurred in the towns of Decani and Djakovica, and two thousand protesters from the KLA heartland in western Kosovo marched to Pristina to demand their release. In the capital, local residents did not join the protest, indicating growing support for UNMIK's effort to demonstrate that no one is above the law. On July 6, 2002, eleven members of the Kosovo Guard, an elite unit within the KPC, were arrested in connection with the postwar murder of Hamze Hajraj, a former Yugoslav police officer and suspected collaborator with Yugoslav authorities, and his family. The KPC response was muted in the face of public indifference to the operation. Commenting on the arrests, the UNMIK police spokesman stressed that action was taken against the individuals involved and not against their organization. SRSG Michael Steiner pledged that the campaign would continue and that those who had committed crimes would be brought to justice.[78]

LESSONS IDENTIFIED IN KOSOVO

Despite the success of the crackdown on organized crime, UNMIK's police leadership remained reluctant to use the SPUs in crowd control, high-risk arrests, and other sensitive situations. This partly reflected the northern European and North American officers' lack of familiarity with the SPU. In many cases, the SPUs were considered a strategic reserve and left alone unless required to handle an emergency. Located in separate compounds, SPU commanders often were not invited to staff meetings and were not always included in planning for operations. This fed a belief in some quarters that the SPUs spent their tours in comfortable camps, relaxing, eating well, and enjoying their recreation facilities, a misperception exacerbated by the UN leave and rotation schedule, which often meant that acquaintances were barely made before officers were on their way to new assignments.[79]

More seriously, it reflected problems in the SPU tripartite command structure. SPU commanders were responsible to the commissioner, the regional commander, and the SPU special adviser. These three frequently competing authorities often failed to communicate with one another be-

---

78. Arben Qirezi, "Kosovo: New Crime Crackdown," Balkan Crisis Report, no. 349, July 10, 2002.

79. Interviews with UNMIK police and OSCE police training officers, Pristina, June 24–26, 2002.

fore tasking unit commanders. This meant that the SPU could not always respond or would have to delay while requesting clarification of priorities. SPU commanders were frustrated by instructions from the commissioner or regional commanders that failed to recognize the complex nature of their organizations. Instructions to "make ten men available on a certain date" begged questions about what type of personnel, weapons, equipment, and vehicles, and for what mission.[80]

The question of who was in charge once the SPUs were called out and ordered to conduct a specific operation also was unresolved. SPU commanders strongly believed that they should be told what to do, but that, as professionals, they should decide how to do it. Senior SPU officers felt they were best qualified to command their men once an operation started. This troubled the UNMIK police leadership, which was unwilling to simply turn things over to generally more junior SPU officers and hope for the best. As during the early days of the MSU in Bosnia, the problem resulted from a lack of doctrine for using SPUs in peace operations. The SPU special adviser's office was the first to recognize the effect of the absence of common understandings and agreed-upon operating procedures on SPU operations. In the spring of 2002, it began drafting a doctrine regarding command and control functions and the techniques employed in crowd control and other missions. Included in this task was the compilation of a glossary of frequently used terms, because the absence of common meanings even for such words as "group" and "team" resulted in confusion.[81]

Two years after the first SPU arrived in Kosovo, the ten SPUs were, at best, underutilized and, at worst, misunderstood or ignored. This was not completely surprising, given that their core mission was envisioned as crowd control in a generally lawless environment. Had the SPU been present at the start of the Kosovo mission, circumstances would have ensured their use to control ethnic violence. By the summer of 2002, the situation had changed dramatically. According to the UN secretary-general's report to the Security Council, the number of cases of murder, kidnapping, arson, and looting continued to decline, while most crime appeared to be economically motivated. Excepting the protests over the arrests of former KLA leaders, demonstrations concerned economic issues, such as teachers' salaries, and were peaceful. Incidents of ethnically motivated assaults and intimidation decreased to the point where they were no longer systematic.[82] After the terrorist attack in New York on September 11, 2001, the United States lost interest in whether

---

80. Interviews with UNMIK police and OSCE police training officers.

81. Interviews with UNMIK police and OSCE police training officers.

82. UN Secretariat, S/2002/779, 4.

the SPUs were used effectively. At the onset of the mission, President Clinton and Secretary of State Albright personally lobbied Spain's king, Juan Carlos, and other leaders to donate constabulary units for service in Kosovo. By the time the number of SPU personnel climbed above nine hundred and conditions quieted, the United States was engaged in operations in Afghanistan and was planning to intervene in Iraq.[83]

83. Interview with police adviser.

6

Biting the Bullet in Iraq

n 2001, its first year in office, the George W. Bush administration did little to follow up on an avowed interest in finding alternatives for military forces in peace operations. Despite early indications from National Security Adviser Condoleezza Rice, Secretary of State Colin Powell, and others that the United States might look for civilian alternatives to relying on the military, the administration did little to improve U.S. capacity for nonmilitary solutions to the problem of achieving postconflict security. Instead, it took a step backward and dismantled the limited framework for bureaucratic decision making that the Clinton administration had created. As in previous administrations, the president's first National Security Presidential Directive (NSPD-1) established a new bureaucratic framework and interagency process for dealing with issues related to national security and foreign affairs. The directive assigned to Rice the traditional powers of the national security adviser as chairperson of the Principals Committee and head of the National Security Council (NSC) staff. Also in accordance with established practice, NSPD-1 abolished the committee structure and cancelled the presidential directives of the Clinton administration.[1]

Among the casualties of the interagency reorganization was Clinton's peacekeeping core group, which had coordinated issues related to the conduct of peace operations and the three presidential decision directives concerned with peacekeeping policy.[2] These directives were imperfect in design and often ignored in practice, but they offered a bureaucratic framework

---

1. Jane Perlez, "Directive Says Rice, Bush Aide, Won't Be Upstaged by Cheney," *New York Times,* February 16, 2001.

2. The three peacekeeping presidential decision directives (PDDs) President Clinton signed were PDD-25 on reforming multilateral peace operations, issued May 1994; PDD-56 on managing complex contingency operations, issued May 1997; and PDD-71 on strengthening criminal justice systems in support of peace operations, issued February 2000.

and policy process for complex contingencies that sought to ensure the active involvement of all relevant government agencies. The directives were not abolished outright but were consigned to a category of directives that required revision after further study. The residual functions of the interagency working group that had been established to oversee Presidential Decision Directive (PDD) 71, which dealt with the role of police including constabulary forces, were consigned to the new Policy Coordinating Committee on Democracy, Human Rights, and International Operations.[3]

Failure to renew the Clinton administration's directives or to immediately replace them left the Bush administration without clear policy guidance on how the U.S. government should address peacekeeping, particularly concerning issues related to police and constabulary forces that fell within the purview of PDD-71. The administration did not have a clear policy concerning how the United States could assist in restoring public order, law enforcement, justice, and the rule of law in postconflict environments. There was no indication of which agency, office, or individual was responsible for leadership or how interagency programs should be coordinated. There was also no policy guidance on funding responsibilities. This proved problematic when the administration announced its intention to reexamine U.S. programs and priorities.[4]

A LARGER DEBATE ON NATION BUILDING

In the policy vacuum created by the Bush administration's failure to renew Clinton's presidential directives on postconflict interventions, Washington agencies began an internal debate over the propriety of U.S. involvement in what were called complex contingency operations, stability and support operations, or multidimensional peace operations. While agency positions were still being formulated, it appeared that those who believed U.S. traditional national interests were unlikely to motivate American involvement in peace operations had a valid point. U.S. military forces primarily existed to defend against threats to the territorial integrity and vital supply lines of the United States and its historical allies. As the world's sole superpower, it seemed unlikely the United States would need to defend its homeland or those of our allies from a direct attack. To many it appeared the United States could afford a definition of its national interests that stopped at the frontier posts

---

3. Telephone interview with NSC staff member, May 22, 2002.

4. Michele Flournoy and Michael Pan, "Supporting Post-Conflict Justice and Reconciliation," paper prepared for the Joint Project on Post-Conflict Reconstruction of the Center for Strategic and International Studies and the Association of the U.S. Army, July 9, 2002, 3.

of those countries it was sworn by treaty to defend. It also seemed safer and intellectually more comfortable to retain the military's Cold War mission of preparing to fight two major theater wars and to leave responsibility for peacekeeping to others.

At the same time, it also seemed clear that traditional American values would not permit the United States to stand idle in incidents of genocide, famine, or other large-scale humanitarian crisis. A survey of the most senior U.S. military officers found surprising support for participation in peace operations. While acknowledging that peacekeeping was difficult and expensive, the interviewees believed U.S. participation was essential for promoting regional stability, strengthening alliances, demonstrating U.S. leadership, promoting economic development, and improving military efficiency and morale. Military leaders who advocated participation in peacekeeping were quick to caution that this did not mean the United States would become the world's policeman or that the United States should take on every fight; the country did stand alone, however, in its ability to provide global leadership and maintain international stability.[5]

In public, Secretary Powell echoed Rice's earlier comments concerning the administration's interest in replacing U.S. troops in the Balkans with police, specifically constabulary forces from European allies. In April 2001 Powell visited Europe as ethnic Albanian insurgents were conducting a violent campaign against Macedonian security forces and nationalist Croats were threatening Bosnia's stability. During a meeting of NATO foreign ministers in Paris, Powell said the Bush administration would not withdraw unilaterally from the Balkans but was considering ways to reduce U.S. deployments, "possibly by replacing soldiers with police officers." The United States was "looking for opportunities to draw down, but not for opportunities to bail out."[6]

THE GLOBAL WAR ON TERRORISM

The debate on nation building and the administration's focus on the Balkans ended with the traumatic events of September 11, 2001. On a brilliant fall morning, 19 Islamist terrorists hijacked four commercial airliners in flight. The hijackers crashed two of the aircraft into the World Trade

---

5. Edith Wilkie and Beth DeGrasse, "A Force for Peace and Security: U.S. and Allied Commanders' Views of the Military's Role in Peace Operations and the Impact on Terrorism of States in Conflict," report of the Peace Through Law Education Fund, Washington, DC, February 2002.

6. Alan Sipress, "Balkans Uprisings Condemned," *Washington Post*, April 12, 2001, A27.

Center towers in New York City, destroying both buildings and killing nearly 3,000 people. After circling over the White House and the Capitol Building in Washington, DC, the third aircraft destroyed a major portion of the Pentagon, claiming another 300 victims. The fourth aircraft crashed into an open field in Pennsylvania during a struggle between the hijackers and the passengers. The hijackers were followers of Osama bin Laden and members of al-Qaeda, which had its headquarters in Afghanistan and operated under the protection of the leaders of the Taliban, the country's extremist Islamic regime.

In response, President Bush, with the full and formal support of Congress, declared a global war on terrorism. U.S. diplomats quickly forged an international coalition, dividing the world, in the president's words, between those that supported freedom and those that supported evil.[7] U.S. forces deployed to countries surrounding Afghanistan as flotillas of U.S. warships collected offshore. In Afghanistan U.S. Special Forces and operatives of the Central Intelligence Agency made common cause with leaders of the Northern Alliance, a loose confederation of ethnic groups opposed to the Taliban. They also formed alliances with and aided disgruntled ethnic Pashtuns, who rallied against the Taliban in the south. In a lightning military campaign that featured precision U.S. bombing and missile strikes on Taliban forces and ground assaults by Afghan fighters, the Taliban were defeated militarily and swept from power.

At the onset of the global war on terrorism, the United States faced an unprecedented security challenge, arising from a global conspiracy based on intolerant ideology, the willingness of adherents to sacrifice their lives, and their determination to use weapons of mass destruction (WMDs).[8] A global search for al-Qaeda operatives was punctuated by terrorist attacks in Asia, Africa, and the Middle East and periodic alerts for new attacks in the United States. Concurrently the Bush administration sounded an alarm concerning the threat posed by an old adversary, President Saddam Hussein of Iraq. In a television address to the nation on October 7, 2002, Bush warned that Iraq "possesses and produces chemical and biological weapons. It is seeking nuclear weapons. It has given shelter and support to terrorism and practices terror against its own people. While there are other dangers in the world," the president said, "the threat from Iraq stands alone because it gathers the most serious dangers of our age in one place."[9]

---

7.   George W. Bush, "The Hour Is Coming When America Will Act," address to a joint session of Congress, *Washington Post,* September 21, 2001, A24.

8.   Alexandra Vondra and Sally Painter, "No Time to Go It Alone: Europe and the United States and Their Mutual Need for NATO," *Washington Post,* November 18, 2002, A21.

9.   "Text of President Bush's Address to the Nation," Associated Press, October 8, 2002.

THE U.S. DECISION TO INTERVENE IN IRAQ

In truth, Saddam Hussein had given the United States a long list of reasons for seeking regime change in Iraq. In addition to invading Kuwait and precipitating the Gulf War, Hussein had invaded other neighboring states, killed huge numbers of Kurds and Iranians with poison gas, administered a brutal police state, attempted to build nuclear weapons, and claimed to have accumulated chemical and biological WMDs. He had murdered or taken revenge against anyone who might stand against him, including his two sons-in-law. He had also sought to assassinate a former American president, President Bush's father. While Hussein's links to al-Qaeda and international terrorism were open to question, he had conducted terrorist operations abroad and might provide extremist organizations with WMDs.[10] Hussein had demonstrated repeatedly that he was capable of bizarre actions, miscalculations, and questionable judgment. There were no constraints on his behavior within the Iraqi political structure. He was also willing to take enormous risks and allow his country to absorb extensive damage and loss of life in his attempts to become the leader of the Arab world.[11]

In Iraq, Hussein exercised power through a sophisticated security structure and a vast network of informers, using extreme brutality to quell dissent. He also skillfully balanced competing forces within the country, playing upon ethnic and religious rivalries and using co-optation and financial inducements. He concentrated decision making within a tight circle of family members, close relatives, his al-Bu Nasir tribe, and those from his hometown, Tikrit. Beyond this ruling group, he relied on patronage, tribal allegiance, ethnic affiliation, and economic leverage. These, along with his willingness to be brutal and his regime's pervasive intelligence apparatus, meant that Saddam Hussein stayed in power for a long time, despite significant internal and external challenges.[12]

Hussein established an interlocking network of military and civilian security organizations with different official missions, but with overlapping and redundant intelligence and security functions. These security services were responsible to Hussein through the National Revolutionary Council, which he chaired. Their redundant responsibilities and vaguely defined relationships ensured that plots against the regime were likely to be detected

---

10. Philip Gordon, Martin Indyk, and Michael O'Hanlon, "Getting Serious About Iraq," *Survival*, vol. 44, no. 3 (Autumn 2002), 9.

11. Kenneth Pollack, *The Threatening Storm: The Case for Invading Iraq* (New York: Random House, 2002), 253–257.

12. International Crisis Group, "Iraq Backgrounder: What Lies Beneath," *Middle East Report* no. 6, Amman/Brussels, October 1, 2002, 9–10.

and that the various agencies would compete with each other. The result was a pervasive and encompassing system that converted Iraq into a police state. According to former CIA analyst Kenneth Pollack, "Everyone in Iraq must assume that he or she is surrounded by security agents, informants, surveillance devices, and would-be snitches. The result is that few Iraqis can summon the courage to take even the first step toward opposition and most live their lives in constant fear."[13]

Hussein also created several civilian security organizations to preserve his rule. The Special Security Directorate (SSD: al-Amn al-Khas), under the leadership of Saddam's youngest son, Qusai Saddam Hussein, had 5,000 members from the president's Tikriti clan; Qusai hand-picked them from other parts of the security apparatus for their loyalty. The SSD's responsibilities included protecting the president and his immediate family and securing the presidential palaces. It also supplied security details for other senior officials. The SSD was charged with the regime's most sensitive security tasks, such as concealing the WMD program, evading the embargo on sensitive technologies, and supervising the military forces responsible for protecting the president. These forces included the Presidential Guard, the Palace Guard, the Special Republican Guard, and the Republican Guard, all of which reported to the head of the SSD.

Between 1973 and Operation Desert Storm, the General Intelligence Directorate (Jihaz al-Mukhabbarat) was headed by Saddam's brother and its powers increased significantly over time. After the war, the Mukhabbarat lost influence and personnel with the rise of the SSD. Its primary missions were foreign espionage and intelligence collection, supervision of Iraqi embassy personnel, covert action, assassinations, and terrorist operations. Domestically its responsibilities included suppressing Kurdish and Shiite opposition, monitoring foreign embassies, and surveilling all other intelligence and security agencies, as well as government ministries, the Baath Party, and the Iraqi military.

The General Security Directorate (GSD: al-Amn al-'Amm) was the oldest and largest of the security services. Its primary concern was internal security; its operatives were located in every jurisdiction and kept abreast of everything that transpired in their area. GSD personnel were responsible for detecting dissent among the general public and monitoring the daily lives of Iraqi citizens, especially prominent personalities. A good part of the GSD's mission was intimidating the population. Its heavy-handed operatives were responsible for most of the official harassment Iraqi citizens suffered.

---

13. Pollack, *The Threatening Storm*, 117.

The ruling Baath Party had an internal security apparatus—the Baath Party Security Agency (BPS: al-Amn al-Hizb)—that oversaw the activities of Iraqis through party security branches in organizations such as universities, factories, and trade unions. The BPS was responsible for security in all party offices, monitoring the activities of party members, and security activities not directly related to the state.[14]

Below the security agencies were the Iraq National Police (INP: Shurta) and border guards that were responsible for law enforcement. Under the monarchy, the INP force had grown to 23,400 personnel by the 1958 revolution. Established with the assistance of British advisers, the INP was under the jurisdiction of the Interior Ministry and performed routine police functions. The force included representatives from all ethnic groups and religious denominations. In the 1960s police academies were established to improve training. The INP had positive relations with the public and enjoyed a reputation for professionalism, political neutrality, and honesty. After 1968, the Baath Party enacted legislation that led to the INP's militarization and close association with the army. The INP was increasingly marginalized and its responsibilities for internal security subsumed within the various security organizations. By the beginning of 2003 the force strength of the INP was approximately 60,000 personnel.[15]

PLANNING FOR THE POSTWAR PERIOD

In a televised speech at the American Enterprise Institute in Washington on February 26, 2003, President Bush offered the first comprehensive view of U.S. aspirations for a post–Saddam Hussein Iraq. According to the president, a "liberated" Iraq would show the power of freedom to transform the Middle East, bringing hope and progress to the lives of millions of people. Bush noted that rebuilding Iraq would not be easy and would require sustained commitment from the United States and other nations; the United States would "remain in Iraq as long as necessary, but not a day more."[16] Meanwhile, the U.S. and British troop buildup in the Persian Gulf topped 225,000, including five carrier battle groups and stealth and B-52 bombers deployed to bases close to Iraq. Press reports indicated that U.S. Special Forces were already operating

---

14. "The Transition to Democracy in Iraq," report of the Working Group on Democratic Principles prepared for submission to the Conference on Democracy and the Salvation of Iraq, London, December 14–17, 2002.

15. "Transition to Democracy."

16. Dana Milbank and Peter Slevin, "President Details Vision for Iraq," *Washington Post*, February 27, 2003, A1.

inside the country, and British and U.S. aircraft had begun strikes beyond the no-fly zone aimed at crippling Iraq's air defenses.[17]

On the eve of U.S. military action to remove Hussein, there were myriad warnings from inside and outside the government that conditions in postwar Iraq would be difficult, confusing, and dangerous for everyone involved. Since the 1950s regime changes in Iraq had been significantly bloodier than those in other Arab states.[18] The CIA and other intelligence agencies persistently warned that postconflict reconstruction would be more complicated than military victory. The CIA predicted that Iraqis were likely to resort to "obstruction, resistance and armed opposition" and that pro-Hussein groups were likely to attempt to sabotage reconstruction efforts.[19] The U.S. Army chief of staff, General Eric Shinseki, warned that an occupation force of at least 300,000 soldiers would be needed to pacify Iraqi.[20]

From outside the government, the Council on Foreign Relations, the Center for Strategic and International Studies, and the U.S. Institute of Peace[21] warned that Iraq's recent history gave every indication that extreme violence would erupt immediately after hostilities ended. Following Operation Desert Storm, returning Iraqi soldiers had ignited massive uprisings among the majority Shiites in the south and the Kurds in the north. Rampaging crowds executed Baath Party members and regime officials and took revenge for past injustices on members of the Sunni minority that had ruled the country since independence. A similarly violent uprising occurred in December 1998 after a four-day U.S. and British air campaign called Operation Desert Fox, which targeted biological weapons facilities and largely empty Republican Guard barracks.[22]

Coalition military units would have to adjust quickly from combat to peacekeeping operations to avoid a new outbreak of ethnic, religious, and tribal strife. Without a total commitment by coalition forces to maintain-

---

17. Susan Glasser and Vernon Loeb, "War Plan for Iraq Largely in Place," *Washington Post,* March 2, 2003, A1.

18. Charles Tripp, *A History of Iraq* (Cambridge: Cambridge University Press, 2001), 7.

19. Peter Slevin and Dana Priest, "Wolfowitz Concedes Iraq Errors," *Washington Post,* July 24, 2003, A1.

20. Slevin and Priest, "Wolfowitz Concedes."

21. Eric Schwartz, "Iraq: The Day After," report of an independent task force sponsored by the Council on Foreign Relations, New York, 2003, 25–26; Robert Perito, "Establishing the Rule of Law in Iraq," Special Report no. 104, U.S. Institute of Peace, Washington, DC, April 2003, 11–12; Bathsheba Crocker, "Post-War Iraq: Are We Ready?," report prepared by the Center for Strategic and International Studies, Washington, DC, March 25, 2003, 7–8.

22. Andrew Cockburn and Patrick Cockburn, *Out of the Ashes: The Resurrection of Saddam Hussein* (New York: HarperCollins, 1999), 4–34.

ing public order, it was likely that Iraq's ethnic and religious factions would again descend into a fury of revenge taking that would plunge large areas of the country into chaos. If such a breakdown in public order occurred, international terrorist organizations and neighboring states could be expected to intervene to support their proxies, protect their coreligionists, and promote their interests. Failure to control widespread civil disturbances would also prevent international humanitarian assistance agencies and non-governmental relief organizations from reaching those in need. Intervention forces, it was feared, might have to deal with areas affected by the release of chemical or biological weapons and to aid those affected.[23]

In the initial phase of the postwar transition, the U.S.-led coalition was responsible for restoring public order, providing security, and ensuring effective law enforcement as part of its obligations as an occupying power under the 1949 Fourth Geneva Convention.[24] The intervention force would require substantial numbers of troops, trained to interact with civilians and provide basic public services. Such a force would include civil affairs officers, military police, medical units, and combat engineers. Troops trained in border control would be needed to ensure that criminals and terrorists did not enter the country and that war criminals and WMDs did not leave.[25] Establishing the rule of law would require two phases. First, the coalition would need to dismantle and disband the interlocking network of internal security services that were used to control the country. Second, it would need to rehabilitate, retrain, and reform the INP so it could assume responsibility for local law enforcement. Given Iraq's population and size, the coalition would need INP assistance to maintain public order. Iraqi police officers could perform this function if they received international supervision, technical assistance, new equipment, and extensive retraining to make the difficult transition to community-oriented policing in Iraq's new democratic society.

Unlike previous peace operations, it was clear in Iraq that the United States could not depend on its allies to provide military police, civilian constabulary, civil police, judicial personnel, and corrections officers. Neither Britain

---

23. Rachel Bronson and Andrew Weiss, "Guiding Principles for U.S. Post-Conflict Policy in Iraq," report of the independent working group cosponsored by the Council on Foreign Relations and the James A. Baker III Institute for Public Policy of Rice University, Washington, DC, December 18, 2002, 1–6.

24. Michael Kelly, "Legitimacy and the Public Security Function," in Robert Oakley, Michael Dziedzic, and Eliot Goldberg, eds., *Policing the New World Disorder: Peace Operations and Public Security* (Washington, DC: National Defense University Press, 1989), 399–445.

25. "Iraq: Looking beyond Saddam's Rule," report on a workshop sponsored by the Institute for National Strategic Studies, National Defense University, and the Naval Postgraduate School, Washington, DC, November 20–21, 2002, 2.

nor Australia, the principal coalition partners, had constabulary forces and the United Kingdom lacked a national police force. It was also unlikely that constabulary and civil police forces would come from NATO, the European Union, or the OSCE, which had staffed police missions in the Balkans. After September 11 NATO was quick to help defend the United States. NATO troops participated in the war in Afghanistan and manned the ISAF. France and Germany, however, opposed military action to remove Saddam Hussein and there was no indication that the alliance would provide constabulary and police if the United States intervened in Iraq.[26] The United States would have to rely on its own resources to ensure postconflict stability.

POSTCONFLICT CHAOS IN IRAQ

Inexplicably, almost nothing was done to prepare for the inevitable burst of civil disorder that began as U.S. military forces entered Baghdad on April 9. Senior Department of Defense (DOD) officials assumed, remarkably, that despite the trauma of war and the removal of Saddam Hussein's regime, coalition forces would inherit a fully functioning modern state with all its institutions intact. They also believed the Iraqis would welcome U.S. troops as liberators and that Iraqis would join coalition forces in quickly neutralizing the Baath Party, the security services, and other opponents of the new order. Pentagon planners assumed that Iraqi police and the regular Iraqi army would remain on duty and would assume responsibility for local security, enabling coalition forces to deal with regime holdouts and pockets of military resistance. They also thought Iraqi technocrats would manage the country's government ministries, public utilities, and other institutions. Instead, Iraqi security forces and all government authority vanished when Task Force 4-64 of the 2nd Brigade of the U.S. Army's Third Infantry Division reached the city's center.[27]

In scenes reminiscent of the sacking of Panama City and the burning of the Sarajevo suburbs, U.S. military forces stood by and watched as mobs looted Baghdad's commercial district, ransacked government buildings, and pillaged the residences of former regime officials. The only exceptions were the Petroleum Ministry and the Palestine Hotel, which housed foreign journalists, where U.S. troops protected buildings and preserved their contents. As described by Anthony Shadid, a reporter for the *Washington Post,*

> Baghdad descended into lawlessness. Scenes of mayhem were repeated across the city. Hospitals and embassies were looted, as were ministries, government offices, Baath

---

26. Michael Dobbs, "Allies Slow U.S. War Plans," *Washington Post,* January 11, 2002, A1.

27. Slevin and Priest, "Wolfowitz Concedes."

Party headquarters and private residences. Ambulances were hijacked, as were public buses that ran their routes until the very moment of the government's collapse. Cars barreled the wrong way down streets deserted by traffic policemen. . . . Mohammed Abboud, piling a pickup truck 10 feet high with booty, declared: "It's anarchy!"[28]

Once it became clear that the small number of U.S. soldiers in Baghdad were either unable or unwilling to intervene, public exuberance, joy at liberation, and economic opportunism quickly darkened into a systematic effort to strip the capital's stores and public institutions of everything of value. Families from Saddam City, the Baghdad slum inhabited by 2 million impoverished Shiites, and gangs of men armed with assault rifles worked their way through government ministries, removing their contents, tearing out the plumbing and wiring, and then setting the buildings on fire. Looters ransacked Iraq's main medical center, the Al Kindi Hospital, and the wards of Baghdad's other hospitals, which were jammed with victims of the U.S. bombing campaign. The mobs removed patients from their beds and carried away medical equipment that had been in use. Even the city's psychiatric hospital, the colleges of medicine and nursing, and the Red Cross headquarters were not spared. So complete was the destruction that the International Committee of the Red Cross said the city's hospitals were unable to treat war wounded and other victims of the conflict. By night, families armed themselves and barricaded their homes to protect them from the Ali Babas, the gangs of thieves that freely roamed the city.[29]

In the vast industrial parks south of the capital, mobs ransacked factories and warehouses, returning home in a parade of cars, trucks, and wheelbarrows piled with stolen goods. In heavy equipment parking lots, thieves hotwired tractors and bulldozers and drove them away. Looters ransacked, damaged, and destroyed Iraq's nuclear facilities and its plants, which were suspected of producing chemical and biological weapons. With only 12,000 soldiers to police a city of 4.5 million, the U.S. military was unable to prevent these crucial sites from being pillaged by ever more systematic gangs of thieves and vandals. In many cases, the destruction looked like the work of professionally trained saboteurs intent on ensuring that U.S. authorities would never be able to determine what the facilities had actually manufactured.[30]

---

28. Anthony Shadid, "A City Freed from Tyranny Descends into Lawlessness," *Washington Post*, April 11, 2003, A1.

29. John Burns, "Loot and a Suicide Attack in Baghdad," *New York Times*, April 11, 2003, A1; Jonathan Weisman, "Iraq Chaos, No Surprise, but Too Few Troops to Quell It," *Washington Post*, April 14, 2003, A28; Dexter Filkins and John Kifner, "U.S. Troops Move to Restore Order in Edgy Baghdad," *New York Times*, April 13, 2003, A1.

30. Barton Gellman, "Seven Nuclear Sites Looted; Iraqi Scientific Files, Some Containers Missing," *Washington Post*, May 10, 2003, A1.

Mobs of looters and more sinister forces attacked Baghdad's major cultural centers. During the initial outburst, crowds burst into the National Museum of Antiquities, destroying and looting its irreplaceable Babylonian, Sumerian, and Assyrian collections. Most of the looters were local people letting off steam, but according to officials from the United Nations Educational, Scientific, and Cultural Organization (UNESCO), the most serious pillaging was the work of organized criminal gangs that bribed museum guards and minor officials for keys to the vaults holding the most valuable works of art. UNESCO director general Koichiro Matsuura said the looting was well planned by professionals, who stole cultural items that highly organized trafficking rings could sell to collectors in Europe, the United States, and Japan. U.S. attorney general John Ashcroft told an Interpol meeting in Lyon, France, that a "strong case could be made that the theft of artifacts was perpetrated by organized criminal groups who knew exactly what they were looking for."[31] Initial reports that the museum's entire collection of 170,000 items was lost proved exaggerated. Careful accounting by U.S. and international experts determined that at least 6,000 artifacts had been removed by thieves who knew the value of the items.[32] Looters and arsonists also attacked the Iraqi National Library and Iraq's principal Islamic library, destroying their priceless collections of manuscripts and archives. The National Library housed a copy of all the books published in Iraq, plus all doctoral theses. It also had books from the Ottoman and Abbasid periods dating back a millennium.[33]

As a result of years of neglect and attacks by looters, Baghdad's fragile infrastructure ceased to function. Electricity failed, water stopped flowing, and telephone service ceased. Shops closed and Iraqis began to run short of necessities. Women were afraid to leave their homes as stories of daylight kidnappings and rapes swept the city. Murders, muggings, and robberies went unreported by residents who could find no one in authority. Hundreds of Baath Party members and informants were gunned down by former victims who were working from lists looted from security service headquarters. Into this power vacuum stepped a variety of opportunists, self-appointed officials, Sunni sheiks, and Shiite clerics. These pretenders attempted to seize control of towns, government ministries, hospitals, universities, and other institutions. The situation became so chaotic that

---

31. Robert McCartney, "Expert Thieves Took Artifacts, UNESCO Says," *Washington Post,* April 18, 2003, A1; Joseph Coleman, "Ashcroft: Looting in Iraq Done by Criminal Groups, Not Just Civilians," Associated Press, May 5, 2003.

32. Guy Gugliotta, "Looters Stole 6,000 Artifacts: Number Expected to Rise as Officials Take Inventory," *Washington Post,* June 21, 2003, A16.

33. Charles Hanley, "Looters Ransack Iraq's National Library," Associated Press, April 15, 2003.

General David McKiernan, commander of U.S. forces in Iraq, issued a statement reminding Iraqis that the coalition "retained absolute authority." The same day, U.S. soldiers arrested Muhammad Mohsen Zobeidi, the self-appointed mayor of Baghdad.[34]

U.S. efforts to restore order and control lawlessness were hindered by a growing number of armed attacks on American soldiers. Baath Party loyalists, remnants of the security services, former soldiers, Islamic extremists, and Arab terrorists ambushed military convoys, sniped at soldiers standing guard duty, and assaulted isolated outposts with increasing sophistication and deadly results. At the same time, military spokesmen and U.S. soldiers made clear their lack of enthusiasm for performing law-enforcement functions. In response to Iraqi demands that the United States restore order, Brigadier General Vincent Brooks, Central Command spokesman, said the U.S. military would help rebuild civil administration but expected the Iraqis to assume responsibility for public order. "At no time," Brooks said, "do we see [the U.S. military] becoming a police force."[35] In a similar vein, Major General David Petraeus, commander of the 101st Airborne, told reporters that "we should discourage looting, but we're not going to stand between a crowd and a bunch of mattresses." Other U.S. commanders said they lacked the manpower and mandate to interfere with Iraqi civilians. Individual soldiers bluntly told reporters that they were neither trained nor equipped to do police work. In Baqubah, soldiers of the 588th Engineering Battalion, 2nd Brigade, 4th Infantry Division were trained in weapons demolition and bridge building, but were ordered to use their M113 armored personnel carriers like squad cars to patrol the city. As one soldier explained, "By the time we get there, the bad guys are gone."[36] With fires still burning in government ministries and the National Library, U.S. military authorities appealed publicly for Iraqi police to return to duty. On April 14, 2003, joint patrols of U.S. soldiers and Iraqi police tentatively made their initial appearance on the streets of the capital. Iraqi police were not permitted to carry weapons and the appearance of some officers produced outrage from citizens who claimed they were guilty of corruption and other abuses under Saddam Hussein. U.S. civil affairs

---

34. Michael R. Gordon and John Kifner, "U.S. Warns Iraqis against Claiming Authority in Void," *New York Times*, April 24, 2003, A1; Scott Wilson, "Iraqis Killing Former Baath Party Members," *Washington Post*, May 20, 2003, A8.

35. "Lawlessness and Looting Spread in Baghdad," Associated Press, April 11, 2003.

36. William Branigin and Rick Atkinson, "Anything and Everything Goes," *Washington Post*, April 11, 2003, A1; Daniel Williams, "U.S. Troops Frustrated with Role in Iraq," *Washington Post*, June 20, 2003, A1.

officers attempted to weed out the thugs while trying to encourage additional officers to join their colleagues.[37]

Military commanders explained that rebuilding the police was one of the tasks assigned to the Office of Reconstruction and Humanitarian Assistance (ORHA), led by retired lieutenant general Jay Garner. ORHA was created on January 20, 2003, under NSPD-24, which assigned responsibility for postconflict planning and implementation to the Pentagon. General Garner was selected because of his previous leadership of Operation Provide Comfort, the post–Gulf War response to a humanitarian crisis created by Saddam Hussein's revenge attacks on the Kurds. ORHA's small staff was composed of personnel detailed from various government agencies, including a police and a judicial expert from the Department of Justice (DOJ). When U.S. military forces entered Iraq, General Garner and his entire 300-member staff were transferred to Kuwait to wait out the war. Security conditions prevented Garner and a small advance team from reaching Baghdad until April 21, twelve days after U.S. forces entered. The remainder of his staff arrived some days later.[38]

ORHA's plan for Iraq's reconstruction was based upon the assumption that Garner's team would find government ministries intact. Instead, Garner said, ORHA found that seventeen of Iraq's twenty-one ministries had "simply evaporated."[39] U.S. officials found the burned-out shells of public buildings, their contents looted and their staff scattered, frightened, and demoralized. ORHA was prepared to deal with oil fires, masses of refugees, the release of chemical and biological weapons, and widespread starvation. The U.S. military, however, had followed a battle plan, which called for pinpoint bombing, immediate seizure of the oil fields, bypassing of urban centers, and a dash to Baghdad to neutralize WMDs. As a result, there was no large-scale destruction of infrastructure or urban fighting, and the refugee crisis and other disasters ORHA planned for did not occur. What did occur was a complete breakdown in public order and the collapse of public services, problems that Garner's team was ill equipped to handle.[40]

---

37. Douglas Jehl, "As Order Breaks Down, Allies Try to Rebuild Iraqi Police," *New York Times*, April 12, 2003, A1; John Burns, "Joint Patrols Begin in Baghdad," *New York Times*, April 14, 2003, A1.

38. Monte Reel, "Garner Arrives in Iraq to Begin Reconstruction," *Washington Post*, April 22, 2003, A1.

39. Interview with Lieutenant General (U.S. Army retired) Jay Garner, Washington, DC, May 2003.

40. Joshua Hammer and Colin Soloway, "Who's in Charge Here?," *Newsweek*, May 26, 2003; Rajiv Chandrasekaran, "Iraq's Ragged Reconstruction," *Washington Post*, May 9, 2003, AS1.

Only a small number of Garner's staff had experience in previous peace operations and still fewer had ever visited Iraq. Almost none spoke Arabic. At their heavily guarded headquarters in one of Saddam Hussein's palaces, ORHA personnel found little or no office equipment, and no provision had been made for interoffice communication by e-mail or telephone. Staff members could communicate only by visiting each other's offices and could not call out from the palace without going outdoors to use a satellite telephone. Living accommodations were primitive, with many people sharing a single room. In the 120-degree heat, there was often no electricity to run fans and no air conditioning.[41]

A FALSE START ON RECONSTRUCTION

On May 1, 2003, President Bush stood on the deck of the USS *Abraham Lincoln,* an aircraft carrier returning to California from the Persian Gulf, to proclaim that major combat operations were over and that the U.S.-led coalition had achieved victory in Iraq. Bush told the 5,000 naval personnel gathered on the flight deck that "no terrorists will gain weapons of mass destruction from the Iraqi regime because that regime is no more." He said that "difficult work remained in Iraq," but the United States would stay until it was finished.[42] Six days later, on May 7, the president attempted to reverse the deteriorating situation in Iraq by appointing former ambassador L. Paul Bremer III to replace General Garner. Bremer had previously served as head of the State Department's Office of Counter Terrorism and ambassador to the Netherlands; he also had worked in New York for Kissinger Associates. Unlike Garner, Bremer reported directly to Secretary Donald Rumsfeld and enjoyed the support of Secretary of State Powell. Bremer came with a reputation for decisiveness among his former Foreign Service colleagues. In commenting on this aspect of Bremer's character, senior Pentagon adviser Richard Perle said Bremer was aggressive by "Foreign-Service standards," but he had "seen hummingbirds that were aggressive by Foreign-Service standards."[43]

Bremer's arrival in Baghdad brought both a more telegenic public image and a new dynamism to what was now called the Coalition Provisional Authority (CPA). Among his first acts, CPA Order Number 1, was to ban those that had held one of the top four ranks in the Baath Party from holding government jobs. This action reversed ORHA's policy that only banned

---

41. Hammer and Soloway, "Who's in Charge?"; Chandrasekaran, "Iraq's Ragged Reconstruction."

42. Karen De Young, "Bush Proclaims Victory in Iraq," *Washington Post,* May 2, 2003, A1.

43. Mike Allen, "Expert on Terrorism to Direct Rebuilding," *Washington Post,* May 2, 2003, A1.

the most senior Baathists from public service. The CPA's decision answered criticism from some Iraqis that former Baathists were being allowed to remain in power. However, it deprived the Iraqi government of up to 30,000 senior bureaucrats, many of whom had been forced to join the party to obtain their jobs. This broad-brush vetting removed an entire level of senior leadership from government ministries, including the police, and created bitterness, mistrust, and confusion. It also further slowed the restoration of government services.[44] The security situation was further exacerbated by the CPA decision, conveyed in CPA Order Number 2, to disband the Iraqi army and to order the few soldiers that had remained in their barracks to return home. This action was taken without promise of pay or a future in the new Iraq. Within days, crowds of former soldiers staged angry protests in front of CPA headquarters. Disbanding the military added approximately 400,000 unemployed young men to an already volatile situation and increased the security challenges facing the U.S. military and the Iraqi police. Disenfranchised former government officials, police, and soldiers proved to be ready recruits for anti-U.S. insurgent groups and organized crime.

In a June 11, 2003, report on conditions in Baghdad, the International Crisis Group (ICG) stated that Iraq's capital was in "distress, chaos and ferment." Two months after the end of military operations, the CPA had failed to provide personal security, restore essential services, or establish a positive rapport with Iraqis. The report noted that Iraqis had seen their public institutions destroyed by uncontrolled looters and saboteurs. They were not safe on the streets or in their homes, as the number of murders, revenge killings, rapes, carjackings, and armed robberies continued to rise without an effective coalition response. It was "conventional wisdom," the ICG said, that the Americans had blundered by failing to protect vital institutions and impose public order in the first days of the occupation. "The subsequent failure to impose order once the extent of the problem became clear," the report said, "can only be considered a reckless abdication of the occupying power's obligation to protect the population." The report concluded that general lawlessness not only posed a constant danger to Iraqi citizens, but also inhibited the restoration of the city's destroyed infrastructure.[45] In Baghdad, Bernard Kerik, a former New York City police commissioner and the CPA's senior police adviser, was ill equipped to respond to the problem. Kerik had no peacekeeping or Middle East experience. His team consisted of twenty-six U.S. police advisers from the DOJ's

---

44. Peter Slevin, "Many More Iraqis Banned from Government Positions: U.S. Is Purging High Ranking Members of Hussein's Party," *Washington Post,* May 18, 2003, A1.

45. International Crisis Group, "Baghdad: A Race against the Clock," Middle East Briefing, Baghdad/Amman/Brussels, June 11, 2003, 1–8.

International Criminal Investigative Training Assistance Program (ICITAP) who were responsible for conducting a nationwide needs assessment and developing a plan of action, while simultaneously reconstituting the Iraqi police, customs, immigration, border patrol, fire department, and medical emergency services[46]—an impossible mission for such a small number of personnel.

The Iraqi Police (IP) was the only institution in Saddam Hussein's interlocking network of intelligence and security services to remain intact at the end of major combat operations; the CPA decision to disband the Iraqi army and security and intelligence networks spared the police and the Interior Ministry. Unfortunately, the IP had been at the bottom of Saddam's bureaucratic hierarchy of security agencies and suffered from years of mismanagement, resource deprivation, and lack of professional standards. A U.S. DOJ assessment team found that the IP's 60,000 members had little understanding of basic police skills. Most of its senior officers had graduated from the national police college, but its noncommissioned officers and patrolmen had little formal education. Under Saddam Hussein the IP had been militarized and its doctrine, procedures, and weapons were completely unsuited to policing in a democratic society. Iraqis saw the IP as part of a cruel and repressive regime and described its officers as brutal, corrupt, and untrustworthy. Iraqi police officers had remained at their posts until U.S. forces entered Baghdad, then took their personal weapons and went home to protect their families. In the civil disorder that followed, looters and arsonists heavily damaged or completely destroyed police infrastructure. Rampaging mobs demolished police stations, stole police vehicles, and walked away with weapons and equipment. Police returned to find their stations gutted or reduced to smoldering ruins.[47]

In the aftermath of the looting of Baghdad, the U.S. military had to publicly appeal for the Iraqi police to return to duty. On April 14, 2003, joint patrols of U.S. soldiers and Iraqi police made their first appearance on Baghdad's streets. Police who returned to duty lacked leadership, organization, and logistic support. In May 2003 a DOJ assessment team determined that the Iraqi police could not restore public order and would require substantial U.S. assistance. The assessment team's recommendation was not acted upon, however, until the growing Iraq insurgency caused the United States to open police training centers in Amman, Jordan, and in Baghdad in December 2003 and January 2004, respectively. The first graduates of these programs began serving in March 2004, but by that time, the level of insurgent and criminal violence had escalated and the situation in Iraq was slipping out of control.

---

46. Amy Waldman, "After the War: Law Enforcement," *Washington Post,* June 30, 2003, A1.

47. Coalition Provisional Authority Interior Ministry, "Iraq Police: An Assessment of Their Present and Recommendations for the Future," Baghdad, May 30, 2003, 4–5.

THE DEPARTMENT OF DEFENSE TAKES OVER
THE POLICE TRAINING PROGRAM

In November 2003 Secretary Rumsfeld requested that Major General Karl Eikenberry assess the shortcomings of the Iraq police assistance program. Eikenberry reported that the CPA training effort was underresourced, disorganized, and incapable of producing a competent Iraqi police force. The report concluded that the U.S. military should take over training for police as well as the Iraqi army.[48] In the spring of 2004, as the CPA's deadline for returning sovereignty to the Iraqis approached, Washington determined that only the U.S. military had the resources to fast-track the police assistance program. In May, Bush signed NSPD-36, which formally transferred responsibility for the program from the State Department to the DOD.[49] A month later, the CPA's work ended and formal sovereignty returned to the Iraqi interim government. Bremer departed Baghdad on June 28, 2004, a day before the announced schedule for transfer of authority to the Iraqis.

In Iraq the U.S. military established the Civilian Police Advisory Training Team (CPATT) under the control of the Multi-National Force–Iraq—later the Multi-National Security Transition Command–Iraq (MNSTC-I)—which was assigned responsibility for training, equipping, and mentoring the Iraqi police. CPATT was led by a British brigadier general with a civilian (DOJ/ICITAP) deputy and included both military and civilian personnel. Its initially small staff was augmented by the U.S. 89th Military Police Brigade, which supplied the manpower to oversee the reconstruction of Iraqi police facilities, handle the distribution of new equipment and vehicles, and run the central maintenance facilities.[50] Transferring responsibility for civilian police training to the U.S. military was unprecedented. In all previous peace operations, State and the DOJ had led police assistance programs.[51] Unfortunately, the transfer of responsibility from State to the DOD and the restoration of Iraqi sovereignty did not involve a meeting of the minds among CPATT, State, and Justice, along with their contract advisers, the U.S. military battle space commanders, and the Iraqis. There was fundamental disagreement on three critical issues: the

---

48. Special Inspector General for Iraq Reconstruction, *Hard Lessons: The Iraq Reconstruction Experience* (Washington, DC: U.S. Government Printing Office, 2009), 133.

49. The White House, "United States Government Operations in Iraq," National Security Presidential Directive 36, Washington, DC, May 11, 2004.

50. Interview with Brigadier General David Phillips, former commander, Civilian Police Advisory Training Team, Iraq, August 21, 2011.

51. Mark Magnier and Sonni Efron, "Arrested Development on Iraqi Police Force," *New York Times,* March 31, 2004.

mission of the Iraqi police, its relationship to U.S. military forces, and its role in countering the insurgency. The State Department and DOJ civilian police advisers wanted to create a community police service that would operate under the leadership of provincial police chiefs. The U.S. military concluded that the security situation required a militarized counterinsurgency police force, and that community-based policing would have to wait. The Iraqis, whose views their U.S. counterparts generally discounted, would eventually act on their own to counter the threat from insurgents and sectarian militias.

The State Department and DOJ police advisers believed the U.S. military did not understand the ethos or practical requirements for training law enforcement officers and was intent on simply putting Iraqi guns on the street to reduce pressure on coalition forces. DOJ civilian police advisers changed the name of the organization from the Hussein-era Iraqi National Police to the Iraqi Police Service (IPS) to emphasize what they believed should be the new police organization's community service orientation: The advisers wanted to create a lightly armed civilian police organization that used community-policing techniques and operated according to Western democratic standards for professional law enforcement. They argued that Iraq's security problems were best resolved by relying on investigations and arrests to incarcerate criminals and terrorists. Since State and the DOJ ran the training program in Amman, the police cadets that returned to Iraq were trained and equipped for community policing. The security environment in Iraq, however, was not conducive to community policing. Many of the Iraqi police cadets had sought training in Jordan for the opportunity to be safely out of the country, if only for a short time.

The DOJ advisers' arguments for creating a community-oriented police service failed to convince their military counterparts. Once the newly minted police officers graduated from the Amman training facility or the police academy in Baghdad, they became combatants in the growing conflict against insurgent and sectarian militia forces, pitting poorly led and inappropriately trained and equipped patrolmen against heavily armed former military personnel, veteran security operatives, and foreign terrorists. The numbers for trained police reported by the U.S. military thus were virtually meaningless, as the police personnel were prepared for a very different mission—that of policing a peaceful area. The Iraqi police's sidearms were useless against insurgents and militia members with AK-47s. The police were subjected to repeated attacks from car bombs and fighters equipped with rocket-propelled grenades and other military weapons.[52] Involvement in the

---

52. Sabah al-Anbaki, "Police Lack Training, Firepower in Fighting Insurgency," *USA Today*, October 25, 2004.

fighting against insurgents and militias turned the police into a primary target for terrorist attacks, aimed at breaking police resolve and demonstrating the danger of cooperating with the coalition.[53] Operating from unprotected facilities, the Iraqi police patrolled in thin-skinned vehicles, lacked body armor, and took increasingly grievous casualties. From 2004 to 2006, the Iraqi police suffered 12,000 casualties, including 4,000 killed, according to Major General Joseph Peterson, the commander of the U.S. Civilian Police Assistance Training Team in Iraq.[54]

THE ONSET OF CIVIL WAR

In early 2004, terrorist attacks by al-Qaeda on Shiite shrines and pilgrims in Baghdad, Karbala, and other cities in Iraq produced bitter criticism from Shiite leaders of coalition and Iraqi security forces and demands to legalize sectarian militias to guard neighborhoods and places of worship. Militias had been banned under CPA Order Number 91,[55] but militia groups, such as the Kurdish peshmerga and the Shiite Badr Brigade, were well established and included tens of thousands of fighters. As sectarian attacks continued, militia forces openly deployed and challenged Iraq's fledging security forces. In Mosul and other Iraqi cities, Iraqi police mutinied under fire, abandoned their posts, and deserted en masse after repeated insurgent and militia attacks. In testimony before Congress on March 5, 2004, Lieutenant General John Abizaid, United States Central Command (CENTCOM) commander, said Iraqi security forces had been rapidly recruited in large numbers and still lacked adequate training and equipment as well as a clear chain of command. This was particularly true of the Iraqi police, the general said, who were not trained or equipped to respond to attacks by organized militia or insurgent groups.[56]

In April, Sunni insurgents launched a coordinated offensive against coalition forces in Fallujah, Baghdad, Ramadi, Samarra, and Tikrit, while the Mahdi Army took control of Najaf and Sadr City in Baghdad. Newly trained Iraqi military and police forces refused to fight or were quickly

---

53. Magnier and Efron, "Arrested Development."

54. CNN World Service, "More than 12,000 Iraqi Police Casualties in 2 Years," October 7, 2006, available at http://articles.cnn.com/2006-10-06/world/iraq.main_1_iraqi-police-police-officers-northern-iraqi-city?_s=PM:WORLD, accessed October 29, 2002.

55. Coalition Provisional Authority Order 91, "Regulation of Armed Forces and Militias Within Iraq," CPA/ORD/02, June 2004/91.

56. Bradley Graham, "Iraqi Forces Lack Chain of Command; Abizaid Has No Timetable for Baghdad to Assume Control of Security," *Washington Post*, March 5, 2004, A18.

overwhelmed. Under pressure from militia groups, Iraqi police units completely collapsed in Fallujah, Najaf, Karbala, and Kut, with some 3,000 police deserting in a single week. Iraqi police and military failures in battle raised serious concerns about U.S. training programs and U.S. intentions to rapidly transfer responsibility for internal security to Iraqi forces. Of the 200,000 Iraqi security forces that had been rushed into service, only 5,000 Iraqi army personnel were fully trained and equipped to conduct counterinsurgency operations. None of the Iraqi police units were trained or equipped to fight organized enemy units armed with military weapons. Clearly, the United States needed to rethink its strategy for developing Iraqi security forces.[57]

Faced with a growing threat from well-organized and heavily armed groups, the U.S. military was determined to create an Iraqi police force that could protect the Iraqi government against the insurgency and hostile militias, and formed heavily equipped police units composed of former Iraqi soldiers trained to conduct counterinsurgency operations. These were not true constabulary *(gendarme)* forces, normally defined as police forces with military capabilities, but military forces with little to no police training, although they were subordinate to the Ministry of the Interior. According to Lieutenant General David Petraeus, then in charge of training Iraq's security forces, there was a need for specialized police units that could bring combat power to the fight and fill the capability gap between lightly armed Iraqi street cops and the Iraqi army.[58] The U.S. military thus recruited special 750-man police battalions composed mostly of Sunnis who had formerly served in the Iraqi army's special forces. These newly created units included emergency response units, based on U.S. special weapons and tactics (SWAT) teams and designed to conduct high-risk arrests; a mechanized police unit, used for rapid response, fixed-site security, and cordon and search operations; public order battalions, intended for crowd control and routine police functions in hostile environments; and mechanized police units that were heavily armed and specially trained for counterinsurgency operations.[59] These units were sent to flash points in Samarra, Fallujah, and Baghdad, where they were expected to fight alongside U.S. military forces.

At the same time, Falah al-Naqib, Iraq's minister of interior, began recruiting special police commando units for counterinsurgency operations independent of U.S. authorities. Unlike its position in Iraq's Defense

---

57. Special Inspector General, *Hard Lessons*, 134.

58. Bradley Graham, "U.S. Says Police in Iraq Need Bolstering: More Arms, Trainers, Backup Units Sought," *Washington Post*, November 25, 2004, A1.

59. Special Inspector General, *Hard Lessons*, 195–196.

Ministry, the United States had few advisers in the Interior Ministry and little control over the recruiting of Iraqi police personnel. When the IPS performed poorly in battles against the Mahdi Army, Naqib turned to his uncle, General Adnan Thavit, for help. A former air force intelligence officer, Thavit had been involved in a failed attempt to overthrow Saddam Hussein and had served time in prison before being released along with thousands of other prisoners before the U.S. intervention. Thavit recruited commando units composed of unemployed but seasoned officers and men from Saddam Hussein's Republican Guard and special forces. These units began conducting patrols and engaged in skirmishes with insurgents and militia fighters.[60]

The appearance of the Iraqi commandos caught the U.S. military by surprise. The police commandos did not look like a coherent fighting force; U.S. soldiers initially called them pop-up units after stumbling upon them in abandoned buildings and bombed-out military bases. Ragged and poorly equipped, with names such as the Defenders of Baghdad and the Amarah Brigade, they were mostly Sunnis with a mix of Shiites and minority groups. But they were personally loyal to their commanders and bound together by tribal and family backgrounds. Numbering as many as 15,000 men, the units had the internal cohesion, experience, and determination missing in the U.S.-organized Iraqi security forces.

The problem for U.S. authorities lay in determining the extent of the units' loyalty to the Iraqi government and how they could be used to help coalition forces counter the insurgency.[61] Initially U.S. military commanders reacted coolly to what the United States officially designated as irregular Iraqi ministry-directed brigades. U.S. commanders were reluctant to provide arms and training because they feared the units might turn against the central government. In fighting against insurgents and militia, however, the units distinguished themselves by their steadiness under fire when regular Iraqi police and army units broke and ran. Writing in the *Washington Post*, columnist David Ignatius described a battle in which Iraqi police commandos stayed with their U.S. adviser, Colonel James Coffman, Jr., when insurgents ambushed them in Mosul. In four hours of intense fighting, the commandos lost four killed and thirty-eight wounded, but drove off the attack. Afterwards, Coffman, who was wounded in the battle, proudly told Ignatius, "Our guys stood and fought!"[62]

---

60. Greg Jaffe, "New Factor in Iraq: Irregular Brigades Fill Security Void," *Wall Street Journal*, February 16, 2005, A1.

61. Jaffe, "New Factor in Iraq."

62. David Ignatius, "Our Guys Stayed and Fought," *Washington Post*, February 25, 2005, A21.

THE CREST OF SECTARIAN VIOLENCE

With their firepower and military prowess, the police commando units partially addressed the problem of inadequate Iraqi security forces. In January 2005 the Iraqi police and army enjoyed temporary success in providing security for national elections, in which eight million Iraqis voted safely. The installation of Iraq's transitional government in May 2005, however, resulted in a change of leadership in the Interior Ministry and the nature of the Iraqi police commando units. Before leaving his post as interior minister in April 2005, Minister Naqib warned Secretary of Defense Rumsfeld that the Shiite political parties that were taking office would hijack the police commando units and use them for their own purposes.[63] Naqib's fears were well founded. Bayan Jabr Solagh, a senior official of the Shiite Supreme Council of the Islamic Revolution in Iraq (SCIRI), was appointed interior minister. Jabr placed leaders of the Badr Brigade, the armed wing of SCIRI, in key positions in the ministry and recruited thousands of Shiite militiamen to replace Sunnis in the special police commando units. At the same time, militia loyal to the radical Shiite cleric Moqtada al-Sadr also infiltrated the ministry. Members of the Sadrist Mahdi Army used police uniforms and their official status to pass through checkpoints and as cover for sectarian violence. During Jabr's one-year tenure, from April 2005 to May 2006, members of the IPS and special police commando units acted as death squads, kidnapping, imprisoning, torturing, and killing Sunnis. Iraqis reported that gunmen in police uniforms routinely abducted people from their homes, cars, and—in one particularly flagrant case—a hospital bed. On their morning patrols, U.S. troops routinely found bullet-riddled bodies in the streets of Baghdad, some showing marks of torture.[64]

Over the summer and into the fall of 2005, there was a deafening crescendo of sectarian violence involving attacks by uniformed police on Sunnis. On August 25, 2005, gunmen wearing police uniforms dragged 36 Sunni men from their homes in the Huriya neighborhood of Baghdad and left their bodies showing signs of torture near the Iranian border. After an investigation, a judge ordered the commander of the Volcano Brigade commando unit arrested for the murders, but the warrant was never executed. The Wolf Brigade, perhaps the most notorious of the units, was discovered to have illegally detained and tortured more than 1,400 prisoners.[65] On July

---

63. Michael Moss, "Law and Disorder: How Iraq Police Reform Became a Casualty of War," *New York Times*, May 22, 2006.

64. "Iraq's Mean Streets," *Los Angeles Times*, September 10, 2006.

65. Solomon Moore, "Police Abuses in Iraq Detailed," *Los Angeles Times*, July 9, 2006.

4, 2004, members of the 759th U.S. Military Police Battalion discovered 170 malnourished and badly abused Iraqi prisoners, mostly Sunnis, at a secret prison facility on the grounds of the Interior Ministry. The Americans wanted to free the captives, but U.S. military authorities ordered them to withdraw and leave the facility in the hands of the Iraqi police.[66] In November 2005, American soldiers discovered a secret prison in Baghdad's Jadiriya neighborhood run by the Wolf Brigade, where 173 malnourished and badly abused prisoners, mostly Sunnis, were held and tortured.[67]

THE U.S. MILITARY'S EFFORT TO CONTROL IRAQI POLICE ABUSES

In January 2006 the MNSTC–I responded to sectarian police violence by launching an effort to reorganize police training and impose discipline, declaring 2006 the Year of the Police in Iraq. In April the MNSTC-I convinced the Ministry of the Interior to combine the U.S.-created public order battalions and the Iraqi-organized special police commando units into a new organization, the Iraq National Police (INP). The commando units became the First National Police Division; the public order battalions became the Second National Police Division. The new INP was subordinate to the Interior Ministry along with the IPS. National police officers were equipped with small arms, medium machine guns, rocket-propelled grenades, and body armor. INP units were given unarmored pickup trucks and sport utility vehicles, leaving them vulnerable to roadside bombs and insurgent attacks with heavy weapons. Plans called for replacing thin-skinned INP vehicles with armored vehicles from various donor countries over time.[68]

Initially U.S. advisers conceived of the INP as a bridge between the IPS, which was responsible for traffic control, crime prevention, and routine police functions, and the Iraqi army. The INP would back up the IPS and take over when the IPS was outgunned and more firepower and armor was required. If the INP could not control the situation, the Interior Ministry would request military assistance. Unfortunately, the sectarian nature of the INP forces and the deep distrust in police commando units from Iraqi citizens and other Iraqi police and military units made it impossible for the INP to play that role. Distrust in the INP extended to its U.S. advisers; a former U.S. Army adviser to the infamous Wolf Brigade told

---

66. Interview with Brigadier General Phillips, August 22, 2011.

67. Moss, "Law and Disorder."

68. Independent Commission on the Security Forces of Iraq, "Report to Congress," Center for Strategic and International Studies, Washington, DC, September 6, 2007, 109.

National Public Radio that his charges would conduct proper neighbor-hood searches when U.S. soldiers were present, but would go back at night to kidnap and kill Sunnis and burn down their houses. He recalled an in-stance when Wolf Brigade members led U.S. advisers into an ambush. His advice to Americans training for similar advisory missions was to "never let your guard down ever!"[69]

National elections for a permanent Iraqi government were held on De-cember 15, 2005, when sectarian violence was intense enough to border on civil war. After the elections, rival political parties negotiated for five months over the choice of a prime minister and the appointment of a new govern-ment. On May 20, 2006, Nouri al-Maliki was named prime minister, but backroom bargaining continued over the choices for key ministries, includ-ing Interior. It was not until June 8, 2006, nearly six months after the elec-tion, that Prime Minister Maliki appointed a new interior minister, Jawad al-Bolani, a compromise candidate chosen because he lacked a political base and did not pose a threat to any faction. Bolani was a Shiite and former air force engineer with no police experience, but he had a reputation as a com-petent administrator. To ensure that the police would not become the tool of any political faction, Bolani was given strong deputies from the Dawa, Badr, and Kurdish parties. His predecessor, Bayan Jabr, was appointed the new minister of finance, where he retained control of the funding for the Interior Ministry and the direct payment of police salaries.[70]

Despite the change in leadership in the Interior Ministry, police involve-ment in sectarian violence continued unabated. By autumn the U.S. military could no longer postpone dealing with the INP commando units' role in sectarian violence and death squad activities. In September, press reports indicated that U.S. officials had warned Iraqi leaders that, under the Leahy Amendment, U.S. law prohibited assistance to foreign security forces that committed "gross violations of human rights." The warnings came after a joint U.S.-Iraqi inspection of a detention facility, known as Site 4, found evi-dence of the Wolf Brigade's systematic use of torture.[71] On October 5, 2006, U.S. military forces took their first direct action to deal with INP commando units' sectarian violence: U.S. soldiers removed the entire 8th Brigade of the

69. Steve Inskeep, "The Challenge of Policing Iraq," *Morning Edition,* National Public Radio, March 28, 2007.

70. Andrew Rathmell, "Fixing Iraq's Internal Security Forces: Why Is Reform of the Min-istry of Interior So Hard?" PCR Project Special Briefing, Center for Strategic and Interna-tional Studies, Washington, DC, November 9, 2007, 8.

71. Richard Oppel, "Iraqi Police Cited in Abuses May Lose Aid," *New York Times,* Septem-ber 30, 2006.

2nd National Police Division from duty and arrested its officers after the brigade was implicated in a raid on a Baghdad food factory and the kidnapping of twenty-six Sunni workers, seven of whom were executed.[72] This was the first step in CPATT's national police transformation program to remove all the INP brigades from service for limited vetting and three weeks of police training—in many cases, the first training of any kind that INP personnel had received.[73] For the remaining eight INP brigades, the transition process, called rebluing, was extended to one month and included training in respect for human rights and democratic policing, plus tactical training in patrolling and checkpoint operations. To improve the INP's public image, the names of national police units were changed. The Wolf Brigade was renamed the Freedom Brigade. The national police were also issued new uniforms with digital patterns that would be difficult to duplicate.

It took over a year to retrain all nine INP brigades, and abuses continued in the interim. Iraqi officials had sought to counter allegations of police involvement in sectarian killings by claiming that the perpetrators were wearing counterfeit police uniforms. On November 14, 2006, 80 gunmen wearing the new digital police commando uniforms raided the Ministry of Higher Education in Baghdad, kidnapping 159 academics and other members of its staff. The attackers arrived in a fleet of 20 police vehicles and had name lists of those they intended to abduct. As the education minister was a member of the Iraqi Accordance Front, a Sunni political party, observers saw the operation as an act of sectarian violence.[74] On March 28, 2007, Shiite police went on a rampage in the northwestern town of Tal Afar, killing as many as 60 Sunnis after a massive truck bomb shattered the market in the majority Shiite community. Police and Shiite militants roamed Sunni neighborhoods firing into homes and at people on the street. The shooting ended when Iraqi army troops occupied the town, arrested 18 policemen identified by the families of Sunni victims, and imposed a curfew.[75] On May 29, 2007, gunmen wearing digital police uniforms cordoned off an area in eastern Baghdad and kidnapped 5 British security guards in a well-coordinated midday operation. Iraq's for-

---

72. Amit R. Paley, "Attacks in Baghdad Kill 13 US Soldiers in 3 Days," *Washington Post*, October 5, 2006.

73. Department of Defense (DOD), "Measuring Stability and Security in Iraq," Report to Congress in accordance with the Department of Defense Appropriations Act (Section 9010, Public Law 109-289), November 2006, 32–33.

74. James Sturcke, "Up to 150 Kidnapped from Baghdad Institute," *Guardian*, November 14, 2006.

75. Sinan Salaheddin, "Shiite Cops Reportedly Rampage vs. Sunnis," Associated Press, March 28, 2007.

eign minister, Hoshyar Zebari, assigned responsibility for the raid to Iraqi Interior Ministry police.[76]

On July 30, 2007, the *Los Angeles Times* reported that Iraq's Interior Ministry had become an "eleven story powder keg of factions" where hostile militias and criminal organizations controlled various floors and settled their differences by assassinations in the parking lot. The article described offices guarded by armed men and officials who feared the elevators and took the stairs accompanied by heavy security. The Interior Ministry was a command center for "militias that kill under the cover of police uniforms and remain above the law." Its third floor was the domain of Prime Minister Maliki's Dawa Party, while the sixth floor housed units controlled by the Badr Organization militia. The intelligence division on the seventh floor directed death squads and secret prisons. The ninth floor housed Kurdish units. U.S. military personnel described the handful of U.S. police advisers at the ministry as confined to the top floor of the building, where they drank tea, drafted policy statements in English, and had no influence with the Iraqis. The *Los Angeles Times* credited Minister Bolani with attempting to rein in the situation, but said he was thwarted by a web of political alliances that prevented reform.[77]

THE U.S. SURGE TO REVERSE THE TIDE OF BATTLE

U.S. efforts to control the INP commando units coincided with the Bush administration's comprehensive review of the U.S. conduct of the war and implementation of the president's strategy for a new way forward in Iraq. In a January 10, 2007, address from the White House library, President Bush announced he was sending an additional 20,000 U.S. troops to quell the sectarian conflict in Iraq. He said spiraling violence was "unacceptable" to the American people, requiring a change in strategy. The Iraqi government also had put forth an aggressive plan, which included appointing new commanders for Baghdad and deploying eighteen Iraqi army and INP brigades across the nine districts of the capital. Iraqi forces would operate from local police stations—conducting patrols, manning checkpoints, and going door to door to gain the trust of the people. U.S. troops would work alongside the Iraqis to help clear and protect neighborhoods from insurgents. To implement the new strategy, the president appointed a new American commander in Iraq, Lieutenant General David Petraeus, author of the U.S. Army's new doctrine on counterinsurgency warfare, which stressed the importance of protecting

---

76. Mark Tran, "Iraqi Police Cannot Control Crime," *Guardian Unlimited*, May 30, 2007.

77. Ned Parker, "The Conflict in Iraq: A Ministry of Fiefdoms," *Los Angeles Times*, July 30, 2007.

local citizens over hunting insurgents.[78] Deploying large numbers of U.S. forces into areas that insurgents and militia groups had previously controlled brought a sharp spike in levels of fighting in Baghdad and Anbar province during the first six months of 2007.

In September 2007 an independent congressional commission report on the security forces of Iraq delivered a scathing critique of the Interior Ministry and the INP. Led by Marine General James Jones, former NATO supreme commander, the commission's fourteen members included retired military officers and DOD officials, as well as several serving police chiefs and former police advisers. The commission made three trips to Iraq, visiting Iraqi facilities and interviewing U.S. and Iraqi officials and Iraqi citizens. The members concluded that the Interior Ministry was crippled by sectarianism and corruption and lacked the leadership and administrative capacity to support the forces under its control. They recommended major organizational changes to improve the ministry's effectiveness. The commission said it also received uniformly negative reports about the INP, which it described similarly as riddled with sectarianism and corruption, distrusted by the public, and operationally ineffective. Noting the poor quality of INP personnel, low levels of literacy, an overwhelming majority of Shiites, and a lack of appropriate leadership, the commission strongly recommended that the INP be disbanded and reorganized under the Ministry of Defense with a new name and responsibility for ordnance disposal, search and rescue, and other unarmed functions.[79]

Improved conditions in Iraq muted the effect of the Jones Commission report in Washington. By September 6, 2007, when General Jones presented the commission's report to Congress, the brigade combat teams that composed the surge were in place in Baghdad. General Petraeus had redeployed U.S. military units into the capital's neighborhoods to protect Iraqi citizens. With the resulting decline in violence, the U.S. military rejected the commission's call to disband the INP and start over. Speaking to the *Washington Post* by telephone, Major General Rick Lynch, the U.S military commander for Baghdad, said the situation was "past the point where we could just fire everyone and start over." He said the surge required both U.S. and Iraqi forces, and the INP was holding areas of the city that U.S. forces had cleared. Removing the INP would leave a security gap that the insurgents would fill quickly. Lynch admitted that some INP units still engaged in sectarian violence and Sunnis who "saw them as the enemy" feared them. However, "the

---

78. George W. Bush, "The President's Address to the Nation," January 10, 2010.
79. Independent Commission, "Report to Congress," 109–115.

two INP units in his area, which had been through rebluing, were great and were doing what needed to be done."[80]

U.S. military officials were encouraged by reforms within Iraq's Interior Ministry and the prospect that training teams from the Italian Carabinieri would soon be involved in retraining the INP. In Baghdad, Interior Minister Bolani had been stung by the Jones Commission's criticism, particularly its call to disband the INP. Bolani assigned a small group of trusted senior police officers to conduct their own evaluation of the INP in light of the report's findings. The Iraqi evaluation team confirmed the sorry state of the INP, but recommended accelerating reforms rather than disbanding the force. Bolani appointed a new INP commander, Lieutenant General Hussein al-Awadi, a highly regarded military officer who previously commanded the Iraqi Army Staff College. Awadi demanded and received assurances that he could fire corrupt commanders and transfer poor performers. He recruited a staff of competent young officers from among the top Army Staff College graduates to supervise a four-step program for transforming the INP into a reliable security force.[81]

Awadi's reform program involved first removing the commanding officers at the division, brigade, and battalion levels who had been implicated in sectarian violence. In all, the commanders of the two INP divisions, seven of the nine brigade commanders, twenty-five of the twenty-seven battalion commanders, and eight hundred rank-and-file personnel were removed from the INP, although no one was arrested or disciplined for their actions. Second, Awadi continued the program of taking individual brigades offline in succession and providing them with the first training in basic police skills they had received. These brigades were then paired with U.S. military units, which were colocated with INP units to conduct joint operations. This enabled U.S. troops to monitor INP activity closely and prevent human rights abuses. It also enabled U.S. forces to serve as role models and provide on-the-job training in planning, patrolling, and other functions. In addition to the partner units, MNSTC-I created forty-one national police transition teams (NPTTs) composed of military and contract civilian police advisers who were assigned to formally monitor the performance of all thirty-eight INP battalions, all divisions, and the INP headquarters. The NPTTs assessed all units to determine equipment levels and readiness and provided training and mentoring.[82]

---

80. Ann Scott Tyson and Glenn Kessler, "U.S. Military Rejects Call to Disband Iraqi Police," *Washington Post*, September 7, 2007.

81. Interview with Lieutenant General James Dubik, former commander, Multi-National Transition Command-Iraq, January 4, 2011.

82. Independent Commission, "Report to Congress," 111.

In the third phase of reforms, individual battalions were rotated through a training program in leadership and advanced police skills conducted by training officers from the Italian Carabinieri, who arrived in Iraq in the fall of 2007. The Italians' participation in the INP training process was the key to transforming the INP from a rogue force into a competent constabulary. On their own, U.S. military and contract police personnel did not have the technical skills or the corporate culture required to transform the INP. At a new, U.S.-built training facility at Camp Dublin near Baghdad's airport, the Italians, led by Colonel Fabrizo Parrulli, offered training in counterinsurgency, counterterrorism, and crowd control. More important, the Carabinieri discussed the difference between the role of the police and the army and served as role models for their Iraqi counterparts. [83]

Upon arrival at Camp Dublin, Iraqi trainees were deprived of weapons, cameras, and recording devices, given a physical examination, and subjected to identification procedures. The Carabinieri training program consisted of basic, intermediate, and advanced courses in both police and military skills, with advanced levels of training reserved for outstanding graduates, who were groomed as future instructors. The training included a leadership package for commissioned and noncommissioned officers on management-related subjects. The Italians also provided training in specialized skills, such as VIP close protection, sharpshooting, and self-defense. The training sought to develop the trainees' physical and motivational skills, instruct trainees in technical subjects, develop a culture of safety in training and operations, and promote respect for human rights and restraint in the use of force. Basic training was provided in two monthlong courses separated by a one-week break. Trainees had to pass a final examination in physical conditioning and police and military skills. While high performers were invited to stay on and become future instructors, poor performers were dismissed from the training for disciplinary violations and inappropriate behavior, particularly failure to comply with regulations for using firearms or failure to attend class. [84]

Perhaps the most important aspect of the Carabinieri training was the extensive amount of time spent with trainees in discussing the role of police in a democratic society and the moral and ethical responsibilities of a police

---

83. James Dubik, "Building Security Forces and Ministerial Capacity: Iraq as a Primer," Report no. 1, Best Practices in Counterinsurgency, Institute for the Study of War, August 2009, 12–13.

84. Training Guidelines for the Iraqi Federal Police Personnel Attending Courses at the Gendarmerie Training Unit, NATO Training Mission-Iraq, Gendarmerie Training Division, unpublished manual, 2011.

officer in performing his duties. The Italian trainers sought to impress upon the Iraqis the importance of behaving appropriately in dealing with the public and respecting the rights and personal dignity of their fellow citizens. To introduce a spiritual element into the training and build relationships with their students, the Italian training teams developed a common prayer that they said every day with the trainees, both to demonstrate their own spirituality and to tap into the religious fervor of many of their students. The prayer was designed to capture the moral authority inherent in the police officer's duty to enforce the law, maintain order, serve others, and keep the peace. The prayer, entitled *The Policeman,* read as follows:

- God is great and merciful. God is the power that moves the universe and lives in all things. God is everything but He is above all the personification of the universal good and the good is the maximum value of social life.
- In the World we don't have to distinguish black men and white ones, cultured and ignorant, Muslim and Christian, because all men are an expression of God. We all are descendants of the Prophet Abraham and we are all God's creatures.
- In absolute meaning, there are no rich men or poor men because a rich man knows all his money cannot buy the thing he needs most. A poor man can feel pleased with himself even if he has little.
- There are people, without distinction of race, that have a very high religious spirituality. There are people that in their personal space—their family and their work—that have great spiritual knowledge.
- In the World a supreme division exists between good and evil. We can distinguish two kinds of human beings: good men who walk along God's path, and bad men who take Satan's way.
- The policeman represents the good in the World. All criminals are evil. In the fight between good and evil, the policeman is a tool of God.
- You are the angels of God and you should believe this every day when on duty. A loyal and honest policeman is the angel of God that fights evil because he represents the good that defeats evil.
- Only if a policeman is a professional can he achieve success. To become a professional, he must train hard and work for the people among the people.
- Unfortunately, the policeman may die in the line of duty. This is a certain sign of the Will of God. If the policeman fully performed his duty, his sacrifice will not be in vain. "Only those who do good will enter Paradise" God says in the Holy Text.

- The Iraqi National Police will have its heroes, living and dead as it always happens. From every drop of blood shed by these unique and true martyrs in the line of duty will arise a new generation of brave men who will live in a better World, full of serenity and prosperity.

The first class of 430 INP cadets completed the seven-week program in transitional police skills in late December 2007. Battalion-sized training rotations of INP cadets continued on a routine basis through the fall of 2009. In the fourth stage of training, units received follow-on professional courses over time.[85]

THE FUTURE ROLE OF THE IRAQI NATIONAL POLICE

Efforts to improve INP performance coincided with a long-running debate in Washington and Baghdad over whether the INP should become part of the Iraqi army. As early as November 2006 the report of the congressionally mandated Iraq Study Group recommended that the INP should be transferred to the Ministry of Defense, where it would benefit from more rigorous U.S. military supervision and could better perform its counterinsurgency mission.[86] Advocates for transferring the INP to the Iraqi army noted that the INP did not have police powers to make arrests, conduct investigations, or collect evidence. Like the U.S. military, the INP could detain suspected insurgents that were held in U.S.- and Iraqi-run prison camps, often for years. However, the INP had no relationship with the Iraqi judicial system, and U.S. authorities, who saw the INP as a fighting force, did not encourage it. As conditions began to stabilize in 2008, detractors wondered why Iraq needed an additional police force to the IPS, which patrolled Iraqi cities and was responsible for directing traffic and controlling crime.

The INP's commander, General Awadi, argued that his organization had demonstrated its value on the battlefield and would develop its ability to deal with organized crime, drug trafficking, and civil disturbances—challenges that would exceed the competence of ordinary police. He pointed out the INP's sacrifices, including the deaths of 1,650 and wounding of 3,000 of its officers over the previous four years. Other supporters believed that the INP was crucial to eventually establishing civilian police primacy for internal security in Iraq and removing the Iraqi army from that role. The INP was the only civilian security force the Interior Min-

---

85. DOD, "Measuring Stability," 340–341.

86. James A. Baker III and Lee H. Hamilton, *The Iraq Study Group Report* (New York: Vintage Books, 2006), 78.

istry could use to confront insurgents and militia groups that continued to carry out attacks, although at significantly reduced levels.[87] Improved leadership and professional skills were evident in the performance of the INP units that were deployed from late 2007 through 2008. The INP also continued to demonstrate its mettle on the battlefield, where it stood and fought alongside the Iraqi army in Basra, Sadr City, Diyala, and Mosul, in contrast to the IPS, which often ran away rather than engaging in hostilities. The Iraqi Interior Ministry worked to fill the ranks of the INP to an authorized level of 44,263 by increasing the number of Sunnis in the force, in order to reach an ethnic and sectarian balance. Recruitment and training of officers lagged, however, as the INP was only able to meet 42 percent of its leadership requirements.

To bolster the case for maintaining the INP, on June 8, 2008, General Awadi introduced a code of ethics for the INP modeled on the Law Enforcement Code of Ethics of the International Association of Chiefs of Police. At a press conference he stressed the importance of the code in establishing performance standards for INP officers based on respect for human rights and the rule of law.[88] By late fall the INP was on track to meet its goal of becoming a national-level rapid response police force that could deal with large-scale civil disturbance and insurgent and terrorism operations. While still primarily located around Baghdad, the INP had begun to deploy to stations outside the city. Prime Minister Maliki directed the creation and deployment of a third INP division as the first step toward stationing the INP in all provinces in Iraq.[89]

By January 2009 the situation in Iraq had changed markedly. The surge of U.S. troops into Iraqi neighborhoods to protect the population, the Sunni awakening, the rise of the Sons of Iraq, and Moqtada al-Sadr's decision to stand down his militia brought a 63 percent drop in civilian deaths compared to 2007.[90] The U.S. brigade combat teams that constituted the surge had returned home the previous July. Under the newly completed U.S.-Iraq Strategic Framework Agreement (SFA) and Security Agreement, Iraq assumed responsibility for its own security and took formal control of combat operations and detention facilities. On February 27 President Barack Obama announced a plan to begin the phased drawdown of U.S. forces from Iraq by August 31, 2010, and the transition of U.S. forces from combat operations to training and support of Iraqi security forces. In July

87. Lennox Samuels, "The Politics of Policing," *Newsweek*, June 3, 2008.

88. Multi National Corps-Iraq, "Iraqi National Police Adopts Code of Ethics," press release no. 20080614-02, June 14, 2008.

89. DOD, "Measuring Stability," 39.

90. DOD, "Measuring Stability," iii.

2009, U.S. troops completed their withdrawal from neighborhood combat posts in Iraqi cities and towns and redeployed to military bases, where they had little contact with the Iraqi people. During the withdrawal, INP units escorted U.S. military units as they redeployed from urban areas to bases in the countryside. The security situation continued to improve, with the number of incidents falling to levels not experienced since early 2004. Insurgent and militia groups retained the ability to conduct high-profile and deadly terrorist attacks, particularly in Diyala and Ninewa provinces and in some parts of Baghdad. Where insurgents and militia groups still posed a challenge, the INP showed increased ability to plan and execute its own operations with limited technical support from U.S. forces.[91]

Commensurate with the INP's improved performance and expanded presence, the Interior Ministry changed the name of the force on August 1, 2009, to the Iraq Federal Police (IFP). According to a spokesman, the new name reflected the objectives of Iraq's national unity government and the plan to establish a brigade headquarters in every province, including the Kurdish north, within two years. The IFP had proved in many areas that it could restore peace and order, with 42,000 personnel serving in four divisions of seventeen brigades, including one dedicated to providing security during the reconstruction of the al-Askari mosque in Samarra. In addition to expanding geographically, the IFP assumed new security missions that resulted in the creation of three new units: the Embassy Protection Force, the Central Bank of ISF protection force, and the Antiquities/Ruins Security Force—the result of Iraqi police officials visiting Italy and noting that the Carabinieri had similar units. The IFP had diversified its forces to achieve a better ethnic and sectarian balance, even as budget shortfalls were expected to make it difficult for the IFP to achieve its newly authorized strength of 60,000 members.

As in the Balkans, mob violence in Iraq demonstrated the need for U.S. military forces to be able to call upon the assistance of police constabulary forces to control rioting, looting, and other forms of civil disorder. As in the Balkans, U.S. military forces in Iraq were unwilling to use their weapons against unarmed civilians and were reduced to standing by while mayhem ensued. Unlike in the Balkans, however, U.S. authorities could not turn to the United Nations or to allies for rapid provision of police resources. After the destruction of the UN headquarters in Iraq on September 22, 2003, the world organization's role was limited to diplomatic initiatives and assisting with Iraqi national elections. It was not until four years after the U.S. inter-

---

91. Terri Weaver, "As U.S. Troops Scale Back, Iraqi National Police Stepping Up Role as a Viable Security Force," *Stars and Stripes*, June 22, 2009.

vention that a contingent of trainers from the Italian Carabinieri arrived and contributed meaningfully to the police assistance program. In the interim, the U.S. military was left to rely on its own resources, contract police advisers, and Iraqis' own efforts to train, equip, and deploy Iraqi constabulary that could control civil unrest, the insurgency, and militia-inspired violence. As the conflict waned in Iraq, the United States turned its full attention to what some called the forgotten war in Afghanistan. There the United States was engaged in a major program to train the Afghan National Police, and the need for an indigenous constabulary had already become apparent.

7

Police Building under Fire: The Afghan National Civil Order Police

fghanistan first sought to develop a modern police force in the 1930s during the reign of Nadir Shah, with the incorporation of the Public Security Ministry into the Ministry of the Interior and the founding of the Academy for Police and Gendarmerie. The academy was staffed with German and Turkish technical advisers, beginning a relationship between Afghanistan and the German and Turkish police that has continued to the present. German advisers were withdrawn at the beginning of World War II, but returned briefly in 1953 and again in the 1960s, when Mohammed Zahir Shah, Afghanistan's last king, created another national police force, again modeled on the European system. Both the Federal Republic of Germany and the German Democratic Republic supplied training and technical assistance. True to its European model, the Afghan force was divided between a civil police that was responsible for law enforcement and traffic control in urban areas and a constabulary (gendarmerie) that was responsible for riot control, border patrol, and suppression of banditry in the countryside.[1]

By the 1960s the Afghan constabulary was a mobile, armed force that operated in rural areas on horses, with some capacity to conduct large-scale operations. In the countryside, the Afghan police relied on tribal authorities and traditional law to resolve routine disputes and maintain order, and on the Afghan army to deal with serious confrontations. Before the Soviet intervention, there was very limited police presence in rural areas. The average district police station had fewer than forty officers, but despite their small numbers, the police were respected and maintained order. The arrival in a village of a lone policeman armed with a walking stick was enough to command compliance with requests to surrender suspected criminals or leaders engaged in politically questionable activity. The ability to

---

1. Afghan National Police Working Group, "The Police Challenge: Advancing Afghan National Police Training," Project 2049 Institute, Arlington, VA, June 13, 2011, 5.

operate in this manner was due less to moral authority than to the doctrine of collective responsibility, holding the tribe accountable for the wrongdoing of an individual, and fear of the army destroying the entire community. The Afghan version of the social contract was that the central government demanded little direct control in exchange for popular tolerance of the regime in Kabul.[2]

Following the Soviet intervention, the Afghan police were organized on the Soviet model, with a two-track system of a career officer corps commanding a force of short-term conscripts who served for two years as patrolmen as an alternative to compulsory military service. Officers were educated at the police academy; conscripts were uneducated, poorly trained, and often mistreated by their superiors. During the war against the mujahideen, the Ministry of Interior forces—the Sarandoy—grew steadily from 8,500 in 1979 to 96,500 in 1988, short of the goal of 115,000. The Sarandoy was a national force that served under the central command of the Directorate of Defense of the Revolution of the Ministry of the Interior. Its personnel engaged in all types of municipal and provincial policing, traffic control, countering banditry, and conducting counterinsurgency operations. They also arrested counterrevolutionaries, deserters, and political opponents of the regime.[3]

Some 5,000 advisers from the Soviet Ministry of Internal Affairs (MVD) took on an ever-expanding role in the training, equipping, and oversight of Afghan police forces and in the planning and leading of operations. The Soviets grew to distrust the Afghans and excluded them in developing plans, often until the point of implementation. As the war expanded, the Soviet advisers focused on developing the Sarandoy constabulary as a counterinsurgency force equipped with a variety of small arms, mortars, and armored vehicles. Once the Soviet and Afghan military cleared an area, the Sarandoy apprehended any remaining insurgents and protected vital infrastructure, such as pipelines, bridges, major highways, and irrigation systems. Within the Ministry of the Interior, police personnel were drawn into the often violent rivalry between the Khalq and Parcham factions of the ruling People's Democratic Party of Afghanistan. They also engaged in armed clashes with units of the Afghan State Information Agency (KHAD), modeled on and heavily supported by the Soviet KGB. During the war, casualties among Sarandoy forces were high, with one Soviet source reporting 1,200 killed and

---

2. Antonio Guistozzi and Mohammad Isaqzadeh, "Afghanistan's Paramilitary Policing in Context: The Risks of Expediency," Afghanistan Analysts Network, Kabul, November 2011, 7.

3. Olga Oliker, *Building Afghanistan's Security Forces in Wartime: The Soviet Experience* (Santa Monica, CA, RAND, 2011), 25–37.

2,336 wounded in one nine-month period. After the Soviet withdrawal in 1989, the police counterinsurgency force fought on for another three years until the Najibullah government fell.[4]

During the subsequent civil war among mujahideen commanders there were no national police in Afghanistan. The Taliban made no effort to organize a Western-style force, instead establishing the Ministry for the Promotion of Virtue and Prevention, loosely modeled on a similar institution in Saudi Arabia. The Taliban's so-called Vice and Virtue Police were notorious for their brutal methods in enforcing an extremist code of Islamist values dictated by Taliban leader Mullah Omar.[5] The ministry was responsible for carrying out Taliban justice by holding mass public executions at the Kabul football stadium. Religious police patrolled the streets arresting men for the improper length of their beards, kite flying, listening to music, and failing to pray. Women were forced to wear burkas completely covering their head and bodies. Widows were not permitted in public without male relatives escorting them, a severe hardship in a country where many women had lost their husbands and sons in war. The violation of internationally recognized human rights by the religious police was a major focus of concern for the international community during the period of Taliban rule.[6]

U.S. RETALIATION FOR SEPTEMBER 11 ROUTS THE TALIBAN

After a four-week bombing campaign, on November 9, 2001, American CIA and Special Forces operatives on horseback joined Uzbek cavalry in Afghanistan's Northern Alliance in an assault on Taliban positions guarding the city of Mazar-e-Sharif. As these forces, loyal to the Afghan warlord Rashid Dostum, charged forward, U.S. aircraft overhead fired sophisticated laser-guided missiles to cover their advance. Photographs of this dramatic mixture of eighteenth- and twenty-first century warfare captured the world's imagination. The Taliban abandoned the city and were attacked from the air as they fled south in disorganized convoys of pickup trucks. Capturing Mazar-e-Sharif provided the Northern Alliance and its new leader, Mohammed

---

4. Oliker, *Building Afghanistan's Security Forces.*

5. Andrew Wilder, "Cops or Robbers? The Struggle to Reform the Afghan National Police," Afghanistan Research and Evaluation Unit, Kabul, July 2007, available at http://areu.org. af/EditionDetails.aspx?EditionId=63&ContentId=7&ParentId=7&Lang=en-US (accessed November 28, 2012).

6. Tom Coghlan, "Fury as Karzai Plans Return of Taliban's Religious Police," *The Independent,* July 17, 2006, available at http://www.independent.co.uk/news/world/asia/fury-as-karzai-plans-return-of-talibans-religious-police-408231.html (accessed November 28, 2012).

Fahim, with a strategic center of operations and a staging area for an assault on Kabul. Within days, warlord-led armies had liberated areas in the northern, western, and central provinces. Forces loyal to Ismael Khan captured Herat in the west after the Taliban garrison fled. Karim Khalili and his fellow Hazara fighters captured the central city of Bamiyan after convincing the Taliban defenders to defect. In New York, President Bush, accompanied by Pakistani president Pervez Musharraf, appealed to the Northern Alliance not to occupy Kabul until a representative national government could be organized. On November 12, 2001, however, the Taliban looted and then abandoned the capital. The next day, thousands of fighters and hundreds of foreign journalists walked into Kabul, welcomed by cheering crowds. The city celebrated its liberation from repressive Taliban rule with music, dancing, and the shaving of beards. A few weeks later, intensive Western diplomacy resulted in the formation of an interim Afghan government led by a southern Pashtun, Hamid Karzai. The leader of the Northern Alliance, General Fahim, became defense minister, and his troops garrisoned in Kabul.[7]

Even before the U.S. intervention in Afghanistan, the Northern Alliance had begun training police as part of a long-term plan for occupying Kabul. Training took place at a police academy near the village of Dashtak in the Panjshir Valley. The majority of the Alliance's 2,000-member police force was ethnic Tajiks, but the police academy director and some of its cadets were from other ethnic groups. Over a three-year period at the academy, recruits were taught eighteen subjects, including law, basic investigation, criminology, and human rights, as well as martial arts and military drill. According to the academy's deputy director, a veteran Afghan police officer, it was important to use police rather than soldiers to maintain order in Kabul.[8] When the Northern Alliance occupied the city, it deployed some 4,000 police. They had only a few vehicles and little communications equipment, and operated from a few dilapidated or damaged stations. They did, however, cooperate with the International Security Assistance Force (ISAF) and helped reduce the number of armed militia fighters in the city. Without waiting for international assistance, the Afghans reopened the old police academy on the outskirts of Kabul. The academy had spacious, wooded grounds, the remains of a large swimming pool, and the ruins of several buildings. A class of ninety-two cadets

7. Ahmed Rashid, *Descent into Chaos: The United States and the Failure of Nation Building in Pakistan, Afghanistan, and Central Asia* (New York: Viking Penguin, 2008), 80–83.

8. William Branigin, "Afghan Rebels Ready Police Force for Kabul: Officers Part of Plan to Control Capital," *Washington Post*, November 7, 2001, A20.

who transferred from the police academy in Dashtak lived and studied in the complex's only habitable structure.[9]

THE INTERNATIONAL EFFORT TO REBUILD THE AFGHAN POLICE

The starting point for rebuilding the Afghan police was the Agreement on Provisional Arrangements in Afghanistan Pending the Re-Establishment of Permanent Government Institutions—the Bonn Agreement—which representatives of the Afghan people signed on December 5, 2001.[10] The agreement established an interim Afghan authority to run the country and provided the basis for an interim system of law and governance. In Annex I, the parties called to deploy an international military force to maintain security in Kabul. In response, UN Security Council Resolution 1386 of December 20, 2001, authorized ISAF's creation for six months to assist the new Afghan government.[11] ISAF deployed in January 2002 and by summer had 5,000 troops from nineteen countries. Its responsibility was limited to securing the capital, where it conducted routine patrols with local police. ISAF's purpose was to provide a "breathing space" during which the Afghans could create their own security forces and judicial system. It was separate from the U.S-led Operation Enduring Freedom, which operated along the Pakistan border and focused on destroying the Taliban and al-Qaeda.[12]

The United Nations sought to limit international involvement in Afghanistan and to encourage the Afghans to assume responsibility for their own political reconciliation, economic reconstruction, and security. Under the leadership of Ambassador Lakhdar Brahimi, the UN mission in Kabul advocated a "light footprint," a euphemism for minimal international oversight and material assistance, particularly concerning the international

9. Doug Struck, "National Police Force Sought in Afghanistan," *Washington Post,* February 5, 2002, A8; Consortium for Response to the Afghanistan Transition (CRAFT), "Filling the Vacuum: Prerequisites to Security in Afghanistan," International Human Rights Law Group, Kabul, March 2002, available at http://www.irgltd.com/Resources/Publications/ANE/2002-03%20CRAFT%20-%20Afghanistan.pdf (accessed November 28, 2012).

10. United Nations Secretariat, Agreement on Provisional Arrangements in Afghanistan Pending the Re-Establishment of Permanent Government Institutions, 2001, available at http://www.un.org/News/dh/latest/afghan/afghan-agree.htm (accessed November 28, 2012).

11. United Nations Security Council, Resolution 1386, December 20, 2001, Press Release SC/7248, available at http://www.un.org/News/Press/docs/2001/sc7248.doc.htm (accessed November 4, 2012).

12. Moira Shanahan, "Security in Afghanistan: The International Security Assistance Force," Peace Operations Backgrounder, Henry L. Stimson Center, June 2002, available at http://www.isn.ethz.ch/isn/Digital-Library/Publications/Detail/?ots591=CAB359A3-9328-19CC-A1D2-8023E646B22C&lng=en&id=31139 (accessed November 4, 2012).

community's approach to ensuring internal security and assisting the Afghan police.[13] The Bonn Agreement did not provide for UN monitoring or training of police, nor did the Security Council authorize a UN police mission, as it had in peacekeeping operations in the Balkans. According to the Bonn Agreement, responsibility for maintaining security throughout the country rested with the Afghans.[14]

At a G8 donors' conference held in Geneva in 2002, international donors set aside a comprehensive security sector reform program in favor of a lead nation donor support framework, under which the security sector was divided into five pillars, with each assigned to a lead nation to oversee and support reforms. The United States was assigned responsibility for building the military; Italy, the judiciary; Britain, counternarcotics; and Germany, the police. The framework was meant to ensure burden sharing, but assignments were made with little attention to expertise, experience, or resources, and there was no mechanism to ensure a coordinated approach to reform efforts. Some donors presumed the Afghan government would supply oversight despite its obvious shortfalls in the required capacity. Once engaged, international donors, including the United States, regressed into train and equip programs that focused on improving the operational effectiveness of Afghan security forces and largely ignored the ministries that supervised and supported the operational forces. No donors focused on the need to strengthen the Interior Ministry, which was responsible for the Afghan police. The German police assistance mission assigned only one adviser to the Interior Ministry in 2003; at the time, the ministry lacked basic administrative systems for personnel, procurement, and logistics and the ability to oversee police operations. The initial failure to reform the Interior Ministry stifled efforts to remake the Afghan National Police (ANP).[15]

The Afghan interim authority, particularly Interior Minister Mohammed Yunus Qanooni, recognized that international assistance would be required to create a new ANP. The interim authority wanted to create a new professional police service with educated officers and trained career noncommissioned officers (NCOs) and patrolmen. Based on their positive experiences

---

13. Liz Panarelli, "The Role of the Ministerial Advisor in Security Sector Reform: Navigating Institutional Terrains," Peace Brief, U.S. Institute of Peace, Washington, DC, April 2009, available at http://www.usip.org/publications/the-role-the-ministerial-advisor-in-security-sector-reform-navigating-institutional-terrai (accessed November 4, 2012).

14. UN Secretariat, Agreement on Provisional Arrangements.

15. Mark Sedra, "Security Sector Reform and State Building in Afghanistan," in Geoffery Hayes and Mark Sedra, eds., *Afghanistan: Transition under Threat* (Waterloo, ON: Wilfrid Laurier University Press, 2008), 193–196.

with German police assistance before the Soviet intervention, the Afghans welcomed Germany as the lead nation for training and equipping the Afghan police. Germany's goal was to create an ethnically balanced force that was familiar with human rights standards and modern police methods and capable of operating in a democratic society.[16]

Given Afghanistan's size and population, creating a national police force was a far greater challenge than anything the international community had attempted in peace operations in Haiti and the Balkans. The Germans developed an initial plan for training the Afghan police based on the European model of creating a police academy that would provide a university-level education for officers and a shorter academic program for NCOs.[17] The Germans announced a commitment of $70 million to renovate the police academy in Kabul, provided eleven police instructors, refurbished Kabul police stations, and donated fifty police vehicles. The first team of German police advisers arrived in Kabul on March 16, 2002. The German Coordination Office opened on March 18 to supervise the reconstruction of the Kabul National Police Academy, which formally reopened on August 22, 2002, with 1,500 officer cadets enrolled in a five-year program.[18] The academy also offered a three-month recruit course for 500 NCOs.[19] According to Interior Minister Qanooni, the interim authority's goal was to create a police force of 70,000 officers.[20] The German approach would have taken decades to train a police force of that size, if ever.

THE U.S. POLICE ASSISTANCE PROGRAM

The United States did not challenge the German approach to police training as inappropriate for Afghanistan. In 2003 it took the more diplomatic tack of creating a separate program to provide in-service training to those currently serving as police, particularly in the lowest ranks as patrolmen. In 2002 an estimated 50,000 men were working as police in Afghanistan, but

16. United Nations Secretariat, Report of the Secretary-General on the Situation in Afghanistan and Its Implications for International Peace and Security, S/2002/278-A/56/875, March 18, 2002, 9–12, available at http://reliefweb.int/report/afghanistan/situation-afghanistan-and-its-implications-international-peace-and-security-sg (accessed November 28, 2012).

17. Amnesty International, "Afghanistan: Police Reconstruction Essential for the Protection of Human Rights," March 12, 2003, available at http://www.amnesty.org/en/library/info/ASA11/003/2003 (accessed November 4, 2012).

18. Government of Germany, closed session briefing, National Defense University, September 16, 2002, attended by author.

19. Interview with official, U.S. Department of State, April 14, 2002.

20. Struck, "National Police Force Sought."

they owed their allegiances to warlords and local commanders, not the central government. Many were former mujahidin whose experiences of acting with impunity left them poorly prepared to serve as police in a democratic society. A few professional police officers remained from the ANP of the Soviet period, but their training and experience were also inappropriate for the new order: They were skilled at protecting the regime in power, but had no understanding of community-oriented police service.[21] Policemen were largely illiterate, untrained, and poorly equipped. At least five senior officials in the interim authority claimed leadership of the police, though there was no effective chain of command. There was also ethnic imbalance, as ethnic Tajiks held most senior positions. The salary for the lowest ranks was less than $24.00 per month, and patrolmen were not paid regularly. This encouraged petty corruption and the sale of loyalties to the highest bidder. In rural areas many local commanders were involved in opium production and trafficking, which meant that factionalism, criminality, and corruption were present in the police at all levels.[22]

The U.S. State Department established a police-training center in Kabul to train the Afghan police assigned in the capital. The Kabul site served as a prototype for seven regional training centers constructed around the country. The State Department's Bureau of International Narcotics and Law Enforcement Affairs (State/INL) led the U.S. police assistance program, but training center construction, instructor recruitment, and project management were contracted to DynCorp International, which had played a similar role in the Balkans. The U.S. program quickly dwarfed the German effort in funding and enrollment, with $224 million dollars invested by 2004. Germany remained the official lead nation, but the de facto U.S. leadership role was uncontested.[23]

At the flagship facility in Kabul, three U.S. and six international instructors plus Afghan staff handled training. Trainees were selected by the Afghan Interior Ministry and were not vetted by U.S. program administrators.[24]

---

21. Tonita Murray, "Police-Building in Afghanistan: A Case Study of Civil Security Reform," *International Peacekeeping*, vol. 14, no. 1 (2007), 108–126.

22. Lieutenant Colonel James A. From, Joseph D. Keefe, Dr. John P. Cann, Christopher S. Ploszaj, and William B. Simpkins, "Policing in Afghanistan—Reform That Respects Tradition: Need for a Strategic Shift," Institute for Defense Analyses, Paper P-4604, May 2010, 8, available at www.dtic.mil/cgi-bin/GetTRDoc?AD=ADA532384 (accessed November 4, 2012).

23. Cornelius Friesendorf and Jorg Krempel, "Militarized versus Civilian Policing: Problems of Reforming the Afghan National Police," report by the Peace Research Institute Frankfurt, no. 102, 2011, 11–12.

24. Sedra, "Security Sector Reform."

The program offered three core courses based on the curriculum used at the Police Service School in Kosovo. An eight-week course covered basic police skills for literate NCOs and patrolmen; illiterate patrolmen took a five-week course and policemen with extensive experience entered a fifteen-day transition integration program. The training centers also offered a two- to four-week course in instructor development. The U.S program greatly accelerated the number of Afghan police that received some training, with the total reaching 71,147 by July 2007. In contrast, the German Police Academy program trained only 3,600 commissioned officers and NCOs in roughly the same period. [25]

The quality of the training that the majority of the graduates of the U.S. program received is open to question. In Afghanistan, contract instructors faced a formidable challenge. Trainees had little or no classroom experience. They sat on hard benches for hours a day in prefabricated classrooms that baked in the summer and froze in the winter, listening to instructors who spoke in English and Afghan translators who were poorly trained and unfamiliar with police terminology. Few of the U.S. instructors were professional police trainers and there was little to no use of adult learning techniques. Since more than 70 percent of the Afghan trainees were illiterate, over 40 percent of those trained received only the fifteen-day program. The inability of recruits to read and write inhibited their ability to absorb information and learn basic police skills, such as taking statements from witnesses, writing incident reports, and maintaining records. [26]

Trainees did not remain at the training centers long enough to absorb much detail or the ethos of democratic policing through contact with the instructors. The U.S. training program also failed to provide the follow-on field training that had been a constant feature of similar U.S. programs in Panama, Haiti, and the Balkans. Afghan trainees were returned to their place of origin with no follow-up to determine whether they were applying their training or to account for the uniforms, equipment, and weapons that were issued at the end of training. Many police were assigned to static guard duty or reduced to serving under untrained and corrupt leaders who possessed little understanding of the role of police in a democratic society. [27]

The international police assistance program also suffered from a lack of common strategic objectives and coordination between the U.S. and German programs. Neither the United States nor Germany concentrated on

---

25. Sedra, "Security Sector Reform," 201–202.

26. Murray, "Police-Building."

27. James Glanz and David Rohde, "Panel Faults U.S. Trained Afghan Police," *New York Times*, December 4, 2006, available at http://www.nytimes.com/2006/12/04/world/asia/04police.html (accessed November 4, 2012).

improving the capacity of the Interior Ministry to supervise, manage, or support the police. Short on resources, the Afghans looked to the United Nations for assistance with meeting operating expenses. In May 2002 the UN Development Program established the Law and Order Trust Fund for Afghanistan (LOTFA) to enable international donors to contribute funds for recurring budget expenses, particularly police salaries. LOTFA was also intended to provide funding for nonlethal equipment, refurbishing police stations, and strengthening police capacity. By 2004 only $11.2 million of the $65 million requested had been contributed. The funding failure meant that the Afghan government could not support the deployment of national police outside the capital. Even in Kabul, Afghan police went unpaid for months, resulting in petty corruption that undermined public confidence. Increasingly, the public regarded the Afghan police with a mixture of fear and disdain.[28]

THE DEPARTMENT OF DEFENSE AND THE COMBINED SECURITY TRANSITION COMMAND

In 2005 the U.S. government transferred responsibility for the police assistance program from the Department of State to the Department of Defense (DOD), following the lead of the U.S. police assistance program in Iraq. Implementation was assigned to the Combined Security Transition Command–Afghanistan (CSTC-A), which also had responsibility for training the Afghan National Army. Within CSTC-A, responsibility for training was assigned to its task force police directorate, while responsibility for reforming the Interior Ministry went to the police reform directorate. While CSTC-A had overall responsibility, State/INL retained contract management authority for police training, mentoring, and Interior Ministry reform. State/INL also continued to provide civilian police trainers and advisers through its contract with DynCorp International.[29]

As in Iraq, transferring responsibility to DOD infused manpower and financial resources but did little to improve the effectiveness of the police assistance program. In December 2006 a joint report by the inspectors general of both the State and Defense Departments found that U.S.-trained Afghan police were incapable of conducting routine law enforcement and that American program managers could not account for the number of ANP

---

28. Laurel Miller and Robert Perito, "Establishing the Rule of Law in Afghanistan," Special Report no. 117, United States Institute of Peace, Washington, DC, March 2004, available at http://www.usip.org/publications/establishing-rule-law-afghanistan (accessed November 4, 2012).
29. Wilder, "Cops or Robbers?"

on duty, nor did they know the whereabouts of vehicles, equipment, and weapons provided to the Afghan government. The report noted that the official Afghan figure of 70,000 trained police officers was inflated; only about 30,000 were actually on duty and able to carry out police functions. It faulted the failure to establish a field training program that could mentor graduates from the regional field training centers and keep track of equipment. Despite the $1.1 billion the United States had spent on police assistance in Afghanistan to that date, the program was understaffed, poorly supervised, and ineffective.[30]

KABUL RIOTS HIGHLIGHT THE NEED FOR A CONSTABULARY FORCE

The shortcomings of the ANP were further revealed by a day of bloody rioting in Kabul on May 29, 2006, when the police could not control the mobs that rampaged through the city following a fatal incident involving U.S. military forces. The riots were the deadliest incidence of street violence since the defeat of the Taliban. At 8 a.m. the brakes of a heavy U.S. military cargo truck failed on a steep incline, sending the vehicle into twelve civilian cars, killing one person and injuring six. An angry crowd quickly surrounded the accident scene and began throwing stones at the U.S. soldiers, who responded by firing their weapons into the air. Rumors that American troops had shot and killed many demonstrators spread swiftly. Within hours, mobs of men and boys were roaming the streets and looting shops. They torched a foreign aid agency, a new tourist hotel, and government buildings. As the violence spread, armed demonstrators exchanged fire with U.S. soldiers, Afghan police, and local security guards. By sundown, 14 people were dead and 138 wounded. The violence revealed a deep undercurrent of anti-American and antigovernment sentiment and highlighted the inability of the Afghan police to control large-scale civil disorder. The chief of police in Kabul said his forces lacked the resources to deal with rioters, such as tear gas, water hoses, shields, and other types of protective gear. He denied that the police had fired into crowds and caused the death and injury of the protesters.[31]

---

30. Inspectors General, U.S. Department of State and U.S. Department of Defense, "Interagency Assessment of Afghanistan Police Training and Readiness," Department of State Report no. ISP-IQO-07-07, Department of Defense Report no. IE-2007-001, Washington, DC, November 14, 2006, available at http://www.dodig.mil/IGInformation/IGInformation-Releases/Interagency%20Assessment%20of%20Afghanistan%20Police%20Training%20 &%20Readiness.pdf (accessed November 28, 2012).

31. Carlotta Gall, "After Riots, Kabul Residents Begin to Point Fingers," *New York Times,* May 31, 2006.

For U.S. authorities, the riot revealed Kabul's vulnerability to large-scale civilian unrest and the threat this posed to the U.S. embassy, military headquarters, and other facilities. In the aftermath of the riots, the U.S. military began working to create an elite constabulary modeled on the French gendarmerie—the Afghan National Civil Order Police (ANCOP)—with an authorized end strength of 5,365 personnel to be achieved by 2010. The force would be divided into four brigades stationed at Kabul, Paktia, Kandahar, and Herat and composed of twenty battalions. ANCOP's mission was to maintain public order in Afghanistan's seven largest cities, provide a mobile police presence in high-threat areas, and serve as a rapid-reaction force to support the Afghan Uniformed Police (AUP) in an emergency or in cases of urban violence. Its members were recruited from all ethnic groups and from units throughout the ANP. An initial sixteen weeks of training emphasized crowd control, urban tactical operations, tribal relations, and ethics, followed by an additional eight weeks of training on special weapons tactics (SWAT), with top students selected for additional SWAT training. ANCOP received better weapons, equipment, and vehicles than the rest of the ANP.[32]

U.S. military authorities recruited for ANCOP from among the best officers currently serving in the AUP. The intention was to create a force that could rapidly acquire new skills and operate effectively in the relatively sophisticated environment of Afghanistan's major cities, where it would have to interact with foreign troops and relief workers. The critical criterion for selection was a sixth-grade level of literacy, an extremely high standard given that more than 80 percent of the ANP were illiterate. Using literacy as a criterion created an elite force almost by definition, though it had unintended consequences for the overall police development program, as withdrawing the few literate members from police units around the country deprived those units of essential personnel. Absent a force-wide literacy training program, there was no way to replace this capacity. Over time, the very high levels of attrition in ANCOP units created a brain drain that negatively affected the ANP overall.[33]

POLICE FAILURES DICTATE THE NEED FOR A REVISED TRAINING PROGRAM

Although ANCOP was conceived of as a riot control force, its initial assignment was to backfill AUP personnel who were removed from their districts for collective police training under a new program the U.S. military had de-

32. Afghan National Police Working Group, "The Police Challenge," 8.

33. Interview with Captain Mark Hagerott, United States Navy, former staff member of NATO Training Mission–Afghanistan, Annapolis, Maryland, September 10, 2010.

vised. In November 2007, CSTC-A sought to correct for deficiencies in the U.S. police assistance program by launching a new initiative called Focused District Development (FDD), which aimed to enhance AUP capabilities by vetting, training, and reequipping all uniformed police in a single district at one time as a unit. The program was designed to correct the problem of newly trained police returning to their duty stations to serve under untrained and corrupt superiors. Under the FDD program, an advance team of U.S. military and civilian police advisers conducted a pretraining assessment in the district, noting the level of police performance, relationship with the population, infrastructure, and threat level from criminals and insurgents. The entire district force of officers and men were brought to a regional center where they received basic training for all untrained recruits, advanced training for police with previous experience, and management and leadership training for senior officers. The unit was then redeployed to its district under the supervision of a U.S. police mentoring team.[34]

Under the FDD program, ANCOP replaced the district-level Afghan police who were away at the regional center. As an elite unit, ANCOP was supposed to be a model of effective police performance for local citizens, raising popular expectations for the AUP. As replacements, AN-COP's better trained, better equipped, and more disciplined personnel compared favorably with the AUP, who were mostly untrained, poorly equipped, thinly spread, and often abusive in their dealings with the public. ANCOP's training in community policing and counterinsurgency tactics, plus its integrated command structure, also made it more effective in conducting operations. Its higher level of literacy set it apart from the general public and contrasted favorably with the largely illiterate AUP. That ANCOP officers were recruited nationally and moved frequently meant the force was not subject to the influence of local power brokers, unlike the AUP, the personnel of which were locally recruited and served in their home areas.[35]

ANCOP's involvement in a district's FDD program began with the participation of an ANCOP liaison officer in the District Assessment and Reform Team (DART), which conducted a six- to eight-week predeployment evaluation of local conditions, including the level of security and the local AUP's status. This was followed by a two-week relief in place, during which ANCOP overlapped with the AUP and joined it in performing its

---

34. U.S. Government Accountability Office (GAO), "Afghanistan Security: U.S. Programs to Further Reform Ministry of Interior and National Police Challenged by Lack of Military Personnel and Afghan Cooperation," GAO-09-280, Washington, DC, March 2009.

35. From Keefe et al., "Policing in Afghanistan," 49.

duties. During this period the AUP briefed ANCOP, which met with U.S. forces operating in the area, local Afghan officials, and tribal elders. This process was replicated when the district AUP returned. ANCOP units arrived in the district with a full complement of personnel, smart uniforms, and all their weapons and equipment, making a positive impression on the understaffed and poorly equipped AUP, the members of which were promised new uniforms and equipment during FDD training.[36]

For the U.S. military, the arrival of ANCOP personnel was a plus, since they were trained to use their weapons, operate radios, and maintain vehicles. ANCOP officers knew how to conduct patrols, search buildings, and run checkpoints. In clashes with the Taliban, they were more confident under fire, knew how to maneuver, and aggressively engaged the enemy. As outsiders, ANCOP officers experienced some tensions with local residents, as they were often from different ethnic groups and sometimes did not speak the local language. More aggressive patrolling and counterinsurgency operations also brought protests in areas where the Taliban were active and people had mixed loyalties. ANCOP personnel often were reluctant to establish relationships with local residents or their U.S. counterparts because they knew they would leave in a short time. Some ANCOP personnel failed to perform up to the standard of the rest of their units, were lazy, or abused residents. On balance, however, ANCOP proved a net benefit for the districts where it served.[37]

For ANCOP, participation in the FDD program was an opportunity to practice its newly acquired skills, develop the leadership potential of officers and NCOs, and improve unit cohesion. During a NATO Training Mission in Afghanistan (NTM-A) review of the FDD program, ANCOP brigade commanders agreed that conducting operations during FDD deployments enabled them to grow in their positions and establish relationships with their personnel. Participation in the FFD program gave ANCOP experience in working with American, Afghan, and coalition military forces, which improved its ability to conduct mission planning and coordinate its movements. ANCOP members were also able to work on establishing relations with local residents and improving their community relations skills. The brigade commanders noted that when an ANCOP unit was identified for an FDD mission it received a full complement of personnel and equipment from coalition sources. They also noted that once ANCOP left, secu-

---

36. Interview with Captain Jordan Settle, former provost marshal, 10th Mountain Division, Wardak province, Afghanistan, January 19, 2012.

37. Interview with Settle.

rity within the district often deteriorated, as the returning AUP could not maintain a comparable level of operations.[38]

RESURGENT TALIBAN TARGET THE AFGHAN POLICE

Among the many reasons that ANCOP was chosen for the FDD program was its capacity as a counterinsurgency force: Advanced tactical training, mobility, military weaponry, and superior police skills made ANCOP the most capable police force available to counter the resurgent Taliban. By 2007 the Taliban had regrouped and returned to Afghanistan in force, engaging in ambushes, small-unit attacks, and acts of terrorism, including more than 140 suicide bombings, some in Kabul. The Taliban were most active in their traditional strongholds in the south, where central government authority was weak and unable to provide basic public services.[39] In 2008, public opinion polls showed that Afghans considered the absence of public security, including insurgent attacks, criminal robberies, abductions, murders, and tribal violence, as the primary problem facing the country.[40] AUP personnel who worked and lived in their communities formed the frontline defense against terrorism and the insurgency and bore the brunt of the violence. Beyond their inadequate police training, they were ill equipped, poorly led, and used inappropriately as an ultralight infantry force against heavily armed insurgents.[41]

The cost of using civil police in combat, for which they were poorly prepared, was extremely high. According to the DOD, some 3,400 Afghan police were killed or wounded between January 2007 and March 2009. With an average of fifty-six officers killed per month, police combat losses during 2008 were three times larger than those of the Afghan army.[42] A Canadian officer characterized the Afghan police as "cannon fodder" in the fight

38. Author's correspondence with Major General Walter M. Golden, Jr., U.S. Army, Deputy Commanding General–Police, NTM-A, January 10, 2012.

39. General James L. Jones (USMC, retired) and Ambassador Thomas R. Pickering, "Afghanistan Study Group Report," Center for the Study of the Presidency, Washington, DC, January 30, 2008, available at http://www.thepresidency.org/storage/documents/FellowsPaperGradingGuidelines/Afghanistan_Study_Group_Report.pdf (accessed November 28, 2012).

40. Seth G. Jones, Olga Oliker, Peter Chalk, C. Christine Fair, Rollie Lal, and James Dobbins, "Securing Tyrants or Fostering Reform? U.S. Internal Security Assistance to Repressive and Transitioning Regimes" (Santa Monica, CA: RAND Corporation, 2006), available at www.rand.org/pubs/monographs/MG550/ (accessed November 4, 2012).

41. Ali Jalali, "The Future of Security Institutions," in J. Alexander Their, ed., *The Future of Afghanistan* (Washington, DC: U.S. Institute of Peace Press, 2009), 28.

42. GAO, "Afghanistan Security," 6.

against the Taliban.[43] In March 2009 U.S. special envoy Richard Holbrooke characterized the ANP as "inadequate," "riddled with corruption," and the "weak link in the security chain."[44] At that time, the ANP had an annual attrition rate of 20 percent from combat losses, desertion, disease, and other causes. If that rate continued, the equivalent of the entire police force would have to be replaced in five years, raising questions about the possibility of building a competent and stable police organization.[45]

THE UNITED STATES ANNOUNCES A NEW POLICY FOR AFGHANISTAN

When President Barack Obama took office in January 2009, it was evident to U.S. officials in Kabul and Washington that the Taliban were resurgent and that U.S. and coalition forces were under strength, inadequately supported, and in danger of losing the war. Following an initial policy review, President Obama announced a new strategy for Afghanistan and Pakistan on March 27, 2009. Speaking from the White House, the president stated that the core goal of U.S. efforts in Afghanistan and Pakistan was to defeat al-Qaeda and eradicate its safe havens. This would be achieved through military efforts to disrupt the terrorist networks that threatened the United States by promoting a more capable and accountable Afghan government and by developing Afghan security forces that could lead the fight with reduced U.S. assistance. The president announced he was sending more civilian development experts and 4,000 additional troops. The United States also would support a rapid increase in the size of the Afghan army and police to 134,000 and 82,000, respectively, in the next two years. Noting that international terrorism threatened the United States' European allies, the president stressed that the United States would request increased contributions of combat forces, trainers, mentors, and equipment from its NATO partners.[46]

---

43. Wilder, "Cops or Robbers?"

44. James Neuger, "Corrupt Afghan Police Targeted in U.S. Policy, Holbrooke Says," *Bloomberg News*, March 21, 2009, available at www.bloomberg.com/apps/news?pid=newsarchive&sid=auJx_dJa9TGg (accessed November 4, 2012).

45. "Policing Afghanistan: A Meeting of the Security Sector Reform Working Group," audio file, Security Sector Reform Working Group, U.S. Institute of Peace, May 27, 2009, available at www.usip.org/newsroom/multimedia/audio/policing-afghanistan-audio (accessed November 4, 2012).

46. White House, "White Paper of the Interagency Policy Group's Report on U.S. Policy toward Afghanistan and Pakistan," Washington, DC, March 27, 2009, available at www.whitehouse.gov/assets/documents/Afghanistan-Pakistan_White_Paper.pdf (accessed November 4, 2012).

One week later, on April 4, President Obama and his NATO counterparts at a summit meeting in Strasbourg-Kehl, France, agreed to a
major expansion of the mandate of the NATO-led ISAF to include
training the Afghan security forces. NATO leaders voted to create the
NATO Training Mission–Afghanistan (NTM-A), which would upgrade
and professionalize the Afghan army and police. The new commander of
the U.S. Combined Security Transition Command Afghanistan (CSTC-
A), Lieutenant General William Caldwell, would lead both organizations by forming a single command. In its first year, NTM-A would focus on increasing the size and improving the quality of Afghan forces,
while building the facilities and providing the specialized equipment and
training to professionalize the force. NTM-A would collaborate with
the EU Police Mission in Afghanistan and the European Gendarmerie
Force to bring together all the major parts of the international police
assistance effort.[47]

The increased emphasis on improving Afghan security forces occurred
amid growing awareness that the U.S. security assistance program had failed
to produce a viable Afghan police force and that the situation was deteriorating. The U.S. police assistance program was plagued by a lack of funding,
a shortage of professional police instructors, and a poor record of coordination with other foreign police assistance programs. Many training facilities
were operating below capacity because of a lack of instructors and trainer-
to-trainee ratios as poor as 1:466 in some locations. Recruitment dropped to
near-record lows. In September 2009 there was actually negative growth in
the ANP, which was troubled by failing leadership, endemic corruption, drug
use, Taliban infiltration, and high levels of attrition in the face of a deteriorating security situation. Most Afghan police were recruited and deployed
without basic training and were paid a nonliving wage far below army and
Taliban compensation. When NTM-A became operational in November
21, 2009, the United States faced a worsening situation that required an immediate infusion of personnel and resources.[48]

The seriousness of the situation in Afghanistan was reflected in President
Obama's landmark December 1, 2009, speech to the cadet corps of the U.S.
Military Academy at West Point. The president recalled that when he took
office there were only 32,000 U.S. troops serving in Afghanistan compared

---

47. "NATO Expands Its Role in Afghanistan," *NATO News*, April 4, 2009, available at www.
nato.int/cps/en/natolive/news_52799.htm (accessed November 4, 2012).

48. NTM-A, "Year in Review: November 2009 to November 2010," Kabul, 2010, 7, available
at http://www.defense.gov/Blog_files/Blog_assets/NTMAYearinReviewFINAL.pdf (accessed
November 28, 2012).

with 160,000 in Iraq. U.S. commanders had repeatedly asked for additional resources and those reinforcements had failed to arrive. The new U.S. military commander in Afghanistan, Lieutenant General Stanley McChrystal, had reported in September 2009 that the deterioration in the security situation was more serious than he had anticipated and that the status quo was not sustainable. The president told his audience that after concluding a careful strategic review, he was ordering an additional 30,000 American troops into Afghanistan. He also would provide the resources necessary to build Afghan capability to both defeat al-Qaeda and the Taliban and protect the country. The president promised to increase U.S. capacity to train competent Afghan security forces, to get more Afghans into the fight, and to accelerate the transfer of U.S. forces out of Afghanistan beginning in July 2011.[49]

Among the first manifestations of the enhanced international effort was the January 10, 2010, decision of the Joint Coordination and Monitoring Board, the formal governing body for allied security assistance, to increase the growth targets for the ANP from 82,000 to 109,000 in October 2010 and to 134,000 in October 2011.[50] The NTM-A and Afghan Interior Ministry subsequently agreed to end the practice of recruiting and deploying untrained personnel in favor of a new model that made predeployment training mandatory for all police recruits. The Interior Ministry agreed to establish new recruiting and training commands to institutionalize these functions. The NTM-A began work on raising police salaries and improving conditions of service for police officers to reduce the high levels of attrition that were undermining the security assistance effort. It also upgraded the number and seniority of international advisers assigned to the Interior Ministry and began to work on improving leadership development and identifying ways to control corruption. It was recognized that the ministry required greater assistance to improve policy development, management practices, procurement, human resources, and logistical support. All these efforts were directed at improving the quality of oversight and support for the Afghan police.[51]

ANCOP was a major beneficiary of the NTM-A effort to improve the Afghan police and the increased U.S. focus on the Taliban. Lieutenant General Caldwell had visited Iraq en route to Kabul and had seen the Iraq Fed-

---

49. "Full President Obama Speech Text on Afghanistan," latimes.com, December 1, 2009, available at http://latimesblogs.latimes.com/washington/2009/12/obama-speech-text-afghanistan.html (accessed November 28, 2012).

50. NATO, "Afghan National Security Forces," media backgrounder, October 26, 2010, available at http://www.isaf.nato.int/images/stories/File/factsheets/1667-10_ANSF_LR_en2.pdf (accessed November 28, 2012).

51. NTM-A, "Year in Review," 5.

eral Police (IFP) in action.[52] Caldwell was impressed with the IFP story of redemption from a rogue force and its capacity to assist the U.S. military in the hold and build phases of counterinsurgency operations. Caldwell pushed against other U.S. commanders' efforts to disband ANCOP because of its high attrition rates, arguing that ANCOP should increase in size and receive improved training. He recognized that the FDD program's requirement of continual deployment and the frequent transfer of ANCOP units were primarily responsible for attrition levels, which had reached 70 to 80 percent. As the United States was bringing in troops to roll back the insurgency, Caldwell saw ANCOP as a bridge between conventional NATO and Afghan military forces and the AUP. ANCOP was trained as a mobile quick-reaction force and could conduct antiterrorist operations. It had experience in community policing from its work in the FDD program and could serve as the lead element in the consolidation phase of counterinsurgency (COIN) operations after the military had secured an area. Although ANCOP had limited numbers, it was generally viewed as an elite force that could gain the respect of local populations, an essential element in the U.S. COIN strategy.[53]

ANCOP HAS AN EXPANDED ROLE AS A COUNTERINSURGENCY FORCE

The first important test of ANCOP as a COIN force came in the February 13, 2010, U.S.-led assault on Marjah, the insurgent bastion in the Taliban's heartland of Helmand province. In the largest ISAF offensive of the war, more than 15,000 troops, led by the U.S. Marines and including British, Canadian, Estonian, and Afghan forces, sealed off an area with 85,000 residents. Capturing Marjah was the focal point of President Obama's strategy of deploying 60,000 additional U.S. troops and thousands of civilian diplomats and development experts into Afghanistan to reverse the tide of battle. Success in Marjah and the rest of Helmand province was seen as essential to giving the Karzai government the time and resources required to rebuild war-damaged communities and bolster public confidence in the provincial and national governments.[54]

In Helmand province, ISAF troops faced a hundred-square-mile area of farmland dotted with small, mud-walled villages and crisscrossed by a net-

---

52. Robert Perito, "The Iraq Federal Police: U.S. Police Building under Fire," Special Report no. 291, U.S. Institute of Peace, Washington, DC, October 2011.

53. Interview with Dr. Jack D. Kem, former deputy to the commander, NTM-A, January 17, 2012.

54. Tim McGirk, "U.S. and Coalition Forces Strike a Taliban Bastion," *Time*, February 13, 2010, available at www.time.com/time/printout/0,8816,1964186,00.html (accessed November 4, 2012).

work of streams, canals, and roads that the Taliban had seeded with thousands of hidden land mines and roadside explosive devices. The Pashtun population had tribal links to the Taliban and little affinity for the Afghan government in Kabul. Families that had fled in advance of the attack told journalists that the Taliban had tried to force people to stay in place to act as human shields. While the fighting was expected to be intense, Marjah was seen as a critical test for the new U.S. commander's counterinsurgency strategy of placing the protection and welfare of the Afghan people above the killing of insurgents. The centerpiece of the Marjah operation was the plan to insert an Afghan "government in a box" to begin providing services and assistance to the local population. Under Lieutenant General McChrystal's strategy of clear, hold, and build, coalition military forces were to remove the main force Taliban units; ANCOP was to join the military in the hold phase and stay to protect the Afghan civilian government personnel in rebuilding the region.[55]

At the outset of the operation, U.S. Marine commanders expected to spend months clearing Marjah of Taliban fighters, but the operation succeeded more quickly than expected. Within two weeks U.S. officials declared that the hold and build phases of the operation were under way. By mid-March, however, there was clear evidence that the Taliban had returned and were conducting an intimidation campaign among the villagers. In April there were reports that the Taliban shadow governor was holding meetings with local elders and that Taliban fighters were taking part in the annual poppy harvest. From mid-May to mid-June, the Marines suffered more deaths in combat than in the first month of the operation. Despite U.S. efforts to open markets, build clinics, and refurbish schools, residents remained wary of contacts with U.S. forces and were reluctant to cooperate and to provide information on Taliban presence. The Taliban stepped up their intimidation campaign, brutally murdering tribal elders who were accused of cooperating with the Americans to demonstrate that the thinly stretched Marines could not protect local residents.[56]

The U.S. misperception that Marjah had been cleared of insurgents meant ANCOP was deployed prematurely to begin the hold stage of the operation. In mid-February the commander of the Marine Second Expeditionary Brigade, Brigadier General Larry Nicholson, urged ANCOP's deployment

55. C. J. Chivers and Dexter Kilkins, "Coalition Troops Storm a Taliban Haven," *New York Times,* February 12, 2010, available at www.nytimes.com/2010/02/13/world/asia/13afghan. html?pagewanted=print (accessed November 4, 2012).

56. Jeffrey Dressler, "Marjah's Lessons for Kandahar," Institute for the Study of War, Washington, DC, July 9, 2010, 3–5, available at www.understandingwar.org/report/marjahs-lessons-kandahar (accessed November 4, 2012).

in northern Marjah so that coalition forces would not be pinned down holding areas they had already cleared.[57] The Americans viewed ANCOP as the most professional and best-trained element in the ANP and recognized that establishing an effective Afghan police presence was essential to gaining popular support. The AUP's brutal and corrupt behavior had been a major grievance of Marjah residents, who told the Marines that if the old police returned the people would fight them and the Marines to the death.[58] On February 20, 2010, an ANCOP battalion with two hundred personnel arrived in Marjah to begin the task of exerting Afghan government control by flushing out the remaining insurgents and maintaining public order. By April, however, it was apparent that this early commitment of ANCOP had been a mistake.

In the face of the Taliban resurgence, ANCOP lacked the numbers, training, and equipment to provide security over a large area in northern Marjah. High levels of attrition in ANCOP units around the country meant that the battalion sent to Marjah was composed of new personnel and understrength units thrown together at the last moment. ANCOP personnel were mostly Dari-speaking ethnic Tajiks who could not converse with the Pashto-speaking residents. U.S. Marines complained that the Afghan police seemed unaware of the rules of engagement and were not trained to conduct operations. ANCOP members refused to conduct night patrols, stand guard duty at midday, or clean their living areas. ANCOP personnel abandoned checkpoints or, worse, shook down motorists for cash and cell phones. Many policemen openly smoked hashish. During the first month an entire ANCOP unit was withdrawn from duty after a quarter of its personnel tested positive for drug use. In armed confrontations with the Taliban, it was obvious that the lightly armed ANCOP was overmatched. The Marines and their U.S. civilian police advisers felt that ANCOP had promise but that additional preparation was required to make it an effective COIN force.[59]

NTM-A INITIATES A PROGRAM TO IMPROVE ANCOP'S PERFORMANCE

ANCOP's poor performance in the early stages of the Marjah campaign provided added incentive for NTM-A to increase its size and improve the

57. Dressler, "Marjah's Lessons."

58. C. J. Chivers, "With Marjah Largely Won, Marines Try to Win Trust," *New York Times*, March 1. 2010.

59. C. J. Chivers, "Afghan Police Earn Poor Grade for Marjah Mission," *New York Times*, June 1, 2010, available at www.nytimes.com/2010/06/02/world/asia/02marja.html?pagewanted=print (accessed November 4, 2012).

quality of its training. ANCOP's authorized strength of 5,365 was never realized, and its actual staffing was normally around 3,500. Attrition rates from desertion and combat losses surged to as high as 70 percent, the highest level in the ANP, which experienced a general loss of a quarter of its force each year.[60] Alarmed by the high attrition rate, NTM-A and the Interior Ministry instituted a program to overcome ANCOP's systemic problems and create the basis for expanding the force to 10,890 personnel by March 2011. Attrition was high because ANCOP's movement from district to district under the FDD program and its expanding involvement in COIN operations created a situation where units were deployed 95 percent of the time by 2010—meaning that ANCOP personnel were in constant motion with the expectation that they would be away from their families for indefinite periods. Afghanistan's lack of modern communication facilities made it difficult for ANCOP personnel to maintain contacts with home. Afghan and U.S. authorities provided little information regarding the length of deployments and few assurances that police serving continually on the front line would be given leave to rest and recover. For ANCOP officers, service conditions were harsh and the risks of injury or death ever present. As the U.S.-led counterinsurgency effort intensified, Afghan police continued to take casualties at far higher rates than the Afghan army or coalition partners.

Beyond the hardships and the danger, there were also positive incentives to leave the force and seek alternative employment. ANCOP's extensive training and relatively higher rates of literacy made its members targets for recruiting by the private security companies (PSCs) that protected foreign embassies, international organizations, NGOs, and businesses. Afghan and foreign PSCs offered higher salaries, better working conditions, and shorter hours, all in a single location. Afghan police and soldiers were not punished for desertion. Under a policy Karzai designed to encourage recruitment and allow security personnel to return home to help with the harvest, there were no penalties for leaving duty stations without permission, or for taking alternative employment. Thus, ANCOP members could leave the force with impunity.

NTM-A's program for stabilizing the force and improving ANCOP's performance focused on three issues: partnership, pay, and predictability. The so-called Three P Program called for partnering ANCOP units with U.S. military counterparts; increased pay and improved procedures to ensure po-

---

60. "Policing Inteqal: Next Steps in Police Reform in Afghanistan," British Army Afghan COIN Centre, Coffey International Development, November 2010, available at www.coffey. com.au/Uploads/Documents/Policing%20Inteqal%20Next%20Steps%20in%20Police%20 Reform_20110927121921.pdf (accessed November 4, 2012).

lice received their salaries; and predictability, or scheduling unit rotations so personnel knew what to expect. In June 2010, U.S. Special Forces A-Teams and U.S. Marine special operations teams were ordered to establish long-term partnerships with six ANCOP battalions before they participated in a major offensive in Kandahar province. This program mirrored a Special Forces program for the Afghan National Army that had successfully countered attrition and improved operations of Afghan army commando units. The unit-to-unit relationship began with a seven-day training program. ANCOP personnel were given refresher training on small-unit tactics, rifle marksmanship, battlefield communication, and operating traffic checkpoints. The goal was to boost unit effectiveness and improve morale. U.S. partnering units were responsible for ensuring that their ANCOP counterparts had the equipment and logistical support they required. Establishing unit-to-unit relationships in combination with the other parts of the Three P Program was seen by NTMA as effectively stabilizing ANCOP units facing deployment into a combat environment.[61]

When the NATO training command was activated in 2009, it was widely recognized that low police salaries, the difficulty police encountered in receiving their pay in areas without banking facilities, and the almost routine practice of senior officers skimming police salaries were major contributors to high attrition. In November 2009 a new pay scale was instituted that raised the basic police salary to $165 per month, with an additional $75 available in hazardous duty and longevity bonuses. The new $240 basic salary was a 75 percent increase, but still less than the financial incentives the Taliban reportedly offered. To reduce corruption and ensure that policemen received their pay on time, the Interior Ministry instituted a program to pay police officers through mobile telephone transfers rather than have senior officers pay their subordinates in cash. Initially, many policemen believed they had received up to a 30 percent raise when they received their full salary for the first time, and several hundred ANCOP police returned to the ranks when the new salary levels were announced.[62]

To improve predictability, NTM-A developed an operational deployment cycle with three phases: refit, train, and deploy. During the refit phase, the ANCOP unit would return to its home base for five to six weeks of

61. Sean Naylor, "Special Forces Training Afghan Police Units," *Army Times*, June 12, 2010, available at www.armytimes.com/news/2010/06/army_special_forces_afghan_police_061110w/ (accessed November 4, 2012).

62. Ray Rivera, "Support Expected for Plan to Beef up Afghan Forces," *New York Times*, January 16, 2011, available at www.nytimes.com/2011/01/17/world/asia/17afghanistan.html (accessed November 4, 2012).

personal leave, repair and replacement of equipment, and general rest and recovery. This allowed policemen to reunite with their families and take care of personal obligations. A six-week training program followed that reviewed basic skills, provided more advanced training, and specifically prepared the unit for its next assignment in either an FDD program or a COIN operation. When the ANCOP unit was deployed, it did so with its full complement of personnel and its standard issue of vehicles and equipment. At least in theory, the unit was fully prepared for its assignment, unlike in the past, when exhausted units were thrown into the fight with little preparation and inadequate resources.

ANCOP also benefited from the addition of professional Italian Carabinieri trainers to the NTM-A program. The first group of thirty-five Carabinieri arrived in January 2010 to supplement the efforts of American contractors who had been providing specialized training. The Italians brought the experience gained in training the Iraq Federal Police and in earlier participation in peace operations in Bosnia and Kosovo. They also brought a disciplined chain of command and a coherent training program that replaced the ad hoc and inconsistent approaches of the American police trainers. According to NTM-A commander Lieutenant General William Caldwell, U.S. contractors were a mix of city cops, highway patrolmen, and deputy sheriffs who brought a range of experiences and a variety of standards. None had ever served in a constabulary force. The Italians introduced a professional approach to training that had been missing; according to Newsweek, the Carabinieri markedly improved the marksmanship of the ANCOP trainees simply by properly sighting their rifles, a basic step that had somehow eluded the American contractors. As serving members of a constabulary force, the Carabinieri understood the importance of treating the population with respect and establishing good relations with those they were sworn to protect. As they had done in Iraq, the Italians spent time discussing the role of police in a democratic society, stressing the importance of values over skills in their interactions with Afghan trainees.[63]

Finally, NTM-A decided to make literacy training mandatory for all Afghan police and military recruits. The initial requirement that all ANCOP members have at least a sixth-grade level of literacy had been abandoned, as attrition drained away the original members of the force and the Interior Ministry needed to quickly recruit large numbers to replace and expand the force. By mid-2011, NTM-A was educating nearly 30,000 Afghanistan

63. T. Christian Miller, Mark Hosenball, and Ron Moreau, "The Gang That Couldn't Shoot Straight," *Newsweek,* March 29, 2010, available at www.newsweek.com/id/235221 (accessed November 4, 2012).

National Security Forces (ANSF) members at any given time. The immediate goal was to raise the entire ANSF to a first-grade level of literacy in the short term with a longer-term goal of third-grade literacy by 2015. The decision was based on the realization—long in coming—that police officers required a basic level of literacy to perform simple functions, such as identifying license plate numbers, reading suspects' identity documents, accounting for their equipment, and ensuring they received the right amount of pay. Literacy was also required for police officers to receive specialized skills training, understand regulations and procedures, and enforce the law. Higher ANCOP literacy levels contributed to public respect for ANCOP units and their status as an elite unit with the ANP.

KANDAHAR PROVIDES A BATTLEFIELD TEST FOR ANCOP

The test of U.S. efforts to improve ANCOP's performance came in the summer of 2010 during the ISAF offensive in Kandahar province. Beginning in late July, Operation Hamkari was conducted by the 101st Airborne and other U.S. forces that were part of President Obama's Afghanistan surge. The operation also included two Afghan army brigades, Afghan army commandos, and units from the AUP, the border police, and ANCOP—the largest ANSF deployment in the history of the conflict. Kandahar province had been crucial in the Afghan war. The province was the home of President Karzai and the Karzai family. The president's half-brother, Ahmed Wali Karzai, was chairman of the Kandahar Provincial Council and the principal power broker in the province. Kandahar was also the birthplace of the Taliban movement, the base of operations for Taliban leader Mullah Mohammed Omar, and the effective capital of Afghanistan under Taliban rule. Previous efforts to evict the Taliban had failed because of the predatory nature of local government and ISAF's failure to commit adequate military forces. Operation Hamkari was intended to provide both the military resources and the political will required to establish Afghan government control.

In recognition of Kandahar's importance, Lieutenant General McChrystal designated Kandahar and the neighboring Helmand province as the main operational theater of the ISAF joint command's campaign plan. The operation was designed to clear strategic terrain that had long given the Taliban a network of strong points, safe havens, improvised explosive device (IED) manufacturing facilities, and bases from which to attack ISAF and Afghan forces and control the population. Operation Hamkari ("Cooperation") was a comprehensive military and political effort to secure Kandahar province, provide development assistance, and establish Afghan government authority. In a three-phase operation, the ISAF first attempted to improve security in the provincial capital, Kandahar City, and then extend its control into adjoining areas, first into Arghandab and later into Zhari and Panjwai districts. The operation began with the construction of a ring of sixteen security checkpoints along the primary roads entering Kandahar City. Each checkpoint was manned by a squad from the U.S. 504 Military Police Battalion, partnering with ANCOP and ANP personnel. By August more than 1,200 ANCOP personnel were manning checkpoints that created a security perimeter around the city. Outside of Kandahar City, the Afghan security forces that took part in the operation included some of the best ANSF units, including the Third Battalion of the 3rd ANCOP Brigade, which deployed with its U.S. Special Forces mentors. Kandahar marked the first time U.S. units partnered with ANCOP on a full-time basis, which increased police professionalism and prevented predatory behavior toward local citizens. The presence of ANCOP in Kandahar City enabled five hundred members of the locally based AUP to deploy to a regional center for six weeks of training in the FDD program.[64]

The ring of checkpoints increased local security but failed to stop infiltration of the city as long as the Taliban occupied the surrounding countryside. In the second phase of the operation, the ISAF moved into Arghandab district, the location of major Taliban strongholds to the north and west of Kandahar City. The district had been a center of resistance against the Soviets. The Taliban took control of the old bunker and tunnel system and used a network of canals and thick orchards that hindered ISAF operations and provided cover for insurgent activity. It was not until September, after constant raids and a major bombing campaign, that ISAF and Afghan forces launched an assault that gained control of the area. Afghan army, ANCOP, and Afghan border police participated in the operation alongside U.S. Special Forces and regular U.S. infantry and artillery units.[65]

The third phase of Operation Hamkari involved a major military operation led by the U.S. 101st Airborne to clear entrenched Taliban positions in the Zhari and Panjwai districts. In this area of abandoned villages, dry streambeds, high walls, and thick tree cover, the Taliban had built a network of fortifications, trenches, tunnels, and bunkers, prepared weapons caches,

---

64. "Elite Cadre of Afghan Police Set Up," *Pakistan Daily Times*, July 7, 2010.

65. Carl Forsberg, *Counterinsurgency in Kandahar: Evaluating the 2010 Hamkari Campaign* (Washington, DC: Institute for the Study of War, 2010), 16–21, available at www.understandingwar.org/report/counterinsurgency-kandahar-evaluating-2010-hamkari-campaign (accessed November 4, 2012).

and planted IEDs. On September 15, 2010, the ISAF moved into Zhari with adequate forces to take and hold the terrain. On September 26, ISAF forces seized the town of Sangesar, the site of Mullah Omar's madrassah and the place where the Taliban was organized in 1994. By November, Taliban fighters had been cleared from the district after heavy fighting. The ANP and ANCOP presence increased as the clearing operations succeeded in removing main-force Taliban units, including large numbers of foreign fighters. An ANCOP battalion with embedded U.S. Special Forces advisers arrived in Zhari to operate checkpoints and conduct patrols. ANCOP worked with the ANP to establish stations in areas cleared of Taliban, playing their assigned role in the hold phase of the COIN operation. Partnering with U.S. forces improved ANCOP's performance and virtually stopped attrition. In Arghandad district, the 3rd ANCOP Brigade reported only one desertion between July and August 2010.[66]

AFTER A DIFFICULT START, ANCOP FINALLY HITS ITS STRIDE

By early 2011, ANCOP had solidified its position as the most respected organization among the multiple police forces that composed the ANP, though this positive evaluation must be understood in relative terms given the troubled state of the ANP overall. According to the UN Development Program's Police Perception Survey of 2011, only 20 percent of those interviewed believed the ANP was ready to take over responsibility for internal security from international forces. Many Afghans reported concerns with police corruption, impunity, drug use, abusive behavior, ethnic bias, and other forms of misconduct. Improvements were noted in police presence, training and equipment, and success in reducing crime, but only 37 percent of those interviewed felt it would improve matters if they brought a complaint against a police officer.[67] At the same time, ANP officers continued to be killed in the line of duty at rates far higher than Afghan soldiers or NATO and coalition military personnel. From October 2010 to October 2011 the *Washington Post* reported that 1,555 Afghan police officers died—twice the number of Afghan soldiers, even as the Afghan military had 35,000 fewer members. U.S. losses during the same period totaled 474. The higher number of ANP casualties resulted from a lack of body armor and armored vehicles, inadequate arms and equipment, and the practice of stationing police

---

66. Forsberg, *Counterinsurgency in Kandahar*, 24–27.

67. "Police Perception Survey of 2011: The Afghan Perspective," UN Development Program–Afghanistan Country Office, 2011, 3–5; "Eight in Ten Afghans Think Police Weak: UN Report Shows," Reuters, January 31, 2012.

in small numbers in exposed checkpoints and other vulnerable locations.[68] During 2010–11, NTM-A saw significant progress in the size, training, literacy, and performance of the ANP, but the challenges the ANP faced were too great to be overcome in such a short period. ANCOP was a bright spot in the dismal police landscape.

The April 2011 National Police Plan described ANCOP as a regionally based and nationally deployable force responsible, along with the Afghan army, for achieving stability and maintaining civil order. According to the plan, ANCOP was responsible for tactically supporting the Afghan National Army during the clear phase of COIN operations and for leading police organizations in the hold phase. It was to remain responsible for replacing the AUP during FDD training and in high-threat and unstable areas. In urban areas ANCOP was to serve as a rapid reaction force to restore public order during civil disturbances and conduct counterterrorism and hostage rescue operations. It was also tasked with supporting counternarcotics and poppy eradication operations when required.[69]

By September 2011, ANCOP was headquartered in Kabul and had five brigades located in Kabul, Kandahar, Herat, Gardez, and Helmand. ANCOP was commanded by Major General Gul Zamarai, an ethnic Tajik and former Afghan army officer who had fought against the Taliban in the Afghan civil war as a tank division commander in the Northern Alliance. ANCOP's total strength was 14,400 personnel, including those in training. At any given time, at least ten ANCOP battalions were deployed to support coalition and Interior Ministry counterinsurgency operations, primarily in southern and eastern Afghanistan. ANCOP had the highest density of coalition partnering during deployment of any ANP element, which improved effectiveness, reduced corruption, and stemmed the high levels of attrition that previously had characterized the force.[70] ANCOP had overcome its initial shortcomings and established itself as the most professional and respected element in the ANP. With its headquarters in Kabul and brigades in Kandahar, Herat, Gardez, and Helmand provinces, ANCOP had become the regionally based and nationally deployable force that its creators had envisioned.

---

68. Joshua Partlow, "Afghan Police Casualties Soar," *Washington Post*, October 11, 2011.

69. "National Police Plan for Solar Years (SY) 1390–1391," Department of Strategy, Ministry of Interior Affairs, Islamic Republic of Afghanistan, April 2011.

70. "Report on Progress toward Security and Stability in Afghanistan," U.S. Department of Defense, Washington, DC, October 2011, 43.

8

Where Is the Lone Ranger When We Need Him?

At the onset of the war on terrorism, it became clear that the U.S. ability to establish sustainable security in failing and postconflict states would rise in importance. Even before September 11, 2001, the Pentagon had begun planning to address a range of new contingencies, including international terrorism; cyberwarfare; transnational organized crime; illicit trafficking in drugs, weapons, and people; and the proliferation of weapons of mass destruction. Such threats were likely to originate in countries experiencing political, ethnic, and religious turmoil. After September 11, it became unmistakably clear that failed states posed a direct threat to U.S. national security. The 2002 National Security Strategy stated that "America is now threatened less by conquering states than we are by failing ones. We are menaced less by fleets and armies than by catastrophic technologies in the hands of the embittered few."[1] The United States could not afford to flag in its attention to messy situations in places traditionally not considered to be vital to U.S. interests. The United States would need the power to rapidly restore stability and create environments conducive to reconciliation and reconstruction. In the words of a former U.S. Army officer, "The U.S. cannot be unprepared for missions it does not want, as if the lack of preparedness might prevent our going. We cannot be like children who refuse to get dressed for school."[2]

To deal with rogue states and international terrorism, the United States needed new forces and a new approach to postconflict intervention: It had to maintain its warfighting ability while becoming more adept at integrating civilian actors and processes. The military's mission remained one of providing overall security, but in postconflict environments, civilian actors also had crucial roles in achieving sustainable security and establishing the rule of

---

1. White House, "The National Security Strategy of the United States of America," Washington, DC, September 2002, 7.
2. Ralph Peters, "Heavy Peace," *Parameters*, vol. 29, no. 1 (Spring 1999), 73.

law. The way forward was presaged by lessons learned from the international community's experience in Bosnia and Kosovo. Paddy Ashdown, the high representative in Bosnia, pointed out that "in Bosnia, we thought that democracy was the highest priority, and we measured it by the number of elections we could organize. In hindsight, we should have put the establishment of rule of law first, for everything else depends on it: a functioning economy, a free and fair political system, the development of civil society, and public confidence in police and courts."[3] The experience in Kosovo confirmed Ashdown's views. In his predeparture press conference on December 17, 2000, Bernard Kouchner, the senior UN official in Kosovo, said the lesson of Kosovo was that "peacekeeping missions need to arrive with a law-and-order kit made up of trained police, judges, and prosecutors and a set of draconian security laws. This is the only way to stop criminal behavior from flourishing in a postwar vacuum of authority."[4]

Dealing with civil disorder in the Balkans proved that the existing doctrine for conducting postconflict interventions—which dictated a linear transition from intervention and peace enforcement through a period of stabilization to a final phase of national institution building—was incorrect. Building rule-of-law institutions needed to begin as soon as the fighting stopped. From the first day that U.S. Task Force Falcon entered Kosovo, U.S. troops faced the same type of law-and-order mission as they did during the post–World War II occupation of Germany and Japan. In Kosovo, U.S. forces were immediately required to arrest local citizens for committing major criminal offenses, detain them, provide judicial review, and establish and run prisons. Those arrested were criminals who had committed murder, arson, and rape. They threatened the viability of the North Atlantic Treaty Organization (NATO) mission, which was to establish a safe and secure environment.[5] Unfortunately, U.S forces had to wait for ten months for the first UN special police unit to reach Kosovo and nearly two years before enough of these constabulary units were in place to completely contain the violence that threatened to disrupt the mission and plunge Kosovo back into civil conflict.

---

3. Paddy Ashdown, "What I Learned in Bosnia," *New York Times*, October 28, 2002.

4. R. Jeffrey Smith, "Kosovo Still Seethes as UN Official Nears Exit," *Washington Post*, December 18, 2000, A20.

5. Alton Gwaltney, "Law and Order in Kosovo: A Look at Criminal Justice During the First Year of Operation Joint Guardian," paper prepared for the Center for Law and Military Operations, Judge Advocate General's School of the Army, Charlottesville, Virginia, July 2001, 1–5.

In Iraq, mob violence reaffirmed the need for the U.S. military to be able to call on the assistance of police constabulary forces to control civil disorder. Confronted with widespread looting in Baghdad, U.S. military forces were unwilling to use their weapons against unarmed civilians and were reduced to standing aside while mayhem ensued. Unlike during peace operations in the Balkans, the United States could not turn to the United Nations or other allies to provide police resources. After the destruction of UN headquarters in Iraq on September 22, 2003, the world organization's role was limited to diplomatic initiatives and assisting with Iraq's national elections. Not until four years after the U.S. intervention did a contingent of trainers from the Italian Carabinieri arrive and meaningfully contribute to the police assistance program. In the interim, the U.S. military was left to rely on its own resources, contract police advisers, plus the efforts of the Iraqis to create indigenous paramilitary forces to control the insurgency and militia-inspired violence. The effort to create indigenous constabulary forces went awry when Iraqi-created police commando units engaged in sectarian violence. With Iraq on the brink of civil war, the U.S. military and a new Iraqi interior minister intervened to purge rogue elements and begin the slow, painful process of creating the new Iraq Federal Police (IFP), a civilian constabulary that effectively supported U.S. military forces in Baghdad during the surge in 2007.[6]

In Afghanistan, mob violence in Kabul again demonstrated the need for a civilian police constabulary that could control civil demonstrations against U.S. military forces. In 2006 the U.S. military and Afghan Interior Ministry created an elite Afghan constabulary unit bringing together the most literate officers from throughout the Afghan National Police (ANP). Over time, this force—the Afghan National Civil Order Police (ANCOP)—proved exceptionally versatile as a rapid reaction force, as backfill for regular police sent away from their districts from training, and as a counterinsurgency force in some of the toughest fighting of the Afghan conflict. Unfortunately ANCOP's success nearly proved its undoing. Selecting the best officers and keeping them continually deployed in harsh environments and dangerous assignments produced high levels of attrition, weakening the force and draining the entire ANP of its most literate and capable personnel. Ultimately a coordinated program of partnering with U.S. military forces, increased pay, and predictability in assignments was required to stabilize the force, ensure ANCOP's continuity, and set the stage for its expansion.

---

6. Robert Perito, "The Iraq Federal Police: U.S. Police Building Under Fire," Special Report no. 291, U.S. Institute of Peace, October 2011, 12–13.

In Bosnia, Kosovo, Iraq, and Afghanistan, U.S. military forces faced civilian rioters and looters—unarmed but violent mobs—that they were neither trained nor equipped to control. U.S soldiers had to choose between standing back or firing into crowds in violation of international law and American values. In each of these operations, the need for appropriately trained and equipped constabulary forces was readily apparent, but such forces did not exist in the U.S inventory. Over time, the United Nations and international allies supplied police constabulary forces in the Balkans. In Iraq and Afghanistan the United States created constabularies using indigenous security forces. These performed a variety of vital functions, including serving as counterinsurgency forces in Iraq and Afghanistan. However, international forces took months if not years to arrive, and local forces were developed through a costly process of trial and error. The requirement for police constabulary forces is evident after nearly two decades of experience. It is surprising, therefore, that in 2012 the United States is no better prepared to field such forces than it was when U.S. soldiers were confronted with rioters in Bosnia or looters in Baghdad.

The failure to develop U.S. constabulary forces for future peace and stability operations was not entirely for want of trying. Over a period of several years, the State Department convened meetings of the Interagency Stability Police Working Group on Options for a U.S. Stability Policing Capability. In what proved to be the group's final meeting, on July 14, 2009, the Department of Homeland Security (DHS), the Marshal Service of the Department of Justice (USMS), and the State Department's Bureau of International Narcotics and Law Enforcement Affairs (INL) and Office of the Coordinator for Reconstruction and Stabilization (CRS) submitted proposals for creating such a force. After the proposals were presented, participants were allowed to cross-examine the presenters concerning their recommendations.[7]

The USMS proposal was based upon the experience of the agency's Special Operations Group in Iraq, which provided security for Iraqi courts and trained Iraqi police counterparts. The USMS would use its own personnel, who could perform the full range of policing functions. It called for providing operational police in the first phase of an operation and police trainers in the second phase, after stability was achieved. Any forces created under its proposal would have dual use and could serve in the United States and abroad. Questions were raised concerning the USMS's legal authority to conduct foreign operations and its desire to exercise control over all aspects of the force's deployment.

---

7. Interagency Stability Police Working Group, Minutes of Facilitated Session on Options for a USG Stability Policing Capability, July 14, 2009.

The DHS proposal relied on obtaining police officers from U.S. state and local police departments that would come together for training and deployment under federal auspices. The federal government would have to reimburse local law enforcement agencies, and extensive preparation would be required so that police from various parts of the United States could become a cohesive force. An interagency executive committee and program office would handle policy and management issues, but DHS said it had no interest in leading either of these entities. Meeting participants questioned the lack of command and control mechanisms and the lack of a standing capacity since recruiting personnel would take time.[8]

For the State Department, the INL proposal noted that the bureau had deployed over 7,000 U.S. police officers in peace and stability operations over the previous twenty years and had unique experience in conducting overseas operations. The proposal called for outsourcing the personnel requirements to a commercial contractor, the model used in all previous operations, and concentrating on training local police rather than providing operational forces. Participants questioned whether the INL proposal was relevant since the goal was to supply forces that could actually perform riot control and other duties.

Finally, CRS proposed to use officers with police backgrounds serving in the Department's Civilian Response Corps, an on-call advisory team that could deploy on short notice, to provide a command structure for any force developed by another agency. CRS did not care which agency provided the force but considered itself responsible for policy oversight and management. After six hours, the meeting adjourned without selecting any of the options.[9]

No agreement was possible because the proposals were not comparable. None of them was comprehensive. Each stressed the strength of the presenting entity, but left out areas where it lacked authority, resources, or expertise. A series of follow-on meetings under the direction of a senior government official determined to achieve a workable result may have led to a decision, but such meetings did not happen. The chairman of the work group was transferred and never effectively replaced. The entire effort came to a halt and was eventually forgotten. In the final analysis, the working group failed to put together a comprehensive proposal that incorporated the lessons learned in U.S. interventions from Bosnia to Iraq. Missing was an actionable model for a U.S. stability force.

---

8. Interagency Stability Police Working Group, Minutes.

9. Interagency Stability Police Working Group, Minutes.

THE MODEL FOR A U.S. STABILITY FORCE

The answer to the problem of creating sustainable security in postconflict environments is straightforward: In addition to robust military forces, an effective U.S. stability force must include civilian police constabulary units; civil police; judicial teams of judges, lawyers, and court administrators; and corrections officers. These public order and law enforcement components are essential to fill the inevitable security gap that opens between the cessation of hostilities and the emergence of a democratic government that can ensure public order through the rule of law. All elements of a U.S. stability force must be assembled and ready at the outset of military operations. They should be under the control of U.S. military authorities because unity of command in the initial phase of an operation is paramount. Civilian control of the civilian elements of the force should, however, be restored as quickly as possible.

As postconflict stability operations have shown, civilian constabulary, police, and law enforcement units deployed in a timely, fully equipped, and well-coordinated manner are an invaluable asset to U.S. military operations. The civilian units help establish police and judicial authority from the outset, freeing the military to concentrate on other duties. Most important, the units help create the vital foundation for the rule of law upon which the other aspects of political, economic, and social reconstruction can build, in an environment conducive to achieving success.

SPECIAL POLICE UNITS

A U.S. stability force should include civilian stability police units similar to those deployed by NATO and the United Nations in Bosnia and Kosovo. U.S. constabulary forces could serve as a bridge between military and civil police forces and handle tasks not clearly set in either camp. Unlike military police, these civilian constabulary units could take on law enforcement functions as well as threats to public order. They could deploy rapidly with their own weapons, transport, communications, and logistical support; respond to situations such as large-scale civil disturbances that require greater firepower than lightly armed civil police have; and assist the police by performing law enforcement functions such as high-risk arrests in cases involving terrorism and organized crime.

The experience of the IFP and ANCOP demonstrated that stability police units can be crucial in the hold and build phases of counterinsurgency operations. In Iraq and Afghanistan, indigenous constabulary units partnered with U.S. military forces to conduct patrols, man checkpoints, interact with local communities, and ultimately replace main force military units in providing local security. Stability police units could play this role at the outset of an intervention when allied or local constabulary forces are not available. They also could provide monitoring and training for local police, increasing the pace at which indigenous constabulary forces could come on line. From Bosnia to Afghanistan, the U.S. doctrine for employing constabulary forces developed in response to the experience of U.S. military forces in increasingly hostile environments. In the Balkans, where U.S. military forces were part of a UN-led peacekeeping operation, constabularies were seen as the appropriate force to deal with unarmed but violent civilian mobs. In Iraq and Afghanistan, where U.S. military forces engaged as combatants in warfare against heavily armed insurgents, the utility of deploying armed, mobile, and flexible police units in areas that had been cleared of main force enemy units became evident, and the mission of these forces was expanded accordingly. In the hold phase of a counterinsurgency operation, specially trained and equipped stability police units could assume a constabulary role. In the build phase, these units could be mentors, handing off responsibility for security to indigenous civilian police.

Organizing stability police units will require drawing together personnel, skill sets, and equipment that are already present in U.S. civilian law enforcement agencies, in special weapons and tactics (SWAT) teams and special operations units. The component parts need to be organized into preformed, trained, and equipped units by a federal law enforcement agency. Locating the force in a federal agency would provide a center for the development of doctrine and training programs for the use of such forces in postconflict scenarios. As a federal law enforcement entity, the force could have dual-use authority, enabling it to respond to natural disasters, terrorist incidents, and other domestic emergencies.

CIVIL POLICE

Civilian constabulary forces can restore public order, but they should not be required to engage in the routine work of traffic control, community policing, and criminal investigation, which are the responsibilities of civil police in democratic societies. They also cannot serve as role models for indigenous civil police. Except in war zones, U.S. law prohibits the military from training foreign civilian police, and both Congress and common sense require the use of U.S. civil law enforcement professionals to serve as role models and trainers for indigenous street cops in an emerging democracy.

Failure to deploy a civil police force with executive authority to enforce a basic criminal code will result in prolonged deployment of military and constabulary forces.

Creating a civil police component for a U.S. stability force will require moving the civilian police program from the State Department to a federal law enforcement agency and federalizing U.S. police personnel, rather than relying upon commercial contractors, to ensure that U.S. police officers in stability operations respond to direction from Washington and are accountable for their actions under U.S. law. Placing both the U.S. civilian constabulary force and the civil police program in one federal law enforcement agency would create an effective civilian police partner for the Defense Department in Washington and the U.S. military abroad. It would give a voice to the police program in the interagency process, freeing the State Department to concentrate on related foreign policy issues and diplomacy. It also would establish a cadre of law enforcement professionals that could develop doctrine, job descriptions, and training programs and interact with their UN and foreign counterparts. Federalizing the U.S. civilian police program would place U.S. police officers in peace and stability operations on par with those of other nations. The United States now has thousands of police officers that have served on UN police missions and in Iraq and Afghanistan. These veterans could form the core of a new, federalized civil police force, recruited specifically for service as part of a U.S. stability force. Federalizing the U.S. civil police program also would ensure that government regulations and standards of conduct apply to the recruiting, training, and management of police personnel. It would give the federal government the control it now lacks over U.S. policemen in peace operations who wear U.S. uniforms and may carry weapons and have authority to use deadly force but who work for a commercial contractor.

JUDICIAL AND PENAL EXPERTS

At the end of conflict, the judicial systems in the Balkans, Afghanistan, and Iraq literally lay in ruins. Courthouses and detention centers were destroyed. Law books and legal codes had been burned. Judges, prosecutors, and court administrators had either disappeared or were too intimidated to serve. Constabulary and police are important, but they cannot function effectively without the other two parts of the justice triad, courts and prisons. Democracies require that a functioning judicial and penal system process those arrested; without this, restoration of public order is compromised. In the long run, a failure to provide a sense of justice for the victims of war crimes, human rights violations, and other criminal activities can compromise sustainable security.

To complete a U.S. stability force, the United States needs to organize justice teams of lawyers, judges, court administrators, and corrections officers, augmented by a headquarters staff, a cadre of paralegals and translators, and a training unit. The teams would have authority to act independently and could decide to handle sensitive cases on their own without reference to local authorities, establishing their own courts and deciding cases. Their primary mission, however, would be to advise and monitor local courts, which would continue to handle all but the most sensitive cases. They would offer international legal assistance and training to local attorneys, jurists, and penal officers and ensure that the courts functioned fairly and effectively. Judicial teams would also help ensure accountability for human rights violations, provide guidance on dealing with accused war criminals, and advise on and assist with the rehabilitation and reform of the justice system. International corrections officers would take over the handling of important prisoners, supervise the release of those imprisoned for political offenses, ensure the humane treatment of prisoners, and assist with improving prison facilities.

In Kosovo and Bosnia, the United Nations discovered that in politically sensitive cases or those involving nationalist leaders or powerful gangsters, local jurists were either too intimidated or too biased to render proper verdicts. The same was true of corrections officers, who were either afraid or unwilling to jail high-profile offenders. Eventually international personnel handled such cases and ensured that offenders were given fair trials and received appropriate sentences. The United States now has a cadre of experienced judicial experts, advisers, and trainers who worked in the Balkans, Iraq, and Afghanistan and can build on their experience in those operations.

SUMMING UP

In *Waging Modern War,* General Wesley Clark, former NATO supreme commander, described the tactics employed by the Stabilization Force in Bosnia and Herzegovina as "using forces, not force." In Bosnia NATO forces were not at war, but they did everything military forces do short of firing their weapons. In addition to effective military forces, Clark concluded that modern war also requires the participation of civilian police that can perform activities ranging from investigating crime to controlling civil disturbances and urban violence. Clark argued that militaries cannot perform such functions effectively and should not be responsible for them. Rather, "nations will have to create a full range of deployable, robust, police-type capabilities, as well as provide a legal and judicial structure to support their responsibilities."[10]

A U.S. stability force would have such a capacity. By including constabulary, police, judicial, and corrections personnel, this force would have full-spectrum capability to enforce peace and maintain stability through introducing the rule of law. Creating a U.S. stability force would:

1. Join together all the elements required to effectively achieve sustainable security under a single, unified authority.
2. Close the security gap that has plagued previous peace operations by providing for a smooth transition from warfighting to building security institutions.
3. Establish police and judicial authority from the outset, freeing the military to perform its functions and speeding the withdrawal of military forces.
4. Establish the rule of law as a platform from which the other aspects of political, economic, and social reconstruction could move forward in an environment conducive to achieving success.
5. Enable the United States to contribute to UN missions and stability operations by NATO, the European Union, and other regional organizations.

A U.S. stability force would bring together a wide range of capabilities for the first time and provide the United States with capacities it needed but did not have in past conflicts. Creating such as force will require interagency cooperation, consultations with Congress, new authorizing legislation, and new funding. It will require overcoming the kneejerk objections that inevitably arise in response to new ideas. It will not be easy. Only the U.S. Department of Defense and the Joint Chiefs of Staff have the influence and resources to lead the effort to create a U.S. stability force.

The U.S. military bore the brunt of the fighting in Iraq and Afghanistan and holds much of the knowhow and lessons learned from more than a decade of war. Therefore the Defense Department must fully engage in an interagency policy process for a stability force initiative to be successful. Civilian agencies such as the Department of Justice and State will also have to contribute their expertise and resources. The previous failed interagency process to create a constabulary force proved that only an integrated, effectively led, and whole-of-government approach can succeed.

Yet the Defense Department and the U.S. military are turning in another direction. With U.S. forces scheduled to withdraw from Afghanistan in 2014, the U.S. military is "pivoting toward Asia," and is in the process of reorient-

---

10. Wesley Clark, *Waging Modern War* (New York: Public Affairs, 2001), 86, 98.

ing its doctrine, programs, and forces toward conventional war.[11] The urge is understandable. Powers such as China and North Korea challenge U.S. military and economic dominance. The 2011 NATO operation in Libya was heralded as a new model for waging high-impact, small-footprint war from above. In times of budget constraints, it is tempting for the United States to refocus on the basics: shoring up traditional alliances, controlling major waterways, and developing high-technology weapons and aircraft. The United States has a comparative advantage in these areas, while asymmetrical conflicts like those in Iraq and Afghanistan were costly to fight. The United States attempted to adopt a similar orientation at the end of the Cold War and in the period immediately preceding the attacks of September 11, 2001. In each of these cases, however, dramatic events required the United States to intervene in conflicts that demanded more than conventional forces and required the ability to deal with civil unrest and irregular forces.

In the decade that followed the onset of the global war on terrorism, the U.S. military had to patch together the ability to establish basic security and the rule of law in conflict environments. The process was iterative and the learning curve steep. Today the withdrawal from Iraq and Afghanistan does not signal the end of the pattern. The United States will continue to face significant challenges from intrastate conflicts, such as those under way in Yemen and Syria. The U.S. military will be called upon to do more than hunt down terrorists using pilotless drones. It will continue to participate in stability operations, including those in countries where regimes fostered or gave safe haven to terrorists. It will also face a range of other contingencies, such as natural disasters, where a U.S. stability force could provide a more effective and less costly response than the U.S. Army brigade combat team that delivered humanitarian assistance in Haiti following the January 2010 earthquake.

After September 11, the United States became very serious about conducting counterterrorism operations. Now it needs to be equally serious about codifying the lessons learned in counterinsurgency operations and building a multidisciplinary stability force that can respond to future contingencies. The United States cannot afford to adopt policies based upon wishful thinking and pretending that the challenges faced in the Balkans, Iraq, and Afghanistan are forever in the past. We owe those who gallantly served in the peace operations and the wars of the last two decades nothing less than our best effort.

---

11. Mark E. Manyin, Stephen Daggett, Ben Dolven, Susan V. Lawrence, Michael F. Martin, Ronald O'Rourke, and Bruce Vaughn, "Pivot to the Pacific? The Obama Administration's 'Rebalancing Toward Asia,'" Congressional Research Service, Washington, DC, March 28, 2012, available at http://www.fas.org/sgp/crs/natsec/R42448.pdf (accessed October 31, 2012).

Index

A

Abizaid, John, on Iraqi security
    forces, 174
Academy for Police and Gendarmerie
    (Afghanistan), 191
Afghan Interior Ministry, 208
Afghan National Civil Order Police
    (ANCOP), 191–218, 221
    attrition rate, 212
    as counterinsurgency force, 209–11
    FDD and, 203–05
    in Marjah, 210–11
    solidified position, 217–18
Afghan National Police (ANP), 221
    attrition rate, 206
    need for international assistance, 196
Afghan police
    casualties, 217
    illiterate trainees, 199
    international effort to rebuild, 195–97
    problems, 198
    salaries, 213
    as Taliban target, 205–06
    training, 208
        by Germans, 197
Afghan State Information Agency
    (KHAD), 192
Afghan U'e (AUP), 202
    Marjah residents' opposition to, 211
Afghanistan, xiv
    constabulary forces need, 1–2
    new U.S. policy, 206–09

public opinion poll on primary
    problem in 2008, 205
al-Qaeda headquarters in, 158
Sarandoy (Ministry of Interior
    forces), 192
Agreement on Provisional Arrangements
    in Afghanistan Pending the
    Re-Establishment of Permanent
    Government Institutions
    (Bonn Agreement), 195–97
Aideed, Mohamed Farah Hassan, 74
airport security in Kosovo, 145
Alamo, 34
Albania, intervention force for
    restoring order, 85–86
Albanian refugees
    return to Kosovo, 122
    violence on return to Kosovo, 134
Albanians, arrest in Kosovo for
    wartime atrocities, 147–48
Albright, Madeleine, 20, 75–76, 81
Alger, Russell, 38
Amarah Brigade, 176
American values, and U.S. response
    to humanitarian crisis, 157
al-Amn al-'Amm (General Security
    Directorate; GSD), 160
Annan, Kofi, 72, 74
    on violence in Kosovo, 135, 136, 138
anti-Americanism, in Haiti, 44
antidemocratic armies, constabularies
    evolution into, 37

Antiquities/Ruins Security Force, 188
arbitration tribunal for Brcko status,
     19
area of responsibility (AOR;
     blue box), 103
Argentina
     MSU personnel from, 99
     MSU personnel return home, 118
     National Gendarmerie, 92–93
     SPUs in Kosovo from, 142
Arghandab district, ISAF in, 216
Arizona Market, 19, 109
Armstrong, John B., 36
Ashcroft, John, 166
Ashdown, Paddy, 220
Austin, Stephen F., 34
al-Awadi, Hussein, 183, 186, 187
Aycock, Bill, 9

B
Baath Party in Iraq, 161
     leaders banned from government
          jobs, 169–70
Badr Brigade, 177
Baghdad
     ICG report on conditions, 170
     infrastructure failure, 166
     looting of, 171
     Ministry of Higher Education raid
          and kidnapping, 180
Balkan constabularies, for controlling
     civilian mobs, 225
Bamiyan, 194
Banja Luka, 19
Barry, Robert, 91
Bass, Sam, 36
Batić, Vladan, 151
Beadle, Elias, 40
Belkacem, Densayah, 116
Berger, Samuel R., 75
Biden, Joseph, 57
Bildt, Carl, 62, 72
bin Laden, Osama, 158
Bjelosivic, Chief of regional police, 10
black market after WWII, 47, 48
blue box. See area of responsibility
     (AOR; blue box)
al-Bolani, Jawad, 179, 181, 183

Bonn Agreement (Agreement on
     Provisional Arrangements
     in Afghanistan Pending
     the Re-Establishment of
     Permanent Government
     Institutions), 195–97
border checkpoints, SPU
     assistance at, 145
Bosnia-Herzegovina. See also
     Multinational Specialized
     Unit (MSU), xii, xiv, 1, 220
     civilian police role, 77
     constabulary forces in, 80
          U.S. proposal for international, 76
     court cases, 227
     downsizing and restructuring
          police, 68
     European insistence on U.S.
          participation in, 72
     international police force and
          refugee resettlement, 84
     Islamic extremists in, 115
     military force structure, 20
     minority protection absent in, 65
     organized criminal elements in
          power structure, 109
     planning for deterrent force, 83–85
     population, 18
     transfer of municipalities to
          federation, 66–72
     war end. See also Dayton Accords, 61
Bosnia, police training, 117–18
Bosnian Federation
     Croat efforts to withdraw, 112
     territory division with Republika
          Srpska (RS), 63
Boutros-Ghali, Boutros, 74
Brahimi, Lakhdar, 195
Brcko Arbitration Decision, xii
Brcko, Bosnia
     arbitration panel decision, 105–06
     conflict between Serb factions, 6
     desertion before conflict, 18
     IPTF force expansion, 70
     mob attacks on bridge, 14–18
     mob violence against peacekeeping
          forces, 5–14
     police station, 11–12

status, 18–22
U.S. force withdraw from bridge, 18
Brcko District of Bosnia and
        Herzegovina, 106
Brcko Implementation Conference
        (Vienna, 1997), 70
Bremer, L. Paul III, 169
bridge watchers, in Mitrovica,
        136–37, 149
Britain, military unit in Kosovo, 123
Brooks, Vincent, 167
brothel, night assault to free
        women in, 118
Brown, John S., 45
Brownshirts (Nazi), 26
Bryan, William Jennings, 41
Bundesgrenzschutz (Federal Republic of
        Germany border guards), 128
bureaucratic framework of
        G. W. Bush, 155
Burgess, Phillip, 11
Bush, George H. W., 54, 56
Bush, George W., 1, 57, 194
    announcement of military surge, 181
    on Iraqi weapons, 158
    victory declaration on USS
        Abraham Lincoln, 169
    view of U.S. aspirations for post-
        Hussein Iraq, 161–64
Bush (George W.) administration, 155
    absence of policy guidance on
        peacekeeping, 156
Butmir II, 99

C
Cady, Jean Christian, 151
Caldwell, William IV, xii, 207, 208, 214
California National Guard, 54
Camp Butmir, Sarajevo, 95, 101
Camp McGovern, 12
Canada
    Canadian Mounties, 25
    SFOR troops in Drvar, 90
Canton Ten (Livno), 90, 96
cantons, responsibility for police force, 69
Carabinieri (Italy), 30–31, 85–86, 99–100
    in Afghan police training program, 214
    expectations for MSU, 100–01

experience with organized crime, 110
    in IMP training process, 183, 184–86
Carolinas, local militia, 33
Carter, Calvin, 40
Carter, Jimmy, 39
Center for Strategic and International
        Studies, 162
Central Bank of ISF protection force, 188
Central Intelligence Agency, predictions
        on Iraq after Hussein, 162–63
China, 229
Citizens' Association of Bridge St.
        Demetrios, 136–37
civil disorder
    in Balkans, 220
    in Iraq
        absence of preparation, 164
        impact on humanitarian
            assistance agencies, 163
    management in U.S., 53
    need for forces to deal with, 2
    security forces trained to
        handle, 22–23
civil police, 225–26
    cost of using in combat, 205
    in Japan, 50
    transferring training responsibility
        to U.S. military, 172
Civil Police Unit, in UNMIK police, 128
civil war, in Afghanistan, 193
Civil War (U.S.), 2
    revenge killings and feuds after, 35–36
    U.S. army constabulary function, 45
Civilian Police Advisory Training
        Team (CPATT), 172
civilian security organizations,
        Hussein creation of, 160
civilians
    military forces' confrontation with, 27
    military police training on
            interacting with, 60
    SFOR soldiers and, 21
Clark, Wesley
    on impact of weak IPTF mandate, 64
    impression of Carabinieri, 86
    invitation to Oakley and Dziedzic, 88
    at MSU field exercises, 100
    on MSU role, 85, 92–93

as NATO Supreme Allied
      Commander Europe, 74
on need for NATO presence
      in Bosnia, 78
visit to Drvar, 91
visit to Sarajevo, 15
Waging Modern War, 227
warning against opposition to Dayton
      Accords implementation, 17
Clay, Lucius, 49
Clinton, Hillary, 82–83
Clinton, Bill
   in Bosnia, 82–83
   certification of U.S. forces
         needed in Bosnia, 87
   meeting on Bosnia, 75–76
   peacekeeping core group, Bush
         cancellation of, 155–56
   U.S. extension of troop presence
         in Bosnia, 82
Clinton administration
   on peacekeeping in Bosnia, 70–71
   role in peace operations, 1
Coalition Provisional Authority
      (CPA), 169
Coeurderoy, Vincent, 112
Coffman, James Jr., 176
Cohen, William, 17, 76, 77
Combined Security Transition
      Command–Afghanistan
      (CSTC-A), 200
communications
   in Bosnia, 7
   needs for SPU, 152–53
   between organizations in peace
         operations, need for, 150
community policing
   Iraqi police cadet training in, 173
   need in Afghanistan, 198
complex contingency operations, 156
conflict prevention, as MSU goal, 96
conflict resolution, military police
         training on, 60
Connatt, Robert, 112
constabulary police forces, xiv, 1, 224
   in Afghanistan, 191
      Kabul riots as indication of
            need for, 201–02

as Brcko solution, 25
characteristics, 2
confusion from mandate
      differences, 124
definition, 25–27, 28
history in U.S., 33–36
history of use, 2
in Kosovo, 121–54
      officers unfamiliar with, 143
need for, 28, 222
role in peace operations, 27
training, 29
UN absence of experience, 129
from U.S. European allies, 23
U.S. experience abroad, 37–44
U.S. in Germany, post-WWII, 44–52
vs. paramilitary forces, 27
workshop on potential roles, 89
Contact Group for Bosnia, 61–62
Coolidge, Calvin, 40
Coppola, Vincenzo, 91, 95
Corps of National Police (Panama), 38
Council on Foreign Relations, 162
counterinsurgencies, need for
      forces to deal with, 2
counterinsurgency (COIN) operations
      in Afghanistan, 209
criminality, xii
Croat national assembly, self-
      rule setup, 112
Croatian Democratic Union (HDZ)
      party, 90, 108, 111
crowd control, gap in, 88
Cuban Rural Guard, 37–38
currency, security for shipments, 146

D
DART (District Assessment and
      Reform Team), 203
Davis, Edmund, 35
Dayton Accords, 16
   Brcko status in, 18–19
   IFOR authority, 20
   implementing, 66–72
   and International Police Task Force, 61
   IPTF responsibilities, 8
   review of civilian implementation, 80
   signing, 65–66

Decani, Kosovo, demonstrations, 152
Defenders of Baghdad, 176
demobilization of U.S. military, 47
Democratic League of Kosovo, 147
Democratic Party of Kosovo, 147
Departmental Gendarmerie
     (France), 29–30
deterrent force (DFOR), 77
DHS. See U.S. Department of
     Homeland Security (DHS)
Directorate of Defense of the
     Revolution (Afghan), 192
displaced Jews, after WWII, 48
District Assessment and Reform
     Team (DART), 203
Djakovica, Kosovo
     demonstrations, 152
     MSU in, 124
Dodik, Milorad, 106
Dole, Elizabeth, 82
Dole, Robert, 82
Dominican Republic, 41–43
     Guardia Nacional Dominicana, 37
     Marine brigade in, 42
Dostum, Rashid, 193
DPKO. See United Nations
     Department for Peacekeeping
     Operations (DPKO)
drug trafficking, legal efforts
     against, 56–57
Drvar, riot, 89–91
Dubrava, Kosovo, 145
dye-filled balloons, U.S. troops use of, 22
DynCorp International, 198
Dziedzic, Michael, 27, 88–89
     Policing the New World Disorder, 88

E
Eberhart, Ralph, 57
Eisenhower, Dwight D., 45
election security in Kosovo, by SPUs, 146
Ellis, Larry, 100
Embassy Protection Force, 188
English language, SPU need
     for proficiency, 148
ethnic Albanian refugees
     return to Kosovo, 122
     violence on return to Kosovo, 134

ethnic cleansing
     of Brcko (1992), 18
     by Serbs, 66–67
     by Yugoslav Interior Ministry's
          special police units, 125
ethnic groups, representation in KPS,
     127
ethnic Serbs, in Drvar, 90
Europe
     Cohen on deficiency in
          commitment, 77
     constabulary police forces in, 29–33
     insistence on U.S. participation
          in Bosnia, 72
     resolution in Bosnian plans, 79–80
European Gendarmerie Force, 207
European Union
     and Kosovo, 122
     Police Mission in Afghanistan, 207
     responsibility for policing Mostar, 85

F
Fahim, Mohammed, 193–94
failed states, threat to U.S.
     national security, 219
Farrand, Robert, xii, 6–7, 17, 109
     responsibility for Brcko, 20
Federal Republic of Yugoslavia, protocol
     on police cooperation, 151
Ferguson, James Edward, 36
Field, Kimberly, 26
Fitzgerald, Peter, 67, 72
Focused District Development
     (FDD), 203–05
food shortages, German civil
     disorder due to, 48
foreign interventions, U.S. history with, 1
France
     constabulary forces in, 28–29
     Gendarmerie, 29–30
     military unit in Kosovo, 122, 123
     NATO call for contributions
          to MSU, 86
     unwillingness to work with
          Pakistanis, 138–39
Frederiksen, Sven, 135
Freedom Brigade, 180
Frontier Battalion, 35

G

Garde d'Haiti, 37, 43–44
Garden Plot, 53
Garner, Jay, 168
Gelbard, Robert, 15, 16–17, 73, 87
  meeting with Clinton, 75–76
Gendarmerie Départementale
  (France), 29–30
Gendarmerie Mobile, 29–30
General Framework Agreement
  for Peace in Bosnia and
  Herzegovina (GFAP), 18, 61
  signing, 66
General Intelligence Directorate
  (Jihaz al-Mukhabbarat), 160
General Security Directorate (GSD;
  al-Amn al-'Amm), 160
Geneva Convention (1949, Fourth), 163
Georgia, local militia, 33
Germany
  training for Afghan police, 191, 197
  U.S. constabulary forces, post-
  WWII, 44–49
GFAP. See General Framework
  Agreement for Peace in Bosnia
  and Herzegovina (GFAP)
Global Relief Foundation, 116
Gnjilane, Kosovo, violence in, 141
Goldberg, Eliot, 27
governance, xii
Grady, Donald, 7–10
Grange, David, 10, 15, 17
Greece, military unit in Kosovo, 122
green box, 103
Greer, James, 15
Guardia Civil (Spain), 32–33
Guardia Nacional de Nicaragua, 37, 39–41
Guardia Nacional Dominicana, 37
Guillaume Sam, Jean Vilbrun, 43
gunboat diplomacy, 37

H

Hadzici, violence prior to transfer, 67
Haiti, xii, xiv
  anti-Americanism in, 44
  Garde d'Haiti, 37, 43–44
  Tontons Macoutes, 26
Hajraj, Hamze, murder of, 152

Hammit, Brad, 26
Haradinaj, Daut, 152
Hardin, John Wesley, 36
Harwood, J.H., 46
Hay, John, 38
Hay-Bunau-Varilla Treaty, 38
Hendricks, Kevin, 14
Herat, ANCOP stationed in, 202
Herzegovacka Bank (Mostar), 112–14
high-risk persons in Kosovo, SPU
  protection for, 146
Hills, Alice, 26–27
Holbrooke, Richard, 63, 206
Hoover, Herbert, 41
housing, for Kosovo SPU, 133–34
humanitarian assistance, 59
  in Haiti, 229
humanitarian crisis, 58
  postwar in Iraq, 168
Hungarians, training by Carabinieri, 118
Hussein, Qusai Saddam, 160
Hussein, Saddam, 158, 159–60
  warnings of impact of
  removal, 162–63

I

ICTY. See International Criminal
  Tribunal for Former
  Yugoslavia (ICTY)
IEBL. See Inter-Entity Boundary
  Line (IEBL)
IFOR. See NATO-led Implementation
  Force (IFOR)
Ignatius, David, 176
Ilidza, violence prior to transfer, 67
illicit trafficking, after WWII, 47
India, SPUs in Kosovo from, 142, 145
INP. See Iraq National Police
  (INP; Shurta)
Inter-Entity Boundary Line (IEBL), 98
Interagency Stability Police Working
  Group on Options for
  a U.S. Stability Policing
  Capability, 222–23
Interior Ministry of Iraq
  factions, 181
  reforms, 183
  United States and, 176

International Association of Chiefs
   of Police, Law Enforcement
   Code of Ethics, 187
International Committee of the
   Red Cross, 165
international community, xi
   source of instability, 1
International Criminal Investigative
   Training Assistance
   Program (ICITAP), 171
International Criminal Tribunal
   for Former Yugoslavia
   (ICTY), 69, 111
   entry to Bosnian police stations,
      114
   MSU support of SFOR investigations
      of war crimes by, 114
International Crisis Group (ICG)
   report, 137, 170
international police force, Cohen's
   proposal for, 77–78
International Police Task Force
   (IPTF), 5, 7, 20
   Bosnian police forces and, 69
   and Dayton Accords, 61
   evacuation, 12–14
   executive authority and, 64–65
   forced evacuation and, 67
   headquarters knowledge of
      planned Brcko police
      station takeover, 8
   lack of support for civilians, 73
   mandate, 61
      need for change, 73–74
      preference for weak, 63, 64
   mob attacks on, 9, 12
   organization, 61
   proposed models, 62
   quality of personnel, 68
   responsibilities under Dayton
      Accords, 8
   view of MSU deployment, 97
International Security Assistance
   Force (ISAF), 194, 209
   deployment, 195
International Supervisor of Brcko, 70
IPTF. See International Police
   Task Force (IPTF)

Iraq, xii, xiv
   Baghdad Police College expansion, xvi
   civil war, 174–76
   constabulary forces need, 1–2
   CPA order to disband army, 170
   independent congressional
      commission report on
      security forces, 182
   Ministry of Higher Education raid
      and kidnapping, 180
   mob violence, need for
      constabulary forces, 221
   national elections for permanent
      government, 179
   ORHA's reconstruction plan, 168
   police lack of preparation for
      conditions, 173–74
   postwar humanitarian crisis, 168
   postconflict chaos, 164–69
   reconstruction false start, 169–71
   sectarian violence peak, 177–78
   transitional government
      installation, 177
   U.S. decision to intervene, 159–61
Iraq Federal Police (IFP), 188, 208–09
Iraq National Police (INP;
   Shurta), 161, 178
   code of ethics, 187
   future role of, 186–89
   improved performance and
      expanded presence, 188
   rebluing transition process, 180
   U.S. efforts to control commando
      units, 181–86
Iraqi commandos, 176
Iraqi National Library, looting, 166
Iraqi Police (IP), 171
   training of, 172–74, 175
   absence, 171
   in basic skills, 183
   spiritual element, 185
   U.S. military efforts to control
      abuses, 178–81
Iraqi Police Service (IPS), 173
Iraqi Security Force development
   effort, xv
Irish Republican Army, 26
Islamic extremists in Bosnia, 115

Israeli national soccer team game against
Bosnia, MSU deployment, 107
Italy
Carabinieri, 30–31, 85–86, 99–100
in Afghan police training
program, 214
expectations for MSU, 100–01
experience with organized
crime, 110
in IMP training process,
183, 184–86
constabulary forces in, 28–29
military unit in Kosovo, 122
platoons for MSU, 85
Izetbegović, Alija, 66

J

Jabr Solagh, Bayan, 177
Jackson, Mike, 122
Janowitz, Morris, 25
Japan after WWI
government, 49
U.S. constabulary forces, 49–52
Jashari, Adam, 145
Jelavić, Ante, 112
Jews, displaced after WWII, 48
Jihaz al-Mukhabbarat (General
Intelligence Directorate), 160
Joint Coordination and Monitoring
Board, 208
Joint Coordination Committee
for the Fight Against
Terrorism in Bosnia, 116
Jones, James, 182
Jones Commission, xv
Jordan, Joe, 9
Jordan, SPUs in Kosovo from, 142
Jović, Slavoljub "Pagi," 149
judiciary system, xiv
need for, 226–27
justice, police for restoring, xi–xii

K

Kabul, 194
ANCOP stationed in, 202
riots and need for constabulary
force, 201–02
Kabul National Police Academy, 197
Kalinić, Dragan, 15

Kandahar
ANCOP in, 202, 215–17
checkpoints on roads, 216
Karadžić, Radovan, 5, 75, 78, 108
Karzai, Ahmed Wali, 215
Karzai, Hamid, 194, 215
Kasich, John, 82
Kauzlarich, Richard D., 15–16
briefing by Farrand, 16
Kent State University, 53
Kerambon, Yves De, 151
Kerik, Bernard, 170–71
Khalili, Karim, 194
Khan, Ismael, 194
Al Kindi Hospital, looters of, 165
King, Rodney, 53–54
Klein, Jacques, 109
on orchestrated violence Brcko
by outsiders, 17–18
Knapp, H.S., 41
Korean War, 50
Kosovo, xiv, 1, 220
constabulary police forces in, 121–54
court cases, 227
crime and ethnic conflict, 134–36
demonstration patterns in, 144
law and order campaign, 147–52
lessons identified in, 152–54
Mitrovica, 136–41
special police units (SPUs), 128–29
violence in 2000 and 2001, 141–42
Kosovo Force (KFOR), 122–25
responsibilities, 123
Trepca control to close lead
smelter, 140
Kosovo Liberation Army (KLA), 127
Kosovo police service, 125–28
Kosovo Protection Corps (KPC), 147
Kosovo Verification Mission (KVM), 121
Kouchner, Bernard, 122, 135, 140, 220
Krajišnik, Momčilo, 10, 15, 16
Kroeker, Mark, 100
Kroll-O'Gara, 113
Kurdish peshmerga, 174

L

Law and Order Trust Fund for
Afghanistan (LOTFA), 199
Leahy Amendment, 179

Lee, Harry, 41
Leso, Leonardo, 95
"liberated" Iraq, 161
Libya, NATO operations in 2011, 229
"light footprint," 195–96
literacy
    of Afghan police, 202
    mandatory training for, 214–15
    of Afghan police trainees, 199
Lithuania, military unit in Kosovo, 122
local militias, 33–36
local police
    for domestic law enforcement, 27
    as problem vs. solution, xiv
Lockhart, Joe, 16
Lone Ranger, 2, 36
Los Angeles, racial violence
    in 1992, 53–54
Los Angeles Times, 181
Lynch, Rick, 182

M
MacArthur, Douglas, 49–50
al-Maliki, Nouri, 179
Marine Corps, in Haiti, 43–44
Marjah, 209-11
Marjanović, Svetozar, 122
Marshall, George C., 45
Martin, Matthew, 11
Matthews, Gary, 142
Matsuura, Koichiro, 166
Mazar-e-Sharif, U.S. attack on, 193
McChrystal, Stanley, xii, 208, 210, 215
McKiernan, David, 167
mediation, military police training
    on, 60
Mexican Rurales, 25
military forces, role in peace
    operations, 27
Miller, Leszek, 150
Miller, Tom, 117
Milošević, Slobodan, 6, 66
Ministry of Higher Education (Iraq),
    raid and kidnapping, 180
Mitrovica, Kosovo, 136–41
    division into Serb and Albanian
        sectors, 136
    MSU in, 124
    violence in, 137–38, 141, 148–51

mob attacks
    in Baghdad, U.S. military
        inaction, 164–66
    in Banja Luka, Ferhadija Mosque
        reconstruction, 117
    in Brcko, 9, 11, 21
        on bridge, 14–18
        U.S. reaction, 22–23
    in Drvar, 90
    in Iraq, need for constabulary
        forces, 221
    in Mostar, on bank auditors, 113–14
Mobile Gendarmerie, 29–30
Moncada, José Maria, 40
Moskos, Charles Jr., 25–26
Mrkonjic Grad, 104
MSU. See Multinational Specialized
        Unit (MSU)
Multinational Specialized Unit
    (MSU), 3, 83–84, 95–119
    ability to deter civil disorder, 107
    advance team, 91–92
    combating organized crime, 108–14
    command and control, 100–02
    counterterrorism, 115–16
    Drvar riot, 89–91
    expansion, 118–19
    final approval, 92–94
    information collection, 102
    Italy lead in commanding, 99–100
    in Kosovo, 123–24
    mandate and organization, 98–100
    maneuver unit, 99
    perspectives on, 95
    recruitment, 85–87
    roles and missions, 87–88
    SFOR wariness about deploying,
        119
    support for SFOR investigations
        of ICTY war crimes, 114
Musharraf, Pervez, 194

N
Nadir Shah, 191
al-Naqib, Falah, 175–76, 177
National Defense University, Institute for
        National Strategic Studies, 88
National Guard, activation after
        Sept. 11 attacks, 55

National Intelligence Council, 147
Global Trends 2030: Alternative Worlds, xiii
National Museum of Antiquities, looting, 166
National Park Police (U.S.), 53
National Police Plan, ANCOP description in, 218
national police transition teams (NPTTs), 183
national security, change by Bush administration, 155
National Security Presidential Directive (NSPD-1), 155
National Security Service (SNS), SFOR raid of Mostar headquarters, 111
National Security Strategy (2002), 219
nationalism in Nicaragua, Sandino and, 41
nationalists in Sarajevo, criminal groups allied with extremists, 108
Native American tribes, Texan clashes with, 34
NATO
  after Sept. 11 attacks, 164
  aircraft, protection of U.S. after Sept. 2001, 115
  North Atlantic Council, 74
  organization of specialized units of European military police, 88
NATO Kosovo Force, 60
NATO-led Implementation Force (IFOR)
  lack of support for civilians, 73
  need for mandate change, 73–74
NATO Stabilization Force (SFOR), 3, 5, 6
  discussions on future, 70–71
  misuse of MSU, 103–04
  mob attacks on, 11
  MSU arrival and, 101–02
  new mission, 84
  procedures and command relationships for civil disturbances, 103
  U.S. debate on extending, 75–76

NATO Training Mission–Afghanistan (NTM-A), 207, 208
  Italian Carabinieri trainers for, 214
  operational deployment cycle for ANCOP unit, 213–14
  program to improve ANCOP performance, 211–15
Netherlands
  constabulary forces in, 28–29
  Royal Marechaussee, 31–32
Neville-Jones, Pauline, 62
New York Times, 79
Nicaragua, Guardia Nacional de Nicaragua, 37, 39–41
Nicholson, Larry, 210–11
nonmilitary capabilities, development, xii
nonmilitary security forces, 1
Noriega Moreno, Manuel, 39
North Atlantic Treaty Organization. See NATO
North Korea, 229
  forces crossing thirty-eighth parallel, 50
Northern Alliance, 158

O
Oakley, Robert, 27, 88
  Policing the New World Disorder, 88
Obama, Barack, 206
  at NATO summit meeting, 207
  plan for phased drawdown of U.S. forces from Iraq, 187–88
  speech to West Point Military Academy, 207–08
Obilić, Kosovo, 145
Office of Reconstruction and Humanitarian Assistance (ORHA), 168
Office of the Coordinator for Reconstruction and Stabilization (CRS), 222–23
Office of the High Representative (OHR)
  communications, 7
  responsibilities under Dayton Accords, 20–21
Ogata, Sadako, 84

Ohio State University, 53
Omar, Mullah Mohammed, 193, 215
Operation Alba, 85–86
Operation Athenia, 113–14
Operation Camel, 47
Operation Desert Storm, massive
    uprisings after, 162
Operation Eagle Assist, 115
Operation Enduring Freedom, 195
Operation Grom, 111
Operation Hamkari, 215
Operation Hollywood Hotel, 115
Operation Joint Forge, 92, 101
Operation Joint Guard, 101
Operation Munja, 111
Operation Panter, 111
Operation Provide Comfort, 168
Operation Puma, 111
Operation Scotch, 47
Operation Uphold Democracy
    (Haiti, 1994), 44
Operation Vulcan, 139
Operation Westar, 111
Organic Law on the Security
    Corp and Forces, 32
Organization for Security and
    Cooperation in Europe
    (OSCE), 121
organized crime
    Albanian, 135
    in Kosovo, 147
    UNMIK campaign against, 151
    MSU for combating, 108–14
Owen, Roberts, 19

P
Pajic, Mladen, 11
Pakistan, SPUs in Kosovo
    from, 138–39, 142
Paktia, ANCOP stationed in, 202
Panama
    Policia Nacional, 37, 38–39
    U.S. military in 1990, 28
Panama Defense Force (PDF), 39
Panjwai district, 216–17
paramilitary forces, 26
    vs. constabulary forces, 27

Parrulli, Fabrizo, 184
payrolls, SPU protection in Kosovo,
    146
peace
    Clinton administration role
        in operations, 1
    implementation in Bosnia, 83
    police for restoring, xi–xii
Peace Implementation Council
    (PIC), 65, 80, 96
peace operations
    alternatives for military forces, 155
    Bush administration absence of
        policy guidance, 156
    use of military forces, 52
peacekeeping troops in Bosnia, warning
    of deadly force use, 17
People's Democratic Party of
    Afghanistan, 192
Pereyra, Juan Isidro Jiménez, 41
Perić, Jozo, 110
Perle, Richard, 169
Petersberg Declaration (1996), on
    federation police forces, 69
Peterson, Joseph, 174
Petraeus, David, xii, 167, 175, 181, 182
Petritsch, Wolfgang, 112, 117
Philippines, insurgency in, 37
Plavšić, Biljana, 5, 75
Ploče, Croatia
    MSU arrival, 95
    roadblock by demonstrators, 103–04
Poland
    military unit in Kosovo, 122
    SPUs in Kosovo from, 142
police forces, xiv
    Afghan respect for, 191
police functions
    opposition to U.S. troop
        performance of, 74
    U.S. military in Iraq and, 167
police leadership, promoting the
    right people to, xvi
The Policeman (prayer), 185–86
Policia Nacional (Panama), 37
Policing the New World Disorder
    (Oakley and Dziedzic), 88

Policy Coordinating Committee on
Democracy, Human Rights, and
International Operations, 156
politicians in Sarajevo, criminal groups
allied with extremists, 108
Pollack, Kenneth, 160
Poplasen, Nikola, 106
Popovic, Vitomir, 19
Posse Comitatus Act of 1878, 55–56
postconflict interventions
Bush administration failure to
renew directives on, 156
doctrine for conducting, 220
Powell, Colin, 155, 157
presidential decision directives
(PDDs), of Clinton, 155n2
prison in Iraq, secret, 178
prison systems, need for, 226–27
Pristina, Kosovo
MSU in, 123
violence in, 141
private security companies
(PSCs), ANCOP member
recruitment by, 212
Prizren, Kosovo, MSU in, 124
public events in Kosovo, SPU
security for, 145
public order, MSU response to threat, 103
Public Security Ministry in
Afghanistan, 191

Q
al-Qaeda, 115, 116, 158
attack on Shiite shrines, 174
Qanooni, Mohammed Yunus, 196, 197

R
racial violence, in Los Angeles
(1992), 53–54
Radio Pale, 10
raising police forces, xiv–xv
Reconstruction in Texas, 34–35
refugees, in Bosnia, protection
of returning, 84
Reinhardt, Klaus, 135
Remón, José Antonio, 39
Renner Transport Company, 110
Republic of Bosnia and Herzegovina.
See Bosnia-Herzegovina

Republika Srpska (RS), 5
Ferhadija Mosque reconstruction,
mob attacks on, 117
monitoring police, 70
Mrkonjic Grad, 104
reaction to Serb death by
American sergeant, 106
SFOR in, 75
territory division with Bosnian
Federation, 63
rescue of IPTF officers in Brcko, 12–14
Rice, Condoleezza, 155
Ridge, Tom, 57
Riza, Iqbal, 73
Robertson, George, 78
Romanian Politia Militari, 99
Roosevelt, Theodore, 38
Root, Elihu, 38
Royal Marechaussee
(Netherlands), 31–32
RS. See Republika Srpska (RS)
rule of law, 220, 228, 229
establishing in Iraq, 163
Rumsfeld, Donald, 169, 172, 177
Rural Antiterrorist Group, 32
Russia, military unit in Kosovo, 122

S
Sacasa, Juan, 41
Saddam City, 165
Sadikovic, Cazim, 19
al-Sadr, Moqtada, 177
Sandinistas, 40–41
Sandino, Augusto César, 40
Santa Anna, Antonia López de, 34
Sarajevo, 66
Bosniak leadership dependence on
smuggled weapons, 108
Office of the High Representative
(OHR), communications, 7
roadblock by demonstrators, 103–04
U.S. ambassador to Bosnia in,
15–16
Saudi High Commission for Assistance
to Bosnia in Sarajevo, SFOR
storming of, 115–16
Schmidl, Erwin A., 25
Schulte, Gregory, 80, 93–94
Scobell, Andrew, 26

sectarian violence, Iraq police involvement in, 179–81
security gap, 27–28, 88
security, imposing and enforcing, xii–xiv
security sector reform program for Afghanistan, 196
September 11, 2001, terrorist attacks, 157–58
and change in MSU mandate, 115–16
impact on U.S. interest in SPUs, 153–54
National Guard activation after, 55
U.S. retaliation, 193–95
Serb authorities
broadcasts on local radio station, 10
claim on Brcko, 19
Serb Democratic Party (SDS), 6
Serb security forces, withdraw from Kosovo, 122
Serb ultranationalist, shooting by American sergeant, 106
Serbia, protocol on police cooperation, 151
Serbs
ethnic cleansing by, 66–67
smuggling and black market activity, 108
SFOR. See NATO Stabilization Force (SFOR)
Shadid, Anthony, 164
Shalikashvili, John, 16, 74
SHAPE. See Supreme Headquarters Allied Powers Europe (SHAPE)
Shiite Badr Brigade, 174
Shiite political parties, after Iraq election, 177
Shiite shrines, al-Qaeda attack on, 174
Shiite Supreme Council of the Islamic Revolution in Iraq (SCIRI), 177
Shinseki, Eric K., 21, 75, 91, 162–63
Silovo, Kosovo, MSU in, 124
Skelton, Ike, 16
Slovenian military police, 99
Smith, Charles, 51
Smith, Leighton, 67–68, 73
Snider, Don, 26
social contract, Afghan version of, 192
Solana, Javier, 74, 76, 80, 87, 89

Somalia, loss of U.S. Army Rangers in, 63
Somoza, Anastasio, 41
Soviet intervention, Afghan police organization after, 192
Soviet Ministry of Internal Affairs (MVD), 192
Spain, 86–87
constabulary forces in, 28–29
Guardia Civil, 32–33
NATO call for contributions to MSU, 86
SPUs in Kosovo from, 142
special police units (SPUs), 224–25
special police units (SPUs) in Kosovo, 128–29
command and control, 130–31
for crowd control, shortcomings, 148
deployment, 132–34
financial arrangements, 131–32
as odd jobs unit, 142–47
from Pakistan, 138–39
Zvecan smelter guarded by, 140
sources for, impact on use, 143
UN selection criteria, 129–30
underutilized or ignored, 153
Special Security Directorate (SSD; al-Amn al-Khas), 160
spiritual element of Iraq police training, 185
sponge grenades, U.S. troops use of, 22
Steiner, Michael, 67, 150, 152
Stevens, Ted, 82
Stimson, Henry, 40
Stolac, 103
Sunni insurgents, in Iraq offensive, 174–75
Sunni men, Shiite attacks on, 177–78
Supreme Commander for Allied Powers (SCAP), 49–50
Supreme Headquarters Allied Powers Europe (SHAPE), 83
Operation Plan 10407, 98
surveillance, by MSU, 110
sustainable security
creating in postconflict environments, 224
U.S. ability to establish, 219
Sylvester, John, 116

T

Taibah International, 116
Tal Afar, 180
Taliban, 158
  Afghan police as target, 205–06
  Kandahar and, 215
  land mines in Afghanistan, 210
  Ministry for the Promotion of
      Virtue and Prevention, 193
Task Force Eagle, 5
Tasovčići, 103
tear gas, in Bosnia, 15
terrorism, global war on, 1, 157–58
Texas Rangers, 2, 33–36
  mythology of, 36
  Texas law referring to, 35
Texas Republic, 34
Thaçi, Hashim, 147
Thavit, Adnan, 176
Three Kingdoms, 101
Three P Program, 212–13
Torrijos, Omar, 39
training
  of Afghan police, 191
    failures as indicating need,
        202–05
    lack of instructors, 207
    U.S. assistance, 197–200
  of Bosnian police, 117–18
  of constabulary forces, 29
    in Sonthofen, Germany, 46
  of Iraq police, 172–74, 175
    absence, 171
    in basic skills, 183
    spiritual element, 185
  Kosovo Police Service School
      (KPSS), 126–27
  of military police, 60
  of MSU, 95–96, 100
  of Northern Alliance, 194
  to serve in SPUs, 130
Trepca mining and industrial facility,
    UNMIK takeover, 139–40
Trespalacios, José Félix, 33
Trujillo Molina, Rafael Leónidas, 42–43
Truman, Harry, 50
Tudjman, Franjo, 66

U

Ukraine
  K-9 teams in Kosovo from, 145
  military unit in Kosovo, 122
  SPUs in Kosovo from, 142
unemployed workers in RS,
    demonstration with
    roadblock, 105
uniforms, of Iraq National Police, 180
United Kingdom
  and forces to manage civil
      disturbance, 86
  multinational brigade in Kosovo, 122
United Nations
  Border Police Unit in Kosovo, 128
  International Police Task
      Force (IPTF), 132
  in Iraq, limitations, 188
  leadership in Sarajevo, reaction to
      MSU deployment, 97
  reimbursement of countries
      for equipment, 132
United Nations Department for
    Peacekeeping Operations
    (DPKO), 66
  Civilian Police Division, 129
United Nations Development
    Program, 199
  Police Perception Survey of 2011, 217
United Nations Educational, Scientific,
    and Cultural Organization
    (UNESCO), 166
United Nations High Commissioner
    for Refugees, 122
United Nations Interim
    Administration Mission in
    Kosovo (UNMIK), 121
  law enforcement confusion, 134–35
  police, 128
  protocol on police cooperation, 151
  violence against, 141
United Nations Mission in Bosnia and
    Herzegovina (UNMIBH), 66
United Nations Protection Force
    (UNPROFOR), 23
United Nations Security Council
    Resolution 1026, 65

Resolution 1031, 66
Resolution 1171, 93
Resolution 1244, 121, 123,
        125–26, 137
Resolution 1386, 195
United Nations Stabilization Force
        (SFOR), and constabulary
        forces role, 95
United States
    armed forces prohibited from law
        enforcement activities, 55–56
    congressional legislation on
        exemptions, 56–57
    constabulary forces
        history, 33–36
        in post-WWII Germany, 46
        in post-WWII Japan, 49–52
    defense appropriations bill, FY
        1998, and funding for U.S.
        troops in Bosnia, 71
    goal of defeating al-Qaeda, 206
    history with foreign interventions, 1
    involvement in peace operations, xii
    in Iraq, absence of allied support, 163
    military unit in Kosovo, 122, 123
    National Guard, 52–58
    need for new approach to postconflict
        intervention, 219
    resolution in Bosnian plans, 79–80
    retaliation for Sept. 11 attacks, 193–95
    stability force model, 224
        benefits from, 228
United States Code
    Title 10, 56
    Title 32, 57
U.S. Combined Security Transition
        Command Afghanistan
        (CSTC-A), 207
U.S. congressional delegation,
        opposition to U.S. troop
        presence in Bosnia, 16
U.S. Department of Defense, 228
    expectations at end of Hussein
        regime, 164
    on paramilitary forces, 26
    responsibility for Iraq police
        training, 172

responsibility for police assistance
        program, 200
U.S. Department of Homeland
        Security (DHS), 57, 222–23
U.S. Department of Justice
    International Criminal Investigative
        Training Assistance Program
        (ICITAP), 73, 96, 126
    Marshal Service (USMS), 222–23
U.S. Department of State, Bureau of
        International Narcotics and
        Law Enforcement Affairs
        (INL), 198, 222–23
U.S. Department of the Army, civil
        disturbance plan, 53
U.S. Institute of Peace, 162
U.S.-Iraq Strategic Framework
        Agreement (SFA), 187
U.S. military
    armed attacks on soldiers in Iraq, 167
    European pressure to continue
        presence in Bosnia, 78
    failure to protect Iraqi institutions,
        170
    lack of mob control training, 222
    military police, 58–60
    move to Korea from Japan, 50–51
    responsibility for Iraq police
        training, 172
U.S. police assistance program,
        limitations, 207
UNMIK. See United Nations Interim
        Administration Mission
        in Kosovo (UNMIK)
urban rioting, forces to control, 2

V
Vedrine, Hubert, 81
Vice and Virtue Police (Taliban), 193
victims, military police training
        on handling of, 60
Villa, Francisco "Pancho," 36
violence, xii
Virginia, local militia, 33
Vogosca, violence prior to transfer, 67
Volcano Brigade commando unit, 177
Vucitrn, Kosovo, 126–27

W

Waging Modern War (Clark), 227
Walker, Michael, 67
war on drugs, 56
war on terrorism, 229
    MSU and, 115–16
warfighting effectiveness, impact of
        peacekeeping roles on, 51–52
warning shots, at Brcko bridge, 14–15
Washington, DC, security for
        demonstrations, 53
Washington Post, 176
Washington State National Guard, 54–55
Watts neighborhood riots (1965), 54
weapons of mass destruction
        (WMDs), 158
Westendorp, Carlos, 87, 91, 105, 106
Western Europe, police and civilian
        understanding about
        demonstrations, 144
White, William, 12
Wilson, Pete, 54
Wilson, Woodrow, 36
Wolf Brigade, 177, 178–79
    evidence of torture, 179
    renamed, 180
Women of Srebrenica return, to
        commemorate wartime massacre,
        MSU deployment, 107

Women's International League for
        Peace and Freedom,
        visit to Haiti, 43
Wood, Leonard, 37, 38
World Trade Organization,
        demonstration against, 54–55
Wyoming Air National Guard, 55

Y

Young Generals (ethnic Croats),
        112–14
Yugoslavia
    European efforts on dissolution, 72
    Interior Ministry's Special
        Police Units, 26
    NATO bombing campaign
        against, 106

Z

Zamarai, Gul, 218
Zebari, Hoshyar, 181
Zhari district, 216–17
Zobeidi, Muhammad Mohsen, 167
Zubaydah, Abu, 116
Zvencan, Kosovo, 137
    lead smelter, KFOR takeover
        to close, 140

About the Author

Robert Perito is the director of the Center of Innovation for Security Sector Governance (SSG) at the United States Institute of Peace (USIP), leading a team that builds security institutions that promote democracy and the rule of law. Prior to joining USIP, he led the Justice Department's International Criminal Investigative Training Assistance Program, supervising programs in Haiti, Bosnia, and Kosovo. Perito was a U.S. foreign service officer with the Department of State, retiring in 1995 with the rank of minister counselor. He served in the White House as deputy executive secretary of the National Security Council under Presidents Ronald Reagan and George H. W. Bush. Perito was an American Political Science Association Congressional Fellow. He was a visiting lecturer in public and international affairs at the Woodrow Wilson School, Princeton University; Diplomat in Residence at American University; and an adjunct professor at George Mason University. Perito received an MA from George Mason University in peace operations policy and a BA from Denver University in international affairs. He attended Columbia University Graduate School of International Affairs. He is the author of *The American Experience with Police in Peace Operations;* co-author of *The Police in War: Fighting Insurgency, Terrorism, and Violent Crime;* editor of a *Guide for Participants in Peace, Stability, and Relief Operations;* and author of reports, book chapters, and articles on Iraq, Afghanistan, and Haiti.

United States Institute of Peace Press

Since its inception in 1991, the United States Institute of Peace Press has published more than 175 books on the prevention, management, and peaceful resolution of international conflicts—among them such venerable titles as Raymond Cohen's *Negotiating Across Cultures;* John Paul Lederach's *Building Peace; Leashing the Dogs of War* by Chester A. Crocker, Fen Osler Hampson, and Pamela Aall; and *The Iran Primer,* edited by Robin Wright. All our books arise from research and fieldwork sponsored by the Institute's many programs, and the Press is committed to extending the reach of the Institute's work by continuing to publish significant and sustainable works for practitioners, scholars, diplomats, and students. In keeping with the best traditions of scholarly publishing, each volume undergoes thorough internal review and blind peer review by external subject experts to ensure that the research and conclusions are balanced, relevant, and sound.

VALERIE NORVILLE
DIRECTOR

About the
United States Institute of Peace

The United States Institute of Peace is an independent, nonpartisan institution established and funded by Congress. Its goals are to help prevent and resolve violent conflicts, promote postconflict peacebuilding, and increase conflict-management tools, capacity, and intellectual capital worldwide. The Institute does this by empowering others with knowledge, skills, and resources, as well as by its direct involvement in conflict zones around the globe.

MEMBERS EX OFFICIO

Michael H. Posner, Assistant Secretary of State for Democracy, Human Rights, and Labor

Kathleen Hicks, Principal Deputy Under Secretary of Defense for Policy

Gregg F. Martin, Major General, U.S. Army; President, National Defense University

Jim Marshall, President, United States Institute of Peace (nonvoting)

Other Titles of Interest from the United States Institute of Peace Press

Assessing the Impact of Transitional Justice
Challenges for Empirical Research
Hugo van der Merwe, Victoria Baxter, and Audrey R. Chapman, editors

376 pp. • 6 × 9
Paper: 978-1-60127-036-8

Customary Justice and the Rule of Law in War-Torn Societies
Deborah Isser, editor

400 pp. • 6 × 9
Paper: 978-1-60127-066-5

Facilitating Dialogue
USIP's Work in Conflict Zones
David R. Smock and Daniel Serwer, editors

172 pp. • 6 × 9
Paper: 978-1-60127-140-2
Ebook: 978-1-60127-141-9

Guiding Principles for Stabilization and Reconstruction
United States Institute of Peace and United States Army Peacekeeping and
Stability Operations Institute

244 pp. • 6 × 9
Paper: 978-1-60127-046-7

The Quest for Viable Peace
International Intervention and Strategies for Conflict Transformation
Jock Covey, Michael Dziedzic and Leonard Hawley, editors

368 pp. • 6 × 9
Paper: 978-1-92922-367-1

United States Institute of Peace Press
http://bookstore.usip.org